The Historical Shape of Faith

THE HISTORICAL SHAPE OF FAITH

by RALPH G. WILBURN

THE WESTMINSTER PRESS
Philadelphia

LIBRARY OF CONGRESS CATALOG CARD NO. 66-12793

Published by The Westminster Press ®
Philadelphia, Pennsylvania

PRINTED IN THE UNITED STATES OF AMERICA

TO MY DAUGHTERS

Contents

Preface

This volume is addressed to what is conceived to be a vitally important question for contemporary theology: What is the nature of the impact of the modern idea of history on the traditional Christian faith? What impact has the modern idea of history had on the traditional Christian understanding of history and of faith's relation to it? How should theology respond to this crucial aspect of its contemporary intellectual environment?

A basic presupposition of this book lies in the conviction that if theological thinking is to be creative and constructive, it must be responsive to the intellectual situation within which it does its work. Theology cannot remain healthy, vibrant, and relevant if it merely clings to the past and repeats its outmoded forms, even Biblical forms and ways of thought. When it does so, what happens is that theology weds itself to scientific beliefs that have long since been outdated: demonology, a three-story universe, belief in the imminent catastrophic terminus of history, etc. Whenever theology permits itself to be enslaved by holding traditional forms to be sacrosanct, it commits the fallacy of absolutizing the relative. To avoid this fallacy and achieve cultural integrity, theology must reinterpret the gospel in the light of the intellectual resources provided by the cultural situation in which it seeks to fulfill its responsibilities. The concern in this volume is restricted to an attempt to develop some of the significant implications for theology in its responsiveness to the influence of secular thought in the philosophical development of the idea of history during the past couple of centuries.

Since the main purpose of this volume is to deal with the

impact of the modern idea of history on the traditional Christian understanding of faith and history, an introductory chapter is called for, stating in broad outlines the eschatological understanding of history that dominated the Western mind from the beginning of the church's existence down until the Renaissance and the Enlightenment. It is not germane to the purpose of this book to enter into a detailed analysis of the historical development of this traditional, eschatological understanding of history. A brief delineation of the basic principles of the traditional understanding of history however is necessary to serve as the historical foundation for the argument of the volume. I have therefore restricted the exposition of the initial chapter to a summary statement of New Testament perspectives on the problem of faith and history, and to Augustine's theology of history. This arrangement is dictated by the fact that at least on this issue it was the New Testament perspective, as modified by Augustine's classic, *The City of God,* which by and large dominated the mind of the Western world until the beginning of the modern period.

The eschatological view of history was eclipsed by the cultural development of Enlightenment rationalism. In this development, eschatology was secularized and replaced by the modern doctrine of progress. In the intellectual climate of the Enlightenment, the traditional Christian faith found itself in crisis. At the same time, however, the fact that many theologians refused to dehistoricize the faith (as the Deists did) itself helped leaders in the latter phase of the Enlightenment to perceive the weakness and even historical fallacy of the spirit of the Enlightenment. Though, to be sure, this was not the only, nor even the major, cause of the decline of Enlightenment rationalism and of the development of modern historical-mindedness. Enlightenment rationalism was broken up from within by the pervasive eighteenth-century movement of skepticism, especially in France; and from without by the force of Romanticism, especially in Germany. Further, because the deep religious hunger of the human spirit eventually tired of being fed nothing but "a mess of ethical and metaphysical crumbs" (Schleiermacher), there emerged the great Evangelical Awakening associated with the Wesleyan move-

ment in Great Britain and the Edwardian movement in the
United States.

Prior to presenting a survey of the birth and development
of the modern idea of history, a consideration of the crisis of
traditional eschatological faith, in the unhistorical climate of
the Enlightenment, is called for, in order to assess the faith-
culture situation in the early phase of modern culture. It was
out of the complexity of this situation that the outlook of
modern historical-mindedness was born.

Two chapters are then devoted to a survey of the philosophical development of the modern idea of history. The first of
these is a general survey of the major phases of this development. The second, which sketches some of the more significant
developments in the science of history in the twentieth century, is restricted to brief summaries of the historiographies of
Benedetto Croce, Arnold J. Toynbee, and R. G. Collingwood.
These three thinkers have been selected because together they
fairly well sum up these historiographical developments. Collingwood (d. 1943) is widely recognized as the most original
and stimulating philosophical historian in twentieth-century
English philosophy. Croce (d. 1952) was without doubt the
most influential Italian philosophical historian of his age. And
Toynbee is perhaps the most popular and influential British
historian of our period.

Following the two chapters that survey the historical development of the modern philosophical idea of history, the
three concluding chapters deal with some of the more significant theological implications of the impact of this modern
philosophical movement on the Christian faith. In Chapter V
I attempt to describe some of the more general implications
of the impact of the historical development on the understanding of the Christian faith. The rise of historical thinking is
perhaps the most significant new element in contemporary
perspective, as compared with new elements of the seventeenth
and eighteenth centuries. The new historical-mindedness has
significantly altered the basic posture of theology. It has finally
shattered the idols of orthodoxy, liberated theology from the
rationalism of the Enlightenment, established a historical approach to self-understanding, and posed new problems of

historical relativism and historicism. In the light of the historical character of all thinking, theology in our day is challenged to wrestle anew with the nature of revelation and with the transcendent dimension of the religious relationship, in order to break through the prison of relativism and historicism.

One basic aspect of the new historical understanding of human life and thought concerns the awareness of the inner-connectedness of all human life and thought in the flow of history, or the historically relational or conditioned character of individuals, communities, ideas, and philosophies. This conditioning inner-connectedness of historic process poses some basic Christological problems. In Chapter VI three such problems are identified and critically dealt with. First, the scandal of particularity in theology's belief in the absolute uniqueness of the historical moment that constitutes its normative center: Jesus the Christ. Second, the problem of how a figure of the remote past can become the source of a vibrant faith in the present. Third, the historical problem of arriving at any certain knowledge of the historical Jesus.

At its inner core the Christian faith takes its shape out of a symbiotic relationship between history and transcendence, for faith's union with the transcendent God is achieved by means of his historical self-manifestation. The revelation in the Christ event, which provides faith with a norm by which all history is judged, is itself grounded in historical events. Hence the perennial problem of the relation of the " Jesus of history " to the "Christ of faith." Through the development of the historical Christianity of the nineteenth century, and the contemporary reaction to it, this problem has become acute once again. Critical contemporary thought about this problem centers mainly about the new quest of the historical Jesus which has emerged among the followers of the Bultmannian school of kerygma theology. My main concern in the concluding chapter is to assess the theological significance of this new quest.

As my sources indicate, I am indebted to numerous thinkers who have been profoundly concerned about the problem of faith and history, and whose writings have provided many germinal seeds for my own thought. I have learned much from the thought of such men as Ernst Troeltsch, Adolf Harnack, H. Richard Niebuhr, Wilhelm Pauck, Rudolf Bultmann, Karl Barth, Paul Tillich, Benedetto Croce, Arnold J. Toynbee, and R. G. Collingwood. For my outline of the development of the modern idea of history, I am especially indebted to Collingwood, whose brilliant survey in this area I have found to be highly illuminating and stimulating.

My gratitude goes to the faculty members of the Divinity School of Yale University for the courtesy extended to me of using their library for the research of much of the content of this volume; to the Offices of The American Association of Theological Schools, for granting me a Faculty Fellowship which helped to make possible a leave of absence from my duties at Lexington Theological Seminary for the research for this volume; and to my colleagues at the Lexington Seminary for sharing the duties of the Dean's office during my absence. I am especially indebted to my secretary, Olive M. Dorman, and to my student, Stephen Jay Brock, for assistance in the composition of the manuscript and for critical proofing.

Portions of this volume were, in substance, given by the author in the M. T. Burt Lectures at Cotner School of Religion and the University of Nebraska, Lincoln, Nebraska, January 3 and 4, 1966. The Lectures were sponsored by Cotner School of Religion and the College of Arts and Sciences of the University of Nebraska.

This volume is designed to be a kind of handbook, especially for college, university, and theological students, and for ministers and theologically concerned laymen. Its modest aim is to acquaint its readers with the development of the modern idea of history in nontheological circles, to show that theology can ill afford to carry on its work in isolation from these philosophical developments, and by focusing critical attention on problems related to the historicoeschatological "center" of the Christian faith in Jesus as the Christ, to deal constructively with these theological problems in the light of conversation with nontheological thinkers in the modern discipline of history.

RALPH G. WILBURN

Lexington, Kentucky

1

The Eschatological View of History in the Biblical-Augustinian Tradition

All religions look through and beyond man's proximate concerns toward life's ultimate. They orient human existence to, and seek reunion with, transcendent reality. Basic differences in religions appear in the ways in which this transcendentalizing of human existence is conceived and effected. In Buddhism (with its Nirvana) and Hinduism (with its Brahman) we get classic types of ahistorical, mystical versions of the transcendentalizing of life. By the use of mystical techniques the religious goal is to banish the illusion of the entire phenomenal world and achieve union with the divine, which as absolutely changeless is conceived as infinitely removed from the flux of finite things.

In classic Greek philosophy we get a similarly ahistorical, but more rational version of this transcendentalizing. The Greeks equated history with the natural order of change and becoming, and sought the liberation of the changeless reason in the transcendental realm of the changeless Absolute (Plato's Ideas and Forms).

Part of the peculiar character of the Christian faith lies in the way in which transcendent reality is conceived, the way it is related to the process of history, and the way this faith achieves the transcendentalizing function. Unlike Buddhism, Hinduism, and the Greek philosophy of religion, Christianity found itself unable to effect the transcendence of faith over finitude by means of any mystical or rational flight from the sphere of historical existence. The Christian faith achieves its victory not by a negation of history but by the redemption of historical existence itself, a redemption in which the sinful distortions of finite existence are conquered.

The positive place of the historical dimension in Christian theology is due partly to Christianity's organic rootage in Judaism. From Judaism a Messianic heritage was derived which provided the basic frame of reference for the Christology of primitive Christianity and which led to the early church's self-understanding as the community of the new covenant, as the goal and consummation of redemptive history.

A Christology that cuts the Christian faith free from all history before the Christ event would therefore be as erroneous as one that severs it from subsequent history and demands that one leap back over the intervening centuries in order to relate himself to Jesus as the Christ. The appearance of Jesus is organically linked both to the Jewish community out of which he came and to the subsequent Christian community of which he is, in some basic sense, the founder.

To an even more radical extent one sees history as integral to the Christian faith in the interpretation of its original historical focus by the doctrine of the incarnation. Here eternity appears in time. God manifests himself in history. The realm of the Spirit is not isolated in a superworld of timelessness, but is present, here and now. The two dimensions of history and transcendence intersect. Neither nature nor history can therefore be thought of as extraneous to the process of redemption. As Herbert Butterfield puts it, "If one moment of time could hold so much as this, then you cannot brush time away and say that any moment of it is mere vanity. Every instant of time becomes 'eschatological.' " [1] Or as Rudolf Bultmann prefers to put it, every instant has "the possibility" of becoming eschatological, a possibility realized in Christian faith.[2]

Christian theology, however, was not at first fully aware of all the historical implications of its doctrine of redemption. The passage of time was required for these to be brought to light. The hope of the "second" coming of Christ was originally conceived as the completion of the "first" coming, the redemptive work of which was only temporarily delayed. As the decades passed, however, and the Second Coming (Parousia) failed to materialize, it was inevitable that the church recognize that it had become a historical phenomenon and that it had a historical mission and destiny.

NEW TESTAMENT PERSPECTIVES

In this introductory chapter we cannot present a detailed analysis of the different perspectives on the problem of faith and history found in the writings of the New Testament. The following brief summary of these perspectives is intended to serve merely as an introduction to this volume. To see the ways in which the development of the modern idea of history has affected the historical dimension of the Christian faith, the latter must first be delineated, at least in terms of its broad outlines.

A basic unity comprehends the different perspectives in the New Testament, a unity rooted in the eschatological understanding of Christian existence. Historical existence is understood in the light of the end of history, by the presence and power of which life's ambiguities and contradictions are overcome, in history fragmentarily and in hope, but perfectly in the final consummation of the Kingdom. Because God is sovereign over all, the fulfillment of faith and hope is definitely coming. Eschatology means the urgency with which life, under the power and lure of the Eternal, presses forward toward its ultimate good (*telos*).

Within the general eschatological outlook of the New Testament writers, however, there is a variety of shifts and emphases, resulting in a plurality of concrete perspectives. In general, four fairly clear perspectives can be identified: (1) the dual eschatology of Paul; (2) futuristic eschatology, expressed, for example, in The Letter to the Hebrews and in Revelation; (3) the movement toward greater historical realism in Luke; and (4) the radical contemporizing of eschatology in John.

In the perspective of Paul, the early church's apocalyptic view of history was retained, with its dualism of cosmic powers correlated with the present age and the future age. The present evil age is under the reign of demonic forces; the future age of righteousness will be inaugurated in a catastrophic way at the imminent day of the Parousia, with its accompanying dramatic events: the descending Lord, the cry of the archangel, the trump of God, the resurrection of the dead, and the Final Judgment (I Thess. 4:16 ff.).

Alongside the apocalyptic view of Paul, however, stood another type of eschatology, which has been described as "realized eschatology," [3] or "an existentialist conception of eschatology." [4] The central focus in this second view of history is the note that the apostle elaborated in a variety of ways, namely, that the decisive eschatological event *has already occurred* — in the death and resurrection of Jesus as the Christ. Therefore, to be in Christ means the end of the old creation and the coming of the new (eschatological) being (II Cor. 5:17), potentially for all men, actually for men of faith. In this latter view of history, the old aeon (under the reign of demonic powers) and the new aeon (of salvation) lie side by side. The relation between the two cannot, therefore, be described in terms of a succession of historical periods. The time of eschatological history, in this view, is not to be regarded as an extension of the time of world history. The time of eschatological existence is existential in character; its central meaning lies in the *quality* of man's relation to God, in the freedom of faith. This time must not be confused with objectively catalogable time computed by *quantitative* elements of measurement borrowed from the categories of space.

These two views of history — the apocalyptic and the existential — exist in tension in the thought of Paul, though as Paul grew older his emphasis on the imminence of the end tended to weaken a bit. The element of truth in apocalyptic eschatology lies in the futuristic thrust of Christian faith and hope, which presses forward to the final consummation of God's work of redemption. To this extent, Paul's retention of apocalyptic inherited from his Jewish tradition is theologically justified. Yet Paul correctly saw that in principle the Christ event radically altered Jewish apocalypticism, for the Christ event brought the Jewish hope of salvation into present realization, its fulfillment into the Now (II Cor. 6:2) of salvation, the *kairos* (Gal. 4:4). Salvation was no longer merely a hope, but in faith a present eschatological reality. (Col. 3:1 ff.)

A second identifiable perspective stands in some contrast to that of Paul. We may take the posture of The Letter to the Hebrews as an expression of this second perspective. Written by an unknown author during the last quarter of the first century, this letter reflects a situation in the church in which the hope of the Parousia had become acutely problematical. The long delay of Christ's Second Coming generated skepticism: the Parousia hope was waning! Christian hands were drooping and Christian knees were weakening. (Heb. 12:12.) The predominant tone of the letter is one of repeated admonition to cling steadfastly to the church's initial confidence — unto the end. (Heb. 3:14; 10:23.)

To be sure, the Pauline note of realized eschatology is not wholly lacking in this letter. But due to the long delay of the Parousia, the Pauline balance between realized eschatology and apocalyptic hope now became unbalanced. And this imbalance seriously affected the confidence of faith. This is perhaps the most tragic aspect of the mistaken belief in the imminent Parousia. The author of Hebrews appears to have had no strong feeling of the nearness of the end, yet he still felt that the Parousia hope was of supreme importance.

Although the Now of salvation is not entirely lacking in the thought of the Hebrews letter, the accent falls on the Then, when Christ will appear a second time, not to deal with sin, but to fulfill the salvation hope of those who wait for him (Heb. 9:28) . The accent falls not on the ultimate reality of our present faith, but on the hope of a future salvation. The Christian life is understood as " a new Exodus " [5] out of this present world, to a heavenly rest.

In Hebrews the force of Paul's existentialist eschatology is thus considerably weakened. While Paul thought of Christians as " risen with Christ " (Col. 3:1 ff.) , the writer of Hebrews thought of them as followers of a heavenly Christ, who at present cling to " the promise of entering his rest" (Heb. 4:1) and who at the end of faithful endurance in history will enter the Sabbath rest. The difference between Paul and the writer of Hebrews is, of course, not absolute, since Paul too clung to the Parousia hope. Yet the difference in emphasis is sufficiently striking that one New Testament scholar has said that the writer of Hebrews was "essentially an eschatologist," whereas Paul was basically "a mystic." [6]

In the main, Erich Dinkler is correct when he argues that in the perspective of the Hebrews letter, "history is taken out of the existence of Christians." [7] Yet not entirely, for the *power* of the future Sabbath rest makes itself felt in historical existence, bestowing courage to endure suffering, abuse, and affliction, as Christian "strangers and exiles on the earth" wait patiently for their suprahistorical reward. The main drift of this letter seems to represent a compensatory glorification of the future at the expense of the present in a way that is hardly justifiable theologically. Such an outlook fails to disclose the full implications of the relevance of the Christian gospel for historical existence.

A third perspective on our problem appears in Luke-Acts. Writing probably in the seventh or eighth decade of the first Christian century, the author was driven to reflect on the delay of the Parousia and the implications of this delay for the church's existence in world history. Luke came to terms with this situation by developing a new concept of church history. He could have resolved the problem of the church's historical situation as did the writer of Hebrews, by simply clinging doggedly to the primitive apocalyptic hope. Instead, he developed a new interpretation of Christian history.

Luke-Acts thus represents the earliest concern to write a history of the church from its historically documented beginnings in the life of Jesus. Luke's explicit purpose was "to write an orderly account" of "the things which have been accomplished among us" from the beginning (Luke 1:1-4). The second part — Acts — traces the development of the church from its beginnings in and expansion from Jerusalem, and its expansion into the Gentile world through the missionary journeys of Paul.

The problematical character of the "wait it out" attitude generated by the hope of the imminent Parousia was implicit from the beginning of the church's existence. If the story of Stephen (Acts, chs. 6 ff.) may be taken as an authentic account of Stephen's outlook and not merely a reflection of Luke's theology, Stephen was one of the earliest to grasp the universal scope of the Christ event. He called for a kind of Christian world mission, which shattered the complacency of the early Hebraic Christian community, a complacency that logically resulted from the hope of the imminent Parousia. William Manson argues [8] that Stephen's manifesto generated a cleavage in the early church. It confirmed the Hebraic Christians in their attitude of passive waiting for the end. While the Jewish-Hellenist leaders who followed Stephen were "scattered," subsequent to Stephen's martyrdom, going out to proclaim the gospel, the Hebrew-Christian apostles declined to participate in this worldwide mission.

The main point of the account of the preaching and martyrdom of Stephen and the subsequent scattering of his Jewish-Hellenist associates was to emphasize Luke's belief that the church has a historic mission: it is to bear its witness, even "to the end of the earth."

Luke formally retained the belief in the Second Coming, but its force was greatly weakened by the comprehensive scheme of salvation history that he developed. The central themes of Luke's theology concern the historical life of Jesus, objectively set forth, the presence and power of the Spirit in the life of the church, and the ministry and mission of the church in history, in the different historical stages of the church's development. Luke developed the concept of different historical periods of salvation history: (1) the period of the Law and the Prophets; (2) the period of Jesus' life and work (the center) ; (3) the period between Jesus and the Parousia, the period of the church. Further, he showed that shifts and changes properly occur in the period of the church due to changes in the historical situation. His portrayal of the foundation period of the apostles and eyewitnesses is deliberately set forth in contrast to the present church situation.

The shift of emphasis in Luke's theology away from the waiting attitude of the primitive church is obviously due to the fact of the church's continuing life in ongoing history. Luke began The Acts with the statement that " it is not for you to know " the date of the last things; he then referred to God's plan and to the Spirit who, as Hans Conzelmann aptly says, " appears as a substitute (alla) for knowledge of the

Last things and makes it unnecessary to know when they will take place." [9] Luke appears to have been the first to develop the phenomenon of the Spirit as a solution to the problems generated by the increasingly distressing delay of the Parousia. By the power of the Spirit the disciples are called to be witnesses "in Jerusalem and in all Judea and Samaria and to the end of the earth " (Acts 1:8).

In Luke's theology, the Last Day has been projected into an indefinite future. The waiting attitude of the primitive church is in large measure overcome; it is replaced by a more positive doctrine of Christian life in history of long duration. Christian ethics still depends on the *fact* of the Final Judgment, but no longer on its imminence. As Conzelmann says, " The longer the time of waiting, the greater the impact of suffering, which makes the expected End 'endlessly' remote." [10] The central theme of Luke's message is thus no longer the imminent appearance of the final Kingdom, but rather the " way " of salvation, during the period of the church's existence in history, however long it may be. Problems related to the daily ordering of Christian life call for consideration. Church existence is no longer a sheer eschatological phenomenon, but is viewed in relation to the church's historical environment. Major concern has to do with the problem of Christian behavior in persecution and martyrdom.

In the fourth perspective on the problem of faith and history in the New Testament, the blunting of the sense of the finality of the cross and resurrection (evident in primitive futuristic eschatology) was boldly overcome by a radical contemporizing of eschatology. In the Gospel of John the accent shifts once again, this time away from the Then of the Parousia to the Now of eternal life. The waiting attitude of the early church is here radically transcended. The conjunction of the two aeons disappears. Existential eschatology is radical and thoroughgoing. Everything turns on the judgment that takes place in Jesus Christ.

By the time the Gospel of John was written,[11] the problem of retaining the mistaken belief in the Second Coming had grown to serious proportions. The deepening disappointment of hope again and again deferred resulted in widespread despair and apathy. Yet this sense of frustration was countered by a theologically dubious fanaticism of some (the Montanists, for example) who arbitrarily closed their minds to the realities of history and clung with vehemence to the Parousia hope.

John proposed a theological resolution of these eschatological difficulties by radically contemporizing the doctrine of the last things, more radically than did Paul. Those who respond to the gospel in faith *already have* " eternal life " (John 5:24). The Final Judgment is not a futuristic event, but a contemporaneous occurrence; it consists in the division of faith and unfaith which occurs now, in the hearing of the message of Jesus (John 3:18; 12:31). That the resurrection is reinterpreted as a depth dimension of the present life of faith, with no relation to a transformation at the temporal terminus of history, is clear in the dialogue between Jesus, Martha, and Mary. Martha understood Jesus' words of assurance in the traditional, apocalyptic sense. She responded that she knew Lazarus would rise again in the resurrection day. Jesus then corrected her interpretation by declaring himself to be the resurrection and the life, and by promising that though the believer die, " yet shall he live," and that he who lives and believes in him shall never die (John 11:23-26).

John attached tremendous weight and significance to the cross and the resurrection of Christ as the final eschatological happening. He located *in this event* the basic happenings formerly regarded as connected with the apocalyptic day: the Final Judgment (John 3:18); the "resurrection from the dead" now transposed and interpreted spiritually (John 5:25-29; 11:23-26); and the return of Christ now regarded as fulfilled by the bestowal of the Spirit on the community of Jesus' followers.[12]

Death, of course, marks the termination of physical existence; but it in no way changes the *essential nature* of the life of the new being in Christ. Death will simply mean the final realization and perfection of the " eternal life " already possessed in faith. The posthistorical perfection of eternal life will be a full participation in the final glory of the Father, the substance of which Christians already possess.

Several observations can be made regarding the significance of the New Testament witness for contemporary theology, on the problem of faith and history. One finds here no "philosophy of history," no logical schema for the periodization of the whole course of history. New Testament faith was content to leave the problem of world history to the mystery of Providence, though faith was persuaded that God is nonetheless working out his purposes in history.

As pointed out above, the dynamic thrust toward the realization of future possibilities for good constitutes an element of truth in apocalyptic eschatology. Yet a growing historical realism gradually compelled the church to modify the primitive form of its hope. Due to the canonical development of Scripture, the Parousia hope was formally retained, but postponed into an indefinite future (Augustine), thereby losing much of the ethical significance that it held for primitive Christianity. As the hope of the Parousia moved to the periphery of Christian thought and concern, Christians gradually became more historical-minded. At the same time, however, the dynamic impingement of life's Ultimate upon the present was transferred from the Parousia focus to the Sacraments and the presence of the Holy Spirit. These shifts in emphases laid the basis for the posture of medieval Christianity.

The movement of the church away from the too unhistorical otherworldliness of its primitive outlook toward a more positive orientation to its place and mission in ongoing history represented a valid theological development; for implicit in this development was a dynamic sense of the church's mission in history. Yet this development was not without its dangers, especially when Constantine and Theodosius bestowed political sanction on Christianity. Religion's attainment of cultural respectability always carries with it the temptation to be sucked into the world's ethos.

At the one extreme, we get the otherworldly, pilgrim concept of church existence; at the other, we get a church that has lost sight of the God relationship and has become a mere pious echo of a secular culture. Both are fallacious ways of understanding faith's relation to historic process. The church is *in* the world; it must therefore refuse the escape hatch of the pilgrim notion. But the church is not *of* the world; therefore it must not be conformed to the world but, rather, seek to transform the world, by the purposes of God for human existence. The church lives out of transcendence. That is, it shares in the transfiguring power of the life and love of God, so that the meaning of this transcendence may find concrete expression and fulfillment within the historical orders of human existence.

Numerous problems, of course, did not fall within the horizon of theological concern of the church during the New Testament period, problems brought to light only by subsequent history. For example, the New Testament writers were not as critically aware as modern thinkers of the problems related to the historical character of all human thinking that is now popularly summed up by the phrase "historical relativism." The modern problem of the relation between the "historical Jesus" and the "Christ of faith" appears not to have assumed the critical proportions that characterize it in our day. This is probably due to primitive Christianity's dominant concern with the "history of salvation," though awareness of this problem was not entirely lacking.[13] Nor was there any grappling with the thorny problem of Christian social ethics, for the apocalyptic hope generated an attitude of relative indifference toward the sociopolitical institutions of the day. Subsequently, the full ethical implications of the gospel had to be thought through afresh in view of the extension of history far beyond what the New Testament writers ever dreamed.

When all negative judgments have been made, however, in regard to the New Testament outlook on faith and history, there remain several basic motifs that are relevant to the work of contemporary theology.

1. *The Christological Motif.* In the Christian faith, salvation is anchored to a central historical focus: the events of the life, teachings, and death of Jesus of Nazareth. Faith believes that in and through these historical events God has acted to disclose himself for man's salvation. The fact that participation in the Christ reality is historically mediated gives an *evangelical definiteness* to the structure of the God relationship of faith.

2. *The Ontological Motif.* This second motif is found in

the tension that results from the dynamic interrelationship of history and transcendence. The alternatives to the New Testament eschatological understanding of existence are, on the one hand, an ahistorical mysticism or rationalism, and on the other, secular philosophies of history, which hold that history carries its meaning within itself. The former represents a radical type of religious transcendence; the latter, a radical immanentism, which finds numerous modern expressions: the evolutionary view of history connected with the modern idea of progress; the humanism of atheistic existentialism; the dialectical materialism of the Marxian view of history.

Christianity recognizes elements of truth in both of these alternatives. With the ahistorical outlook it recognizes that the source of the meaning of history is not to be found in history per se, for this meaning derives from the transcendent Creator-Redeemer God. It is not we, but he who informs history with ultimate purpose and meaning. Yet with historism Christianity recognizes that compensatory otherworldly idealism is a most unsatisfactory kind of meaning, and that authentic existence is possible only if its meaning is realizable in history.

At the same time, the Christian eschatological view of history is opposed to both the alternatives mentioned above and seeks to include in its synthesis of history and transcendence what each of the alternatives omits. Life can possess ultimate meaning only in the eschatological view. Secular philosophies of history eliminate the dimension of transcendence and are left with no logical basis for holding existence to possess any all-embracing, ultimate meaning, while traditional rationalism (and similarly mysticism) seeks to overcome the partialities and the becomingness of history by the liberation of the changeless reason in the transcendent realm of the Absolute.

3. *The Anthropological Motif.* A third basic motif lies in the existentialist eschatology of the New Testament which embodies the anthropological significance of God's supreme act of revelation. The apostle Paul never tired of emphasizing that to exist as a Christian means to live life in the freedom of the Spirit. This freedom of existence in faith means liberation from the mistakes of one's past, a liberation achieved by accepting God's acceptance and by living life anew, out of the

power of God's love (Rom. 5:5). Creative freedom also means freedom *for* God, for his Kingdom of "righteousness and peace and joy in the Holy Spirit" (Rom. 14:17). By the power of the Spirit (love) one is released from the inhibiting bonds of self-centeredness, released for a life of service in love. Man's true destiny is thus found in eschatological faith, which alone turns his freedom into a source of new life, "delivering the real essence of his existence,"[14] and making possible the fulfillment of his destiny, even amid the frustrations of existence.

4. *The Dynamic Motif.* Whatever distortions were engendered by the apocalyptic aspect of New Testament eschatology, implicit in it was a sense of dynamic thrust toward future possibilities for good. The form which this prophetic eschatology assumed is evident in the New Testament awareness of the frontier between church and Kingdom. This frontier established a distinction between the "already" and the "not yet" of the realization of man's destiny.

The New Testament has much to say about the "already" of faith's inheritance.[15] The church is an eschatological community, a community that participates in "the powers of the age to come" (Heb. 6:5). Yet the "already" of the church's being becomes sadly distorted if it is not held in dynamic tension with the "not yet" of its destiny. To the extent that the church is an imperfect manifestation of love and righteousness, it cannot be identified absolutely with the Kingdom.

The church must live in the dynamic tension. It must refuse two temptations that have dogged its footsteps. The one temptation is to absolutize the status quo; the other is to become radically otherworldly and develop an escapist religion. The former allows the "already" to swallow up the "not yet," thereby forfeiting the blessedness of hope. The latter permits the "not yet" to eliminate any positive significance of the "already," thereby losing the relevance of the Kingdom goal for historical existence. Both distortions terminate with a static view of history. This failure results in the loss of the ability to use the Kingdom ideal as a fulcrum by which to move history.

Faith is as it ought to be only if it "[strains] forward to what lies ahead" (Phil. 3:13). The goal of Christ's Lordship is universal in character; it is to embrace all creation in an ultimate unity. (Eph. 1:22-23; I Cor. 15:25-28.) The ultimate character of this Lordship gives to the church its most profound task. It is the ultimate basis of the validity of Christian ethical action. It is what makes Christian ethics religious, in the ultimate sense of the term. It is what bestows upon the church its brightest hope and its deepest spiritual strength.

5. *The Resurrection Motif.* A final motif of the New Testament is found in faith's victory over the nonbeing that characterizes historical existence. This nonbeing is symbolized most powerfully by death. In historical existence everything seems to be forever wasting away; nothing abides. The "time" of historical existence is perpetually perishing. As Isaiah put it:

> All flesh is grass,
>   and all its beauty is like the flower of the field.
> The grass withers, the flower fades,
>
> . . . .
>
>   surely the people is grass.
>
> — Isa. 40:6-7

The heart of man is dazzled by a perception of beauty, so that with Goethe's Faust, he cries out, "Stand still; thou art so beautiful." Yet the grandeur quickly passes, and like a butterfly slipping through the fingers of a child's hand, the glory disappears. All of life seems to be like this: our pleasures, our successes, our creative labors. The rich and abundant quality of our experience vanishes, its joy fades, and its beauty is swallowed up by an aching, hungry void.

Faith's victory over the tragic transiency of historical time is dramatically expressed by the symbol of the resurrection. This symbol means that the negativities of human existence are overcome by the power of the Eternal, whose creativity in the beginning pushed back the chaos of nonbeing and created the world, whose grace overcomes the negativities of man's sin, and the power of whose eternity transcends the all-consuming flux of historical time.

> "The grass withers, and the flower falls,
>   but the word of the Lord abides for ever."
>
> — I Peter 1:24-25

The resurrection symbolizes the hope of eschatological faith, generating a vision beyond the categories of knowledge to conceptualize. It symbolizes the eternalizing of our fleeting existence and the eternalizing of our ending, finite lives. We cannot get beyond Luther's statement that the Christian knows *that* he hopes, but not *what* he hopes. But eschatological faith experiences the ultimate power of the transcendent God, by which faith overcomes the anxiety arising out of awareness of man's finitude. It is given to faith to know that somehow the values realized in the brief span of historical existence cannot ultimately be lost, but in God's mysterious way are gathered up into an eternal abidingness.

AUGUSTINE'S THEOLOGY OF HISTORY

With the passage of time the church's awareness of being an empirical movement in world history deepened and increased. The growth of this awareness was augmented by the fact that the central authority of the church gradually came to focus in the living voice of the episcopate, for thereby the sense of the importance of the church as a historical institution came into prominence. The early Pauline idea of the church as a Spirit-controlled type community gradually faded as the church developed external sanctions and securities by structuring its being about the office of the bishop. As the church did this it was inevitable that attempts be made to legitimize the institutional church by setting down, in scientific fashion, a chronicle of bishops, reaching back to the apostolic period. Such attempts were made, for example, by Irenaeus [16] and Eusebius.[17] Eusebius wrote objective church history, thereby correlating the history of Christianity with world history.

Despite the problematic character of the Parousia belief and despite the church's rejection of Montanism as heretical (mainly because it stood in opposition to episcopal authority), throughout the second and third centuries the feeling pervaded the consciousness of the church that the Last Day was not very far away. This feeling is reflected in the Didache [18] and in the writings of Ignatius,[19] Polycarp,[20] Barnabas,[21] and Irenaeus.[22] Barnabas established a mathematical schema for a chronicle of world history: the six days of creation meant that God would finish all things in "six thousand years." [23]

In A.D. 221 Julius Africanus published his chronicle of the world, dating the appearance of Christ in the flesh in the year 5500 of world history, and predicting the apocalyptic end of history in A.D. 500.[24] Hippolytus of Rome (d. ca. A.D. 236) accepted the six-thousand-year theory, but calculated that 5,738 years had elapsed and that the Last Day would occur in 262 more years.[25] Lactantius (d. ca. A.D. 320) similarly estimated that world history would continue for about two hundred years.[26]

With these developments the idea of total world history made its appearance, a concept not to be found among the ancient Greek and Roman historians. Not until Augustine (d. A.D. 430), however, do we find a Christian scholar who tackled the problem of faith and history with critical thoroughness. The rich fruit of his fourteen years' reflection on the problem is found in his famous treatise *The City of God*. Augustine's portrayal of the *Civitas Dei* and the *Civitas Terrena* reflects the relation between Christianity as an eschatological community and the contemporary sociopolitical situation. Yet it also reflects the inner conflict of Augustine's own being, which is generalized into the basic ontological conflict that constitutes the heart of the drama of all history.

By a profound restatement of the Biblical perspective, Augustine overwhelmed and eliminated the classic cyclical view of history. In the latter view, history is understood as an endless round of recurring cycles. Human generations follow the natural law of periodicity, without beginning and without end, with no real purpose and no future. In the Biblical-Augustinian view, history has a definite beginning and an ultimate end. The eschatological event of faith means also that something happens *which never happened before,* something that liberates one from his former "misery" and bestows on him "eternal bliss." [27] By thus distinguishing man's essential being from the being of nature, and by delineating the transcendent dimension of man created in the image of God, it has been said that Augustine discovered personality and thereby also history.[28]

By the power of Biblical faith, Augustine thus replaced the analogy of the cycle by the analogy of the arrow. But the progression of the eschatologically historical arrow is uneven throughout the City of God's pilgrimage on earth, due to the fact that its members are never wholly freed from man's estrangement from life's Ultimate. Christian pessimism, however, is irradiated with hope, for while man's ultimate beatitude is not present in his life, in patience he waits for it in the future, and is thus " blessed by hope." [29]

Augustine's understanding of the ultimate meaning of history focused in Jesus Christ. As the God-man, Christ is both the way and the destination of man — " God our journey's end, and man our way unto it." [30] In the incarnation the disclosure of the universal way of salvation was decisively *defined* but not *confined,* for in essence, though not in fullness, this Logos-light has been granted by God's mercy to man throughout all history.[31] The humility of Christ (God in the *forma servi*) shatters man's sinful pride and teaches him that humility is the way and sphere in which all goodness is perfected.[32] This meaning of the incarnation became the key to Augustine's understanding of the perennial conflict between the *Civitas Terrena* and the *Civitas Dei.*

The two societies originate in two kinds of love. The *Civitas Terrena* finds its definitive principle and force in self-love and pride which even dared to despise God. The *Civitas Dei* finds its definitive principle and force in the love of God, which is the essence of humility. Pride generates lust for sovereignty and domination, for its essence lies in a self-centered love of power. Humility generates outgoing goodwill for others, for its essence lies in a God-centered power of love.

Both societies have a historical development. But the development of the City of God represents no progressive victory over the earthly city, such as one finds, for example, in Joachim of Fiore's vision of the final historical " Age of the Spirit." According to Augustine, the two societies " are confused and comixed " until the Last Day.[33] The forward movement of the conflict represents an augmenting of the tension — until the Parousia.

Both societies share in common the temporal goals of human

morality, good citizenship, and civic peace. Both societies utilize temporal goods and share in common man's mortality and finitude, yet to different ends. The heavenly society regards temporal goods as means to an eternal end. The earthly city regards temporal goods as the *only* good, thereby distorting them into the end (*telos*) of life. In this way the misery of the *Civitas Terrena* only increases the more.

Augustine was the heir of two traditions in the Christian heritage: (1) the ecclesiastical-dualistic tradition, and (2) the philosophical-apologetic tradition. The latter was best represented by the broad humanism made possible by the Alexandrian Logos doctrine, which viewed all extra-Christian value and truth as germinal seeds of the cosmic Logos. The former, represented by the ethics of Tertullian, made a sharp, absolute cleavage between the pre-Christian life under the reign of sin, and the new realm of grace under Christ. With his many-faceted mind, Augustine was somehow able to incorporate both of these traditions into his theological system.

Due to the twofold heritage of these traditions, Augustine was able to maintain, yet at the same time relativize, the antithesis between the *Civitas Dei* and the *Civitas Terrena*. Man's sin is simply a "corruption" of a fundamentally good nature.[34] The Romans are less bad than others, because of the Roman love of human glory.[35] On the other hand, members of the City of God on earth are not wholly free from self-love and pride,[36] though they do strive for perfection.

By relativizing the antithesis of the two societies, Augustine could regard the earthly society as *essentially* the world of sinful humanity outside of Christ, while at the same time arguing that in its political and natural organization the *proper end* of the earthly society is to protect and to promote the City of God. In its inner essence the earthly city is evil; yet in the providence of God it serves a good end, for law and order are necessary for the promotion and spread of the gospel.[37] It was only subsequent to his controversy with the Donatists, however, that Augustine went so far in his synthesis of church and state that he contended that, as a final resort, it is proper for the sword of the state to be used to instill a wholesome fear into persons prone to join schismatic sects, and to punish heretical dissenters, in the hope of leading them to surrender to the true faith.

It would be erroneous, however, to construe Augustine's idea of the two cities in a way which *equates* them with the institutional church and the state.[38] They are, rather, two types of human existence, eschatological and secular. It is nevertheless true to Augustine to interpret the church as the City of God *insofar* as the church participates in the liberating power of the Spirit. The state is similarly the earthly city, *insofar* as it embodies the principles of self-love and lust for power. It would probably be correct to say that for Augustine, the state is fraught with *representative* significance for the *Civitas Terrena*. Yet at the same time the state holds *typological* significance for the *Civitas Dei;* Jerusalem as a political community is thus " holy " only in the typological sense.[39]

The grand finale of the drama of history will occur at the Parousia. Though Augustine had little patience with " empty-headed " apocalyptic date setters, he still believed in the literal terminus of history at the Parousia. The idea of a " bodily " resurrection taxed Augustine's intellectual powers.[40] Some may find comfort in his belief that excessive obesity and embarrassing skinniness will be duly corrected at the resurrection. Yet the " end " of the miracle of the resurrection is the matter of supreme importance: " To enjoy God, the unchangeable good, without any molestation, and to remain in Him forever without delay or doubt, or deceit of error." [41] The destiny of the *Civitas Dei* will thus vindicate God's eternal mercy. The destiny of the *Civitas Terrena* will be that, with resurrected bodies suitably adapted to their destiny, members of this society will be damned to suffer in eternal fire, thereby vindicating God's justice. Thus, according to Augustine, the inequities and ambiguities of history will ultimately be resolved. In the Last Day, God's judgments (now also present but in large measure hidden from human eyes) will be fully disclosed. Then all shall behold the felicity of the saints and the misery of the wicked.

By the power of the Biblical faith Augustine transcended the cosmic dualism of his early years among the Manichees and generated a persistent belief in the unitary coherence of all things, under the power of the Creator-Redeemer God. Though rationally undeveloped, there was present in his thought the idea of the unity of the whole of world history. He recognized certain positive ways in which different cultures and historical epochs contribute to the divine plan of world history. He saw evidences of this plan in the diversity of languages, nations, and laws, by which men seek to establish and preserve earthly peace.[42] It has been argued that Augustine was the first thinker to develop the idea that the whole of history represents an actualization of a divine purpose, and that, therefore, every nation has its own unique mission to fulfill in the drama of world history.[43] One must, however, guard against overemphasizing Augustine's "philosophy of history," for world history held no intrinsic interest for Augustine, an eschatological pilgrim bound for the promised land.

Augustine's idea that the unity of history centers in Providence stands in significant contrast to many modern views of history's unity. Hegel held a rational view of history's unity, elaborating Reason as an imminent principle working itself out in the dialectical development of history. Karl Marx absolutized the factor of economic value and made it the rational center of his dialectical materialism. As Robert W. McLaughlin says,[44] Augustine saw history from above; Hegel from within; Marx from below.

While Augustine's faith in Providence was not wholly blind,[45] he underscored the Biblical belief that man's rational grasp of its unity can at best be only partial and fragmentary. Faith answers the question posed by life's evils by clinging to the belief that God does nothing without reason, but frankly admitting that divine reason infinitely transcends human reason. At the same time, however, Augustine felt it to be not inappropriate for faith to seek as much understanding as possible. He therefore advocated the Neoplatonic doctrine that equates evil with nonbeing and good with being, a doctrine that interprets human vices as mere privations (or corruptions) of the good.[46] It is questionable whether this Neoplatonic interpretation of evil in terms of ontological negativity is wholly consistent with Augustine's more Biblical view of moral evil as something positive, namely, the rebellion of finite wills to the will of their Creator. Yet Augustine clung to both views.

Augustine also struck out a Stoic solution, tackling the problem of evil by arguing for a concept of the universe as an aesthetic, teleological unity. Aesthetic unity demands contrasts. What we call evil, either moral or physical, thus constitutes the minor chords in the symphony of the universe.[47] As Augustine's thought grew more Biblical, this Stoic solution took on a more Biblical character. God's goodness and power are such, said Augustine, that he would not permit evil to exist were he not able to bring good even out of evil.[48] Evil qua evil is not good. But the fact that evil exists alongside the good is itself a good. Otherwise, the existence of evil would not be permitted by the omnipotent God.[49]

Augustine never wholly abandoned his rational attempts to resolve the problem of evil. The force of these arguments was considerably weakened, however, by his mature emphasis on the perversion of the will through original sin and by the dominant otherworldly orientation of his idea of man's destiny. How can one think of the world as an orderly whole if some attain eternal salvation while others do not? The *really* good life would seem no longer to be existence in God's aesthetically good creation. The *real* good is, rather, to be rescued from " the mass of perdition "[50] of this present world and saved for the world to come. Augustine was finally obliged to rest back on the notion of the inscrutable decrees of divine election. Here his reflections on theodicy terminated. While Augustine never wholly lost the sense of this-worldly aesthetic joy, in the oscillation of his mind between such joy and sorrow over the sin-corrupted world the latter finally prevailed and became the more dominating mood.

Augustine seems never to have rationally resolved the paradox of divine sovereignty and human freedom, though he wrestled with the problem throughout his life. In the struggle against the Pelagians, he was led to affirm absolute predestination. Both the demands of God and the power of will to fulfill them are gifts of God.[51] But the absoluteness of predestination is softened a bit by the distinction Augustine drew between " prevenient " grace and " cooperative " grace. Grace *operates without us* to make us willing; but once we have the will to the good, grace *cooperates with us*.[52] The absoluteness of divine sovereignty is further modified by Augustine's explicit statement that God is *not* the giver of evil wills.[53] Yet in the very next breath he affirmed that *all* wills are subject to God, since they have no power except as God gives it to them. It is clear, however, that even Augustine balked at making God the *direct* cause of human defects and corruptions. Created good, he argued, man is corrupt by choice.[54] To say the least, Augustine failed to make altogether clear how the two beliefs logically cohere: (1) all power of will is of God; (2) the power of an evil will is not of God.

A few summary statements can be made regarding the general significance of Augustine's understanding of faith and history. First, a realistic analysis of human selfhood confirms the Biblical-Augustinian teaching regarding the self-centered predicament that lies at the root of man's ontological estrangement. One has but to scratch the surface of any self to discover the inner demon of self-love or pride, to use Augustine's key terms for sin.

Second, not only in regard to sin, but also to grace, Augustine spoke of realities in his own experience. This experiential character of his theology is given expression in the phrase by which he often summed up his all-consuming concern: " God and the soul." And this God relationship was profoundly altered by his experience of the Logos incarnate in Jesus the Christ. One may take issue with specific details and aspects of Augustine's Christology, but he cannot deny that Augustine's thought was profoundly determined by the Biblical perspective which finds the center of history in the eschatological Christ event.

Third, the positive significance of Augustine's theology of history for subsequent views of history in Western culture is not always adequately appreciated. The Biblical-Augustinian theology of history is the historical source of its perverted, secular forms of expression both in the modern gospel of progress and in the Marxian materialization of eschatological history. Both of these modern " gospels " are eschatological in the sense that they view history under the idea of dynamic development toward a goal. Secularized views though they are, they derive whatever spiritual force they possess from the dynamic idea of history released in the Western world by the Biblical-Augustinian outlook on human existence.

Fourth, while Augustine said more about the mystery of Providence than he had a right to say, especially in his rigid predestinarianism, his recognition of the dimension of mystery behind the drama of history is well taken. Augustine was not opposed to discovering all that can be learned about the "general laws" of history through empirical investigation. There may well be "recurrent patterns," as Arnold J. Toynbee suggests. However, in view of the failure of rationalistic views of history adequately to account for the meaning-defying surds of history, Augustine's belief in the mystery of Providence becomes more plausible if the idea that there is a meaning to the whole drama of history be given credence. As a reply to the high pretensions of rationalism (Hegel's system, for example), there is real point to Charles N. Cochrane's retort that "it constitutes an audacious anthropomorphism, a kind of sky-writing which projects upon the cosmos a merely human rationality and translates it into an account of nature and of God." [55] To say the least, Augustine's awareness of the limitations of human reason is eminently more sound than the high pretensions of rationalism.

Fifth, we may here leave aside the ancient Hindu view that held the phenomenal world to be totally without meaning. The contemporary alternatives to the Biblical-Augustinian eschatological understanding of history are: (1) the humanistic view which says that history contains or makes (existentialism) its own meaning, and (2) the subhuman view of Communism, which absolutizes the material aspect of human existence.

Should the technocratic ideology of modern materialism win out in the contemporary spiritual struggle of man, one shudders to contemplate the horrible shrinkage of human values that would ensue. An eschatological interpretation of human existence does not, of course, stand in conflict with the development of scientific technology. Used as means (and not end), the latter possesses positive significance for the fulfillment of life. But a technocratic ideology that not only stifles spiritual growth but destroys the very roots of religion is quite another matter. It is this technocratic ideology which in our day is competing with the gospel for the possession of the mind of man.

Christianity has much more positive affinity with the alternative of humanism, though Christianity holds that the type of humanism which seeks its source *only within* history is a truncated humanism. With no ontological context or transcendent source of meaning, human history is, in the final analysis, reduced to a meaningless, even farcical, episode on one of the minor planets. For where the whole is without meaning, any momentary meaning created by man is radically precarious and in the final analysis nullified.

On the negative side, a few crucial questions must be raised. First, while agreeing in general with Augustine's eschatological view of history, does not the dominant otherworldly character of his type of eschatology blunt the dynamic historical possibilities of eschatology? His theology was not as otherworldly as Christian Gnosticism, for in many ways he found ultimate meaning *in* historical existence. Christian hope gives meaning and direction to the whole of existence. Love of God and neighbor infuses existence with eschatological quality and determines the ethical structures of existence.[56] But the question is: Did Augustine adequately develop the relevance of eschatology for existence? Did he adequately envisage the possibilities of historical approximations to the Kingdom of God?

The historical realization of life's *telos* always remains ambiguous and problematical. Agreed. But much too otherworldly are Augustine's statements that the supreme good is not to be found in this life,[57] that in history we have no hold on salvation and can only wait for it in hope,[58] and that the church merely wanders like a stranger on earth.[59]

In making this negative judgment one should not fail to appreciate the historical forces which generated this otherworldly distortion of Augustine's eschatology. His thought was strongly shaped by the Neoplatonic idea of the many as only quasi real, as compared with the transcendent One, the really real. His *City of God* was written in the midst of the degeneration and collapse of the Roman civilization. And Augustine too shared deeply the pervasive feeling of ancient Catholic Christianity regarding the evils of mortality and decay, and the prevailing tendency to think of salvation mainly as resurrection to immortality beyond history. Hence, the present blessings of Christian existence could only be viewed as promise and pledge of eternal life, but not as containing the *final reality* of faith. Christian existence was thus reduced to a prologue to man's destiny, a mere preparation [60] for the main event.

Second, the unity of history finds its source in a reality that transcends history. Agreed. But a question must be raised regarding the dialectic of judgment and mercy in terms of which Augustine explicated the nature of this transcendent reality. Here we touch again his doctrine of predestination, which stems from his belief in the absolute omnipotence of God.

Augustine gave exegetical reasons for his doctrine of predestination. At those who objected to his doctrine he could even throw the " infallible Scripture " in a blunt and unreasonable way.[61] But deeper than Scripture were his theological and philosophical reasons, which demanded that God's wrath *and* mercy be vindicated in objective ways. Heaven and hell were therefore demanded by the inner nature of the divine.[62]

Augustine erred at this central point because he failed to derive his doctrine of election exclusively from the Christological center. Had he done so, he could have avoided many knotty problems in his doctrine of election. Karl Barth has correctly observed that the decisive finality of God's self-revelation in Jesus Christ is obscured and overshadowed by the inscrutable will of Augustine's hidden God, with his eternal decree of reprobation. Barth has supplied [63] a much needed corrective of the Augustinian tradition by radically subordinating the idea of election to the single, wholly unified will of God disclosed in Jesus Christ. Such a Christological approach to the problem eliminates the idea of eternal decrees of election standing independently of, and behind and above, the merciful will of God in Christ. Correctly to speak of election is therefore to speak of the gospel, and *only* of the gospel.

The principle of unity in history is found in the purpose of

God. Agreed. But the moral disunity of history should not be construed in such a way that this conflict is read back into the heart of God, thereby making it impossible to conceive of God as a unity. The conflict should, rather, be understood as a conflict between God's will for man's redemption and man's rebellious freedom. The principle and ultimate meaning of historical existence is God's creative love. The source of moral disunity lies in man's responsible ignorance and in the moral turpitude of his will.

Third, in moments of deepest reflection Augustine was aware of the relativity of historical existence, including the empirical church. This Biblical-Platonic awareness led him to see that the *Civitas Dei* is an eschatological reality that cannot be actualized in history. In one passage he complained vigorously against the doctrine that identifies the Kingdom with "the church which is at this time." The church is only a gathering of persons for " a future and eternal life." [64] Only in eternity, beyond history, is the *reality* of the heavenly society to be found.

Through the Donatist controversy, however, Augustine was led to attribute to the *institutional* church, with its infallible dogma and saving Sacraments, qualities that in his more spiritual moments of reflection he was willing to apply only to the *spiritual* community constituted by grace, on the one hand, and by faith, hope, and love, on the other. The concept of the church that was the heartthrob of Augustine's own soul focused in the reality of God's immediately experienced grace and the response of faith, hope, and love. At heart, Augustine remained a mystic, not a Sacramentarian. But as Adolf Harnack has aptly said, "Augustine subordinated the notion of the Church and Sacraments to the spiritual doctrine of God, Christ, the gospel, faith and love as far as that was at all possible about 400 A.D." [65]

Augustine was too unhistorical in his understanding of the church. He therefore introduced new errors into the understanding of faith's relation to history. By drawing a veil (so to speak) over the historical relativity of all doctrinal and ecclesiastical forms of church expression, he helped to perpetuate the illusion of an infallible church and thereby (quite contrary to the main emphasis in *The City of God*) helped to establish an idolatrous attitude in the inner citadal of faith itself. It is one of the ironies of history that Augustine, who so eloquently exposed the basic sin of pride, himself paved the way for the sin of ecclesiastical pride in medieval Christianity.

By and large, the Biblical-Augustinian view of faith and history prevailed throughout the medieval period and the sixteenth-century Reformation of the church, both Protestant and Catholic. The most significant reinterpretation of the traditional perspective, during the medieval period, is perhaps to be found in the theology of Joachim, the apocalyptic prophet of Fiore (d. ca. 1202), whose efforts at a spiritual reform of the church were largely unsuccessful. Joachim and the Joachimites were unable to reform the Augustinian view of history, which had dominated the mind of the church for more than seven centuries. The revolutionary implications of Joachim's teachings, however, were drawn out by his followers among the Franciscans of the thirteenth and fourteenth centuries, who saw in the figure of Joachim the spiritual counterpart of John the Baptist, and in Francis of Assisi the " new Messiah " of the New Age.

It is not germane to the purpose of this volume to set forth Joachim's doctrine of the three ages of salvation history, corresponding to the three Persons of the Trinity. Joachim's mathematicoprophetic imagination produced a complicated series of wheels within wheels, as he spun out his view of history. His understanding of faith and history grew out of his lively interest in the apocalyptic teachings of the Biblical writings, his allegorical method of exegesis, and his readings in traditional patristic exegesis and chronography.

From Adam to the Parousia, salvation history was, for Joachim, a developmental process, in which a lower form of spiritual existence gives way to a higher form. Such a developmental view enabled him to maintain a conservative attitude toward the institutional church while yet taking a prophetic outlook on the future, in which he saw the Papal Church giving way to the formation of a wholly spiritual church, the final eschatological community to be fully realized in the third historical age, the Age of the Spirit. It was his calculation that the final age would dawn about A.D. 1260.

Contrary to Joachim's intention, the final result of his spiritual thrust toward a betterment of human existence in the future is found in the secularization of Christian eschatology and in the modern doctrine of progress. The secular counterpart of Joachim's Age of the Spirit is found in Francis Bacon's New Atlantis. One may perhaps say that the birth and growth of modern science was the remote outcome of Joachim's prophecy regarding a new age in history; but the new age turned out to be a far cry from the final age of Joachim's vision. He was certainly correct in discerning that something new was about to happen, but as to the character of the new age, he missed the mark considerably.

With the Renaissance came a transition from an ecclesiastically dominated culture to a broader type of culture in which religion assumed a different place in the entire cultural enterprise. Religion now found itself obliged to compete with the steady, vigorous growth of nonreligious intellectual concerns, which though not directly opposed to religion, were competing with it for the interest and attention of individuals and groups. In modern culture, born during the Renaissance, science, politics, art, music, and philosophy are no longer under the control of the church, nor indeed should they be.

The humanism of the Renaissance generated a fresh and vital interest in history, which focused in its adulation of ancient classical culture and literature. The Renaissance, however, did not develop a new idea of history. It was, therefore, inevitable that the Renaissance should revive the ancient Greek cyclical view of history. The humanism of the Renaissance, however, put new blood into the heart of the church and helped to make possible the Protestant Biblical reform of the sixteenth century. Also, in recovering the Greek love for the beauty of natural forms, the Renaissance pointed up a woeful lack in the traditional otherworldiness of the Christian faith.

In the religiophilosophical aspect of Renaissance humanism, the religion of modern rationalism was in process of formation, which reached its flowering period during the Enlightenment. It was present during the period of the Renaissance, in the main, only in its beginnings. Yet the negative reaction to the historical particularism of the Christian doctrine of revelation was already manifest in the Renaissance, coupled with a strong impulse toward a broad, universal humanism. One of the most popular ways of dealing with this conflict was that advocated by Erasmus, who became perhaps the most influential exponent of Renaissance humanism. Erasmus proposed a reinterpretation of the symbols of the Christian tradition. They were to be viewed as *suggestive symbols* of a natural, universal morality. By this method Erasmus hoped to give full validity to the spirit of rational universalism, yet without wholly rejecting the particularism of the Christian tradition.

In the transition from the Renaissance to the Enlightenment, the spirit of rationalism moved beyond the Erasmian method. The religion of reason finally attempted to liberate itself completely from any and all historical particularisms, retaining in any religion only what is in common to all. This more thoroughgoing type of rationalism is found, for example, in Herbert of Cherbury (1583–1648), the " Father of English Deism." The philosophical influence of the humanism of the Renaissance led finally to the negation of eschatology and of the concepts of transcendence and providence. Of the two great ideals of Augustine, the City of God and ascetic holiness, the Renaissance interest in man's universal humanity destroyed the first and its unbounded exultation in this-worldly life eliminated the second.

II

The Crisis of Faith in the Unhistorical Rationalism of the Enlightenment

The Renaissance had only an academic interest in the past, or found in its historic sources a sort of Romanticist release from the drabness of church dogma and the bonds of its authority, which too long held in restraint the freedom of the human mind. The Renaissance represents the transition of European culture from domination by ecclesiastical tradition to a broader outlook on human existence. The concept of Universal Humanity was the formative ideal that inspired the intellectual labors of the Renaissance. As is evident in the illustrious figure of Desiderius Erasmus, however, there was not as yet a total break with the Christian tradition, even if Erasmian humanism proposed a symbolic reinterpretation of traditional symbols.

A BREAK WITH THE PAST

The rapid development of the new, physical sciences of the seventeenth century and the creative thrust toward the future which its success generated finally gave birth to a full-orbed rationalism, which lost the sense of organic relationship with the past and took delight and pride in its own scientifically enlightened thinking, setting the latter in bold contrast to the dark period of the "middle" ages. Insofar as the men of the Enlightenment had any view of history, it was a view that set the present age of scientific thought in sharp contrast to the past, which they construed as a prescientific era of religious superstition. The general character of the Enlightenment must thus be regarded as a gradual secularizing of human culture, and the evolving concept of progress during the Enlightenment as a gradual secularizing of the teleology of Christian theology.

The Enlightenment must therefore be regarded as a radical new phase of Western culture. J. B. Bury has well written:

Ubiquitous rebellion against tradition, a new standard of clear and precise thought, which affects even literary expression, a flow of mathematical and physical discoveries so rapid that ten years added more to the sum of knowledge than all that had been added since the days of Archimedes, the introduction of organized co-operation to increase knowledge by the institution of the Royal Society at London, the Academy of Sciences at Paris, Observatories — realizing Bacon's Atlantic dream — characterize the opening of a new era.[1]

At the beginning of the new movement the man who perhaps did more than any other to influence the future development of Western thought was René Descartes (d. 1650). Descartes attempted to provide the philosophical basis for a fresh, clear-cut beginning in the human quest for knowledge. He affirmed two basic axioms: (a) the invariability of the order of nature, and (b) the all-sufficiency of reason. But the " reason " that Descartes glorified is not discursive reason, not reason in dialogue with the past but, rather, first, the reason of inner intuition, then deductive reason. To begin with, he will accept nothing but an indubitable rational intuition. In his famous *Meditations on the First Philosophy* he proceeds by way of a methodological doubt. He will doubt everything that can be doubted until, by this method, he arrives at something that is indubitably certain. On this certitude he will then build his entire knowledge of self, the world, and God, by way of logical deduction, constant analysis, checking and rechecking, by a critical Baconian procedure. Descartes's method is a curious combination of a variant version of Augustine's doctrine of an " inner light " and Bacon's critical methodology.

In the first of the three *Meditations,* Descartes proceeds to sweep away everything that can be doubted. Seated before the fireplace, in robe and slippers, relaxed in his comfortable chair, he asks himself: Can the reality of all these things of one's perceptual experience be doubted? They *seem* real enough, to be sure. But perhaps they are but a dream; for while one is dreaming the perceptual illusions of the dream *seem* to be very real indeed. It is only when one awakens that he is made to realize that it was but a dream. Perhaps, then, the entire of my perceptual experience of the objective world is nothing but a dream, from which I have not yet awakened. Descartes admits that there is no way to prove that the dream theory of phenomenal existence (a theory highly developed in the metaphysics of Hinduism) is not true. *How can I be sure that my perceptions do not deceive me?* I confess, he says, I cannot. So he tosses overboard the entire of his perceptual experience — nothing indubitably certain here!

What have we left? Well, objective world or no objective world, the mathematical truth, for example, that $2 + 2 = 4$ would seem to remain indubitably certain. Aha! says Descartes. Perhaps indeed this is not so certain as at first blush it appears. How does one know that $2 + 2 = 4$? May it not be possible that $2 + 2 = 5$, and that some evil cosmic demon has beguiled me into thinking that $2 + 2 = 4$? *How can I be sure that my mathematical reasoning doesn't mislead me?* I confess, he says, I cannot be absolutely sure.

It is interesting that today mathematical truth has been drawn into the orbit of relativity. It is not absolutely true that $2 + 2 = 4$, for 2 c.c. of one fluid added to 2 c.c. of another fluid, in the case of some fluids, produces a chemical change such that the total volume is perhaps $3\ 96/100$ c.c., rather than 4 c.c. Also, mathematical formulas that hold good in one geometry are not valid in another geometry. Mathematics now operates in an age of relativity.

Descartes has now swept away, by methodological doubt, the whole realm of perception and the entire realm of reasoning about the world. He writes:

> I shall now suppose, not that a true God, who as such must be supremely good and the fountain of truth, but

that some malignant genius exceedingly powerful and cunning has devoted all his powers in the deceiving of me; I shall suppose that the sky, the earth, colours, shapes, sounds and all external things are illusions and impostures of which this evil genius has availed himself for the abuse of my credulity; I shall consider myself as having no hands, no eyes, no flesh, no blood, nor any senses, but as falsely opining myself to possess all these things.[2]

In the second *Meditation*, Descartes then asks: What have we left? Anything at all? Yes, he says, amidst this immense ocean of doubt *one thing* remains, one tiny island of certainty remains unshakeably secure, namely, the phenomenon of doubting. True, all life may be a grand dream; but if it is, there must be a dreamer, since a dream without a dreamer is unthinkable. There cannot be a doubt without a doubter. In this way, Descartes felt that he had finally hit upon an indubitable intuition of the thinking, doubting ego. *Cogito, ergo sum!* I think; therefore I (a thinking subject) am. And the more I *doubt,* the more *certain* I am that I, a doubting subject, exist.

Descartes, however, was not fully aware of the presupposition of his methodological doubt. He thought he was beginning with *nothing but doubt,* and that by this doubting method he arrived at a point of intuitive certitude. This, however, was not the case. That it was not the case becomes evident if we ask Descartes: Why can't there be a doubt without a doubter? Why is a thought without a thinker impossible? He would reply that such a state of affairs is a fundamental contradiction. To which we would retort: So what? Are contradictions to be ruled out a priori? Descartes would have to answer: Certainly! And this answer would show that he really began with a hidden presupposition of faith, not doubt, as he led us, and perhaps also himself, to believe. He began with faith in Aristotle's rational principle of contradiction. Indeed, he expressed his faith in reason in bold form: " Let him deceive me as much as he will, he can never cause me to be nothing so long as I shall be thinking that I am something." [3]

Here we have a classic example of the basic faith of seventeenth-century philosophical rationalism. The basic presupposition of this modern school of philosophy is that what one must think must be; and negatively, what one cannot think cannot be. Reason, in itself, is held to be a reliable index to reality, so that it is freed from any basic obligation to sense experience.

We cannot here enter into a discussion of the conflict between this philosophical rationalism and empiricism, the other major philosophical school of the seventeenth century, which found leading exponents in such figures as Bacon, Locke, and Hume. Our main concern here is to indicate how Cartesian rationalism cut itself free from the accumulated wisdom of the ages, in a radical and thoroughgoing way. Descartes thought that historical sciences are not science at all, and he proposed to begin *de novo*. He felt that the historian who pretends to know the history of ancient Rome "knows less of it than a cook at Rome, and to know Latin is to know no more than did Cicero's servant girl." [4] Descartes was proud of the fact that he had forgotten Greek, which he had learned in his early education under the Jesuits. He was, of course, a mathematical genius and correctly perceived the role that mathematics was to play in the development of the new physical sciences.

In his own metaphysics, especially in his doctrine of God,[5] Descartes was in debt more than he realized, at least far more than he confessed, to Anselm's ontological argument and to Aristotle's argument for the existence of God as the Final Cause, an argument framed in terms of the concepts of potentiality and actuality. Descartes's arguments for the existence of God bear evidence of Scholastic influence. But the main point we wish to make concerns the spirit of Cartesianism. Sharing in the zest of the new sciences, this spirit was forward-looking. Descartes's doctrine of the invariability of the laws of nature relegated the traditional idea of divine Providence to the limbo of outgrown concepts. And his confidence in the supremacy of reason constituted an open challenge to the principles of authority and tradition that had tyrannized the minds of men. As Bury puts it, " Cartesianism was equivalent to a declaration of the Independence of Man." [6]

During the Renaissance the new, secular-humanistic spirit was enamored with the ancients, with Greece and Rome. The ancient classics were held in high reverence. The forward-looking moderns of the post-Renaissance period saw the need for breaking the hold of this authority of the ancients if progress was to be realized. Francis Bacon and others had begun this iconoclastic task by repudiating the validity of Aristotle's use of final causes in the study of nature. Yet Bacon still maintained a high respect for classical literature. The break with the past was more decisive and final in Descartes. He advocated a final and complete break with the past. He wished to construct an understanding of reality from *pure reason alone,* which in no regard whatever borrowed from the dead past. The past is dead; let it stay buried. We propose to build in the present and for the future on nothing but the power of pure reason. The first title of Descartes's *Discourse on Method* was *The Project of a Universal Science Which Can Elevate Our Nature to Its Highest Degree of Perfection.* It was Descartes's all-consuming belief that the material and moral progress of the human race was dependent not on history, but on modern science and modern philosophy. This was the spirit that inspired the work of Descartes and set the tone and temper for the great Enlightenment, which reached its flowering period in the eighteenth century.

THE ANCIENTS AND THE MODERNS

Bury provides us with a lucid description of the hundred years' literary war generated by the forward-looking spirit, represented by Descartes and subsequent leaders of the Enlightenment.[7] The Renaissance idealized the Golden Age of the classics of Greece and Rome, and tended to view the course of subsequent history as a period of corruption and degeneration. Descartes was a representative voice of a spirit that in the early seventeenth century had begun to challenge the thesis of degeneration.

The main scene of this controversy was in France, but the issue was already raised by a volume called *Miscellaneous Thoughts* published in 1620 by Alessandro Tassoni in Italy.

Tassoni gave the ancients their due, but in his comparative treatment of them with the moderns, the moderns fared better. Taking his clue from Tassoni, Boisrobert, a French dramatist, delivered a lecture before the *Académie française,* February 26, 1635, in which he made " a violent and apparently scurrilous attack on Homer." [8] From that time forward Homer was " a special target for the arrows of the moderns." [9]

The sense of the dignity and ability of modern man thus steadily increased, and the Renaissance glorification of the ancients gradually waned. Said Molière, " The ancients are the ancients, we are the people of today." [10]

George Hakewill, of England, published a six-hundred-page volume to refute " the common error touching nature's perpetual and universal decay." Hakewill felt that comparatively speaking, the Renaissance glorification of the ancients was an exaggeration, and he was strongly persuaded that the theory which regards historic process as one of degeneration is entirely false. It was his firm belief that modern man is not only not inferior to the ancients, but that in many areas of human endeavor he is indeed superior. He even argued that modern man is superior in the matter of morality. Bury says that he developed this idea " at great length into a severe and partial impeachment of ancient manners and morals." [11]

Hakewill's attack on the morals of the ancients was to find more effective literary expression in the following century in the cynical wit of Voltaire. Voltaire registered his high estimate of Enlightenment man as compared to the ancients. He argued that in only a few areas were moderns inferior to the ancients, and that there are spheres " in which the moderns are far superior to the ancients." [12]

Voltaire never tired of heaping criticism on the ancient Jews, the terrible immorality of their history as recorded in their own Sacred Scriptures, and on the evils of ecclesiastical history among the Christians. He portrayed the Jews as an " ignorant, crude people " who derived what good they had by copying it from surrounding nations.[13] These " grumbling Jews, these unjust children of Jewish vagabonds," [14] committed such " pious sacrileges " as Jephthah's sacrifice of his own daughter, and Samuel's using " a sacred chopper " to dismember King Agag.[15] They spared neither age nor sex in the cities they captured; they were indeed, said Voltaire, a "barbarous" people.

The centuries of ecclesiastical Christianity received from Voltaire equally severe criticism. Of all religions, he wrote, it would seem that Christianity should inspire the greatest tolerance, "although up to now the Christians have been the most intolerant of men." [16] He described the doctrinal disputes in Christian history prior to the age of Charlemagne, showing how theological speculation constantly "occasioned the spilling of human blood." [17] The lesson we should learn from these centuries of "horrible discord" is "that we should pardon each other's errors; discord is the great ill of mankind; and tolerance is the only remedy for it." [18]

THE "GOSPEL" OF THE DEISTS

In England the rationalistic revolt against historical religion found its most vocal and popular expression in the movement of Deism. The first phase was one in which the historical revelation was retained but reinterpreted as a "supplement" to natural religion, yet a "supplement" to be verified by natural religion. This was the position of John Tillotson, Archibishop of Canterbury (d. 1694), and essentially also the position of John Locke. Here reason stands at the controlling center, but is not yet held to be omnicompetent, since revelation provides us with a body of truths that reason of its own natural power cannot discover. John Toland, Locke's Irish disciple, in his book *Christianity Not Mysterious,* followed Locke in defining the category of revelation as "above reason" in an equally narrow way.

In this intellectual climate, defenders of the historic Christian faith felt obliged to bolster their faith by a "rational" appeal to the evidences from miracle and prophecy. But no sooner was this done than a more cunning rationalism exposed the irrationalism of these arguments. Men like Anthony Collins (d. 1729), Thomas Woolston (d. 1733), and David Hume (d. 1776) tore these arguments into shreds.

Matthew Tindal (d. 1733) is usually regarded as "the great apostle of Deism." With his book, *Christianity as Old as the Creation,* published in 1731, the year following Woolston's discourse on miracles, the Deistic movement in England reached its high-water mark. Tindal argued that true religion consists in a firm purpose to do whatever good we can, and that we become acceptable to God in this, and in no other way. He wrote:

> Natural religion, which is of the greatest importance to mankind, and is a perpetual standing rule for men of the meanest, as well as the highest capacity, carries its own evidence with it, those internal inseparable marks of truth; but can that be said of any religion which depends on tradition? [19]

Tindal's faith in the omnicompetence of " the Light of Nature " [20] or the " Religion of Nature and Reason " [21] led him to argue that revealed religion differs from natural religion only in the mode of communication, the former being external, the latter internal.[22] But that historical revelation is essentially superfluous follows clearly from Tindal's conviction that the religion of nature is " absolutely perfect, universal, and immutable," [23] and that therefore historical revelation " can neither add to nor take from its perfection." [24] Further, the truth or falsity of a religion of historical revelation must be judged by " the Religion of Nature and Reason written in the hearts of every one of us from the first Creation." [25]

Tindal was not only aware of the fact that his rationalism severed the bond of faith's dependence on its evangelical historic source. The climate of his age gave him a strong feeling of certitude, so that he took rational pride in *reducing* historical Christianity to nothing but " the re-publication of the Religion of Nature," the alternate title he gave to his book. As Norman Torrey says, " The implication was all too obvious that revelation was not only useless but often pernicious." [26]

Voltaire leaned heavily on the English Deists and developed essentially the same faith in the universal light of reason. Describing what he obviously regarded to be the best religion, Voltaire wrote:

> Wouldn't it be one that taught a good deal of morality and very little dogma? The one that tended to make men just, without making them absurd? The one that

wouldn't command belief in impossible, contradictory things, insulting to the Divinity and pernicious to mankind? . . . The one that taught nothing but the worship of God, justice, tolerance, and humanity? [27]

Voltaire and the Deists' ruling belief was the notion that " common ideas of morality " (of the eighteenth century of course!) had been written on the human heart universally and were " as old as creation." It is, of course, clear to us today that this is a highly dubious notion and that they were far more in debt than they realized to the traditional Judeo-Christian faith for these so-called " common ideas of morality." They too were *historically conditioned* in their ideals, but failed to recognize this fact adequately, though our judgment should not be overly severe, for the " historical sense " was yet to appear on the horizon of Western thought. It was only in the latter part of the eighteenth and in the nineteenth century that men began to realize the problematical character of the so-called " universal light of reason."

In the earlier phases of the impact of modern rationalism, especially in the latter part of the seventeenth century, there were, of course, numerous Christian minds who felt the force of the new rationalism and adjusted their traditional Christian faith less radically to the modern temper of mind. The Cambridge Platonists, for example, instituted a revolt against the Aristotelianism that had long held the fort at Cambridge. Leading figures here were men like Benjamin Whichcote, Henry More, and Ralph Cudworth. These men steeped themselves in the ancient classics, thus carrying forward the spirit of the Renaissance. They were followers of Plato and Plotinus, and at the same time broad churchmen, who operated with an irenic spirit, attempting to hold the boat steady, against the inroads of Hobbseian materialism and relativism, Cartesian rationalism, and the rising tide of skepticism and agnosticism.

But in the middle of the eighteenth century there came, as E. E. Aubrey puts it, " a blatant rationalism which spun its own webbs of speculative thought as recklessly as ever the medieval Scholastics did." [28]

The New Interest in History in the Latter Eighteenth Century

The new turn in modern rationalism came about the middle of the eighteenth century. It became clear to its exponents that the modern secular theory of progress needed to be buttressed by an appeal to facts, and this opened the way for a new look at history, for the development of a new " philosophy of history," and for a history of civilization. Up until that time, the rationalistic and humanistic pride of the Enlightenment and its optimism toward the future had inspired many of its exponents to forget the past.

Alfred Cobban contends that to label the rationalism of the Enlightenment " unhistorical " is " a superficial error." [29] Yet even Cobban is forced to admit that seventeenth-century rationalism provided " an unsuitable climate for the growth of history." [30] Cobban might have given more adequate recognition to the fact that this " unhistorical " thinking was not wholly transcended even in the eighteenth century. Indeed, even in the latter part of the eighteenth century Chevalier de Chastellux still held the historically unjustifiable belief that the past history of man held little more than " a mass of acquired ignorance." In order to be happy, therefore, there is " far greater need of forgetting than of remembering," since the great object of enlightened men should be to " raise the edifice of Reason on the ruins of opinion." [31] Chastellux wrote a two-volume general history, *On Public Felicity, or Consideration of the Lot of Men in the Various Epochs of History,* published in 1772. In this work the author argued that public happiness was an ideal to be achieved in the future, and that it could not be achieved without a decisive break with the past. Hence, he was inspired to " retrace the unhappiness of humanity " in the past, to show how bad it was, and thus to underscore the rationalist plea for a clean break with the past.

Prior to Chastellux' work, Voltaire's *Essai sur les moeurs et l'esprit des nations,* published in 1751, and a work on universal history projected by Turgot a few years earlier, represent the beginnings of this new interest in history, an interest that had waned considerably with the rationalistic eclipse of the

Renaissance. Voltaire wrote his work in deliberate opposition to Bossuet's ecclesiastical version of history, *Discours sur l'histoire universelle,* published in 1681. Bossuet portrayed history under the ruling motif of Providence. Voltaire wrote his history from the point of view of modern secular rationalism. He proposed to speak of Jews as he would of the Scythians and the Greeks, giving them equal significance. Voltaire was resolved to eliminate any notion of Providence and to portray the history of civilization in terms of the scientific principle of cause and effect, and immediate human motives.

Voltaire's history was written not out of any sense of the organic continuity of eighteenth-century Europe with the Judeo-Christian tradition. With this tradition, he had definitely and irrevocably broken, by intention at any rate. He wrote his history from the perspective of a philosopher and historian. He complained that up until his time, the luster of the Roman Empire had tended to blind historians, so that they " treated all other men as if they had no existence." [32] The celebrated Bossuet was inexcusably narrow, for when " he happens to mention the Mohammedans, he speaks of them only as a deluge of barbarians." [33]

Voltaire's point of beginning is most significant. His first chapter is on China. Through the reports of French missionaries, China had recently come within the horizon of Occidental knowledge. While Voltaire poured out severe criticism of the immorality of the Jews, and portrayed the Dark Ages of man's history under the domination of church dogma and ecclesiastical tradition as " those ages of barbarism and ignorance," [34] he had many words of praise for the " splendor " of Chinese wisdom, especially its morals, which had subsisted above four thousand years.[35] Recognition is also given to China's exceptionally orderly government and to numerous technical aspects of ancient China: its fine silk, its manufacture of paper, its porcelain, and " that beautiful varnish which we begin now to imitate and to rival in Europe," [36] its invention of printing in the days of Julius Caesar, etc.

Confucius received very high praise at the hands of Voltaire, who kept hung on the wall of his bedroom a picture of Confucius (*Sancte Confuci ora pro nobis*) . [37] Confucius held " the

purest ideas" that man can form of the Supreme Being.[38]
With a cynical touch, Voltaire qualified this statement by add-
ing the phrase "unassisted by revelation."

While recognizing that the contradictions of human nature
are manifest in China as elsewhere, Voltaire nevertheless
summed up "the wisdom which has presided over the constitution of China these four thousand years" by saying that on
the whole, "the spirit of order and moderation, a love for the
sciences, the cultivation of the several arts useful to life, and
a prodigious number of inventions to facilitate the acquirement of those arts, constituted Chinese wisdom." [39] Indeed, the
spirit of China is "the most ancient monument of reason in
the whole world." [40]

By beginning his history with China, and following this with
a chapter on India, Persia, and Arabia, Voltaire gave expression to the fact that his interest as a historian was not ecclesiastically limited as was that of Bossuet, but that he was universal
in his outlook.

Aside from he treatment of China, few other nations received great praise. Indeed, it was Voltaire's belief that most
of human history was scarcely more than a history of crimes,
and that the history of opinions is "hardly anything but a
collection of human errors." [41] Compared with all that had
happened in the past, "the beginning of the sixteenth century (Europe) . . . exhibits the noblest objects to our view
that the theatre of the world ever afforded." [42]

Voltaire's historical method was quite simple. It was mainly
an objective inquiry to learn as much as possible of "the
customs of nations" and "to study the human mind." [43] As
such, the work is remarkably well documented. But Voltaire
did not merely record facts; he also interpreted their significance. His work represents a moral interpretation of history,
for he constantly measured and judged the customs and morals
of the past by the standard of eighteenth-century European
morality.

Although there is a vast amount of historical information
in Voltaire's work, it was the fact that Voltaire obviously aimed
to glorify the present "enlightened" age of reason and progress in science and art by showing its bold contrast to the

irrationalism and superstition of the past that more than anything else made his history so popular. As Löwith says, " The enormous success of Voltaire's essay is due mainly to the fact that it provided the rising bourgeoisie with a historical justification of its own ideals by suggesting that all history was leading up to the eighteenth century." [44] For as Voltaire himself observed, " It requires a vast many ages to perfect human nature." [45]

In view of this new interest in history during the latter eighteenth century, one would be wrong to label the Enlightenment as entirely antihistorical. When we describe the general spirit of the Enlightenment as " unhistorical rationalism," we do not mean that it was antihistorical in the sense that it embraced no interest whatever in history. Such a historical judgment would obviously be false. We mean first, that it was not an age of great historiography. Men such as Hume and Voltaire made insignificant attempts to develop more fruitful methods of historical research. The Enlightenment was unhistorical in the sense, to use Cobban's own words, that there were prevalent " positive and stronger factors which prohibited a concentration of attention on historical scholarship." [46] Although not wholly indifferent to history, the men of the Enlightenment " thought that there were better things." [47]

Second, the spirit of the Enlightenment was " unhistorical " in a deeper sense, a sense in which perhaps the phrase " antihistorical " is not too strong an expression. The Enlightenment so completely identified the past with the reign of barbarism, irrationalism, and religious superstition, and the present as the age of reason that its exponents can rightly be said to have been modern-minded rather than historical-minded.[48] They were antihistorical in the sense that they were not wholly free from the illusion of finality. For this reason, men such as Hume and Voltaire lacked a genuinely historical perspective on human existence. Instead of seeing religion, as they did, as something that held no positive value whatever, a genuinely historical view of human history would be characterized by greater objectivity and by an earnest effort to understand every great historical force and movement as fulfilling a positive function in relation to human existence. A genuinely historical view seeks to penetrate to an understanding of what basic human need or needs these forces fulfilled. But this is precisely what men like Voltaire and Hume did *not* do. Collingwood is correct: " The historical outlook of the Enlightenment was not genuinely historical; in its main motive it was polemical and anti-historical." [49]

Nevertheless, highly inadequate as it was, the new interest in history represents a significant turning point in the development of eighteenth-century rationalism. The modern faith in reason began to weaken as a result of mounting attacks from skepticism. The philosophers decided to devote themselves to more profitable enterprises than philosophy, enterprises which would no longer bring down on their heads the uncomfortable charge that in destroying religion they were destroying morality as well. Hence, the philosophers turned historians and began to survey the whole colorful terrain of human history.

The purpose which motivated the writing of these histories, however, was to illuminate and clarify " the constant and universal principles of human nature " (Hume) . Obviously, little could be learned from this kind of study of history, for the rationalists knew what they were looking for before they set out on their historical quest. They had already created their notion of universal humanity, " man in general," in their own image and after their own likeness, prior to the historical survey. But as Becker says, we can forgive these *Philosophes* for deceiving us with all their talk of studying history in order to discover " the constant and universal principles of human nature," since " they are, even more effectively, deceiving themselves." [50]

Although not quite as detached in their attitude toward history as were the positivistic historians of the nineteenth century, who conceived their task to be merely determining the facts, the men of the Enlightenment nevertheless moved a long way toward the spectator view of history. Hume wrote, for example, " To see all [the] human race, from the beginning of time, pass, as it were, in review before us; appearing in their true colours, without any of those disguises, which, during their life-time, so much perplexed the judgment of the beholders. What spectacle can be imagined, so magnificent, so various, so interesting? " [51]

With the Enlightenment's predominant concern for immediate practical reforms in morals and politics, what study they did make of history was not made to engage in any existential encounter with history, and certainly not with any thought whatever that they might, out of such encounter, be led to alter their fundamental views of man and the world. Rather, as Hume put it, they were " sufficiently interested in the characters, and events, to have a lively sentiment of blame or praise." [52] That is, the study of history was pursued " primarily for the purposes of propaganda." [53]

Positive Values in Our Enlightenment Heritage

It is not our purpose here to offer a full critique of the spirit of the Enlightenment, but rather to assess its significance in relation to the historical understanding of human existence and to the faith-history dimension of Christian theology. As we do so, however, we must not overlook the many positive values of the Enlightenment. To be sure, the developments of the past couple of centuries have led us today to take a more sober and more realistic view of man's abilities, especially in the realm of moral and social improvement. This is for us vastly more problematical than it seemed to be to the men of the Enlightenment. Also, Freudian psychology, epiphenomenological and even biological theories of mind, and the demonic use of " reason " by modern totalitarian political regimes have made the Enlightenment faith in the supremacy of " reason " vastly more problematical for us than it was for the men of the eighteenth century.

Nevertheless, the Enlightenment holds much positive significance for us today. The belief in a basic humanity common to all men, the respect for human rights, the high regard for human personality, and the plea for " liberty, equality, and fraternity " — these are the very foundation stones of our democracy.

Praiseworthy also is the eighteenth-century impatience with an otherworldly theology that failed to generate any profound

impulse for the betterment of man on earth. To be sure, the
"soft" rationalists (such as Helvétius and Condorcet) were
somewhat superficial in their view of man and overoptimistic
in their confidence that the only sin was ignorance, and that
all the social evils which it bred could be abolished by the
process of education. But there were also many "hard" rationalists who had some reservations about the idea of "the
perfectibility of man" that was in the air. Men such as Locke,
Hume, Voltaire, and Kant, in various ways recognized that
there were limits to the powers of human reason. Nevertheless,
they believed that men do possess a measure of real freedom,
and that if they would use this freedom in a responsible manner, many political evils could be remedied, needed social reforms could achieve a beneficent measure of success, and old
superstitions "could be argued out of existence." [54]

Of positive significance also is the eighteenth-century opposition to the depressing yoke of creedalism and ecclesiastical dogma, to which one was formerly obliged to give assent
whether he perceived its truth or not; the plea for rational and
personal integrity in the matter of religious beliefs; the enthusiastic devotion to the new enterprise of science; and the
insistence that human art can be as creative and magnificent
in our day as it was among the ancients, perhaps more so.

It is true that the Deists' concept of man's relation to God
was quite vague and nebulous, and even contained the seeds
of an eventual godless view of human existence, as the subsequent secularizing of modern culture shows. An "absentee"
God inevitably becomes irrelevant to the daily issues of human
existence. Rationalism forfeits the immediate relation with
God called "faith," turns the dialogue of faith into an an-
thropocentric soliloquy, and thereby proves the truth of
Pascal's remark that "without the Mediator all communication with God is removed." [55] Nevertheless, most of the eighteenth-century rationalists still possessed a modicum of religion, which enabled them to maintain a reverent attitude
toward life's Ultimate.

The rationalist notion of "common ideas of morality" held
universally by all men is somewhat fictitious; yet the rationalists deserve our praise for holding morality and virtue in very

high regard, and we are much in their debt for the values of a humane, sensitive, and tolerant civilization, at least for the idea of such a civilization. In many ways, their glowing optimism, their faith in the possibility of genuine progress, and their many "projects" for human betterment represent a decided advance in the history of Western culture.

FALLACIES IN THE UNHISTORICAL OUTLOOK OF RATIONALISM

Although we do not forget the great positive values that we have inherited from the Enlightenment, from the point of view of theology and the context of our main concern in this volume, several negative judgments must also be made.

First, the most serious fallacy is connected with the *Philosophes'* woeful lack of awareness that their ideas and ideals were, after all, historically determined. Without being aware of it, they were greatly in debt to, and heirs of, the intellectual climate of the medieval period of Western civilization, which they so blatantly labeled "the Dark Ages." The Deists eliminated the medieval fear of God, but retained its religious reverence of Deity. Indeed, the idea of monotheism, which the Deists cherished, was derived mainly from the Judeo-Christian faith, not from an objective observation of nature's orderly movements.

Many of the rationalists thought that they derived the idea of one Supreme Being from the teleological argument; but Hume exposed the fallacy of this belief by his devastating critique of the teleological argument. Hume showed that the validity of the teleological argument rests on the hidden assumption of the validity of the principle of analogy, that is, the assumption that the world is analogous to Bishop Paley's watch. But how now can one justify this assumption? From the fact that one cannot have a watch without a watchmaker, does it follow that there can be no world without a world-maker? Who says that the entire mysterious, infinite universe is analogous to the art of human contrivance? On the contrary, "does not the great disproportion bar all comparison and inference?" [56] The dissimilitude between the author of the universe and a human architect " is so striking that the utmost you can here pretend to is a guess, a conjecture, a presumption concerning a similar cause." [57]

But Hume's criticism of the teleological argument for the existence of God goes deeper still. He repudiated the validity of the very idea of a First Cause (the world being regarded as its effect). The causal axiom is merely a scientific category of judgment by which we apprehend the relation of one event to another event, *in the time series*, through repeated experience. Immanuel Kant, of course, retained the *prescriptive* interpretation of the causal axiom, as an a priori category of the knowing mind in terms of which whatever events are experienced must of necessity be experienced. But Hume labeled this prescriptive use of the causal axiom mere psychological propensity, and stressed the *descriptive* use of the axiom. Hume defined a cause as " an object, followed by another, and where all the objects similar to the first are followed by objects similar to the second "; [58] or " an object followed by another and whose appearance always conveys the thought of that other." [59]

For Hume, then, causality is reduced to nothing but observed antecedent and consequent, and as such contains the two elements of continuity and contiguity. The idea of an absolutely First Cause (God) violates the element of contiguity. Therefore, said Hume, the idea of a First Cause is meaningless. A single experience of an event or object provides no basis for a legitimate use of the causal axiom. A single event or object cannot properly be called either cause or effect. We can legitimately utilize the notion of cause and effect only when we have *two or more contiguous, temporally related events*. Now, the universe as a whole is of the nature of a single event or object, for there is only one cosmos. It is, therefore, not legitimate for one to think of the universe as an effect at all. Hume wrote:

> I much doubt whether it be possible for a cause to be known only by its effect . . . or to be of so singular and particular a nature as to have no parallel and no similarity with any other cause or object, that has ever fallen under our observation. It is only when two *species* of

objects are found to be constantly conjoined, that we can infer the one from the other; and were an effect presented, which was entirely singular, and could not be comprehended under any known *species*, I do not see, that we could form any conjecture or inference at all concerning its cause. If experience and observation and analogy be, indeed, the only guides which we can reasonably follow in inferences of this nature; both the effect and cause must bear a similarity and resemblance to other effects and causes, which we know, and which we have found, in many instances, to be conjoined with each other.[60]

But now, even if one may be permitted to brush aside these formidable objections to the teleological argument and to grant the legitimacy of its use of the causal axiom and the validity of its presupposition of analogy, Hume points out that the kind of God which this argument yields is far from the God of religious faith. Since "like causes produce like effects," the God of this argument, said Hume, may well be limited, finite, and imperfect, since the effects are such. "Many worlds might have been botched and bungled, throughout an eternity, ere this system was struck out: much labor lost: many fruitless trials made: and a slow, but continued improvement carried on during infinite ages in the art of world-making." [61]

Since the effects are plural, furthermore, perhaps deity also is plural instead of one. Just as many men join hands in the art of ship-building, so perhaps many deities joined hands in the art of world-building. And since the effects are generated, perhaps deity is also, in which case we are back with the theogony of ancient times.[62] In a word, said Hume, a man who follows the teleological argument "is able, perhaps, to assert, or conjecture, that the universe, sometime, arose from something like design: but beyond that position he cannot ascertain one single circumstance, and is left afterwards to fix every point of his theology, by the utmost license of fancy and hypothesis." [63]

In the light of Hume's critique of the teleological argument, one is tempted to suspect that the Deists did not derive the idea of the Creator-God from the order of nature. Though they may not have been fully aware of it, it would seem that like the medieval theologians and philosophers, they were "rationalizing" a belief in God which in fact derived elsewhere, namely, from the Judeo-Christian faith.

The Deists rejected the miracles of the Bible and held up for cynical ridicule the notion of the six-day creation; yet they clung to the greatest miracle conceivable: the miracle of the creation of the world by God. To be sure, in rejecting the doctrines of historical revelation and the incarnation, they significantly altered Christian monotheism and ended up with the "absentee" God. For with their view of life's "end" set on earth instead of heaven, and with the task of perfecting man's essentially perfectible nature taken out of the hands of God and placed in the hands of man, it was inevitable that the sense of God's immanence in history fade in the perspective of rationalism. But though they discarded the traditional idea of heaven, they still believed in the immortality of the soul.

In spite of the rationalistic boast to having achieved liberation [64] from the clammy hand of church dogma and tradition, in spite of all their cynical wit and caustic skepticism, " there is more Christian philosophy in the writings of the *Philosophes* than has yet been dreamt of in our histories." [65]

Second, the rationalists were so enthusiastic in their newly won intellectual freedom, so resolved to propagate the new gospel of the "universal light of reason," so unhistorical in their knowledge of man, that they failed to see that this vital center of their gospel was indeed more than a little fictitious. It strikes a twentieth-century reader as more than a little naïve to hear the Count de Volney define natural law in the following way:

> The regular and constant order of facts by which God rules the universe; the order which his wisdom presents to the senses and reason of men, to serve them as an equal and common rule of conduct, and to guide them, without distinction of race or sect, towards perfection and happiness.[66]

This belief in "a regular and constant" order of nature sounds like a quasi-secularized version of the Thomist doctrine of natural law. Subsequent developments in physics have seriously challenged this notion. Indeed, David Hume himself already did so by observing that the so-called principle of causality is really nothing but the temporal antecedence and consequence *in our experience* of nature. Natural law is nothing but a statistical correlation of these observed antecedents and consequents. A natural law is thus nothing but a scientific hypothesis that possesses a greater or lesser degree of probability, depending on the extent of the examined evidence and on the critical care of the process of examination. And as Becker says, how can the rationalist " be so sure that he knows what perfection is, or would be happy if he had it? "[67]

Third, closely related to the preceding observation is the failure of the rationalists to see that they and their ideas were as thoroughly embedded in the relative process of history as is the " climate of opinion " of any other historical epoch. They were indeed just as *unhistorical* in their gospel as were the orthodox, against whom they were in revolt. The orthodox thought of the Bible, so to speak, as insulated from the relativities of history. They therefore regarded Biblical doctrines as infallibly true. The Deists similarly thought of their " Bible of Nature " as providing them with a set of moral truths that were similarly insulated from the relativities of historic process. Subsequent developments in the historical understanding of human existence have shown these " gospels " of both orthodox and Deist to be illusions.

The Enlightenment thus went astray precisely at the central point of its faith in reason. Collingwood points out [68] that from its fundamental belief that past history has been in the main a period of irrationalism, " but is capable of being converted into something rational," it generated two impulses: the backward look that portrayed history " as the play of irrational forces," and the forward thrust that because of its faith in the powers of reason, at times took on a utopian quality.

Montesquieu and Gibbon, along with Voltaire, represent the backward look, while Condorcet is perhaps the most vocal exponent of the forward thrust with a utopian quality. Montesquieu developed the thesis that geographical environment is the major causal principle of explanation of the differences between peoples and nations. Hence, historical institutions would be interpreted not as products of human freedom and reason, but as the results of purely natural causes. Edward Gibbon believed that irrationality was the real force of history, which he regarded as " the triumph of barbarism and religion." There was, however, a touch of the Renaissance in Gibbon's outlook, for he clung to the notion of a golden age in the past: the Antonine period.

With such an unhistorical outlook on history as this, one must say that the rationalists of the eighteenth century held an unhistorical conception of their own age of reason. According to their views of human existence, the appearance of modern rationalism was sheer miracle. It had no historical causes, for they certainly never thought of the preceding irrationalism and barbarism as *historical causes* of such rationalism. This criticism touches the very heart of the historical fallacy of the Enlightenment, whose leaders were unable to explain historically what was believed to be of supreme importance, namely, their own faith in reason. Since they had no adequate theory of historical causation, they " could not seriously believe in the origin or genesis of anything whatever." [69] Still, although the historical causes they did hit upon in their historical studies were trifling, similar to Pascal's remark that if Cleopatra's nose had been longer, world history would have been different, they nevertheless did search for some, and in this way pointed toward the development of a more adequate view of the historical causal nexus of events.

Fourth, from the standpoint of theology, perhaps the most important observation to make is to indicate how the historical character of the Christian faith was, in large measure, lost sight of in the transformation that it underwent during the reign of rationalism. Insofar as the representatives of the Enlightenment were concerned with religion, they launched a powerful attack on the traditional connection between religion and history. They developed a contemptuous attitude toward those who permitted themselves to get bogged down in one historical strand of religion. They would never condescend to be bound to something that happened once. Fichte contended that not the historical but only the metaphysical saves. Against the theological idea of the solitary incarnation of God in Jesus as the Christ, Strauss argued that the Idea " is not wont to lavish all its fullness on one exemplar, and be niggardly towards all others." [70] One recalls also the oft-quoted saying of Lessing to the effect that the *eternal* truth of religion can never be proved by *historical* facts. This is, of course, true, but a great deal depends on how one construes its meaning. History is not the *proof* of religious truth, yet it may well be the indispensable *medium* of it. But the Enlightenment turned it the other way round and negated religion's connection with history. " Universal Reason " (a Cartesian phrase) was its broad ideal. History was regarded as unessential to real religion; indeed, it possessed little more than propaganda value. Away with all particularisms! Bring in the glad day of universal natural religion! These were the watchwords of the Enlightenment.

Some, of course, like Kant, held a modified type of rationalism which recognized that at an earlier period of man's development a historical revelation was perhaps necessary. It served as a kind of crutch on which to lean until such a time as reason could maintain itself.

Kant had some reservations in regard to the modern idea that the world is steadily forging ahead from bad to better. He criticized Rousseau for his evolutionary optimism, insisting that " the history of all times cries too loudly against it." [71] Yet at the same time, Kant also felt that what appears to be highly complicated if we look merely at individuals " may yet be understood as a steady, progressive, though slow, evolution of the original endowments of the entire species." [72] Such an evolution of the entire human species is the controlling idea of Kant's essay " Idea for a Universal History with a Cosmopolitan Intent."

Kant's philosophical solution to the problem of history was determined by his belief that the course of history is analogous to that of nature, and that " all natural faculties of a creature are destined to unfold completely and according to their end." [73] His philosophy of history was similarly written under the notion of final causes. And since nature does nothing in vain (?), so we may presume that, in the long run, history will

gradually unfold and realize man's true destiny as well. Hence,
Kant felt highly optimistic about the Enlightenment. What is
Enlightenment? Kant answered:

> *Enlightenment is man's leaving his self-caused imma-*
> *turity.* Immaturity is the incapacity to use one's intelli-
> gence without the guidance of another. Such immaturity
> is self-caused if it is not caused by lack of intelligence,
> but by lack of determination and courage to use one's in-
> telligence without being guided by another. *Sapere Aude!*
> Have the courage to use your own intelligence! is there-
> fore the motto of the enlightenment.[74]

Kant believed that there still remained many hindrances
which prevented men from using their own minds in the matter of religion. But the spirit of freedom was on the march,
and he was able to see definite indications " that this field of
endeavor is being opened up for men to work freely and reduce gradually the hindrances preventing a general enlightenment and an escape from self-caused immaturity." [75]

Because for Kant, religion is not to determine morality but
is, rather, to be determined by it, he was able to assimilate
historic Christianity into his metaphysic of morality only by
way of depriving Christian symbols of their objective significance and interpreting them as symbolic expressions of the
essential, rational-moral truth of humanity in its ethical perfection. Hence, the incarnation of God in Jesus Christ was
reduced by Kant to nothing but an archetypal Idea of " mankind in its complete moral perfection." [76] The traditional doctrine of the Trinity — Father, Son, and Holy Spirit — disappears, and in its stead we get the Deist trinity — God, freedom,
and immortality. The true church, to be carefully distinguished from the empirical, visible one, is, according to Kant,
a " sublime idea of an ethical commonwealth." [77] It must be
distinguished from a church of historicoecclesiastical faith, of
which there are several, " whereas only pure religious faith,
which bases itself wholly on reason, can be accepted as necessary and therefore as the only one which signalizes the *true*
church." [78]

It is clear, of course, that no actual, historical church can be established and maintained by such a purely moral creed as that advocated by Kant. Kant recognized this fact, and seemed to say that for a time it was in a way necessary that ceremonial service (worship) be substituted for the true service of God centering in moral activity alone. But he believed that the former could and should gradually give way to the latter. It is not misleading to say that what he hoped for was for morality to replace religion, religion rooted in redemptive history, at any rate. Kant wrote:

> Hence a necessary consequence of the physical and, at the same time, the moral predisposition in us, the latter being the basis and interpreter of all religion, is that in the end religion will gradually be freed from all empirical determining grounds and from all statutes which rest on history and which through the agency of ecclesiastical faith provisionally unite men for the requirements of the good; and thus at last the pure religion of reason will rule over all. . . . The integuments within which the embryo first developed into a human being must be laid aside when he is to come into the light of day.[79]

From these and similar passages it is clear that for Kant the organic dependence of faith on historical revelation is really destroyed. He called for a gradual transition from church-faith to " the pure religion of reason," the religion of an ethical state on earth. As Edward Caird said, " Church-faith . . . is a ' useful vehicle '[80] for conveying to men a truth which, finally, by a true enlightenment, will be freed from the need of any such assistance."[81]

The difficulty that Kant had in assimilating Christianity into his philosophical system lies partly in the fact that while the New Testament deals with the human problem in terms of the historical, corporate dimension of human existence (" As in Adam all die, so also in Christ shall all be made alive," I Cor. 15:22), Kant's view operated in terms of rugged individualism. In this, of course, Kant shared the eighteenth-century atomistic view of man, which was subsequently overcome by the newer insight that there is no such isolated individual, and that individuality is formed in the matrix of community. Kant's idea of the autonomy of the moral will makes the moral life intelligible only as a subjective self-determination apart from any dependence on, or any assistance the will might receive from, other objects or persons. It is easy to see why Kant encountered difficulty with the social dimension of the community of redemption " in Christ." The New Testament conception of the church as the " body of Christ " could hardly be taken into the Kantian system, for Kant conceived the moral being of each man to be centered in himself and to exist in a self-determined inward realm (autonomy) that bars the entrance of an other.

One reads the Pauline writings of the New Testament to be made to realize that Kant must have been aware of a severe clash between his own philosophy and the theology of Paul. The kind of autonomy for which Kant stood unflinchingly was for Paul the very source of man's sinful predicament, namely: unbelief, in which one removes the center of his being from the divine center to which it belongs; and *hybris,* the act by which one makes himself the center of himself and his world.

Kant defined the will as a principle or force of causality, and freedom as " the quality of this causality through which it can be an efficient cause *independent of extraneous determining causes.*" [82] This *freedom* of self-determination, Kant set in bold contrast to the *necessity* by which nonrational beings are moved to action by *external* causes. " What else can freedom of the will be?" Kant asked, " but autonomy; that is, the property of the will to be a law unto itself?" [83]

Paul just as unflinchingly opposed any view of the moral life that portrays the individual as alone in his sin and responsible for it, and as alone in his effort to achieve righteousness. But Kant was mistaken: this immediate dependence on God as an Other, for the goodness of self does *not* mean heteronomy. What Kant failed to see was that the theonomy of the faith relationship resolves the antithesis between autonomy and heteronomy, for God is at once the Supreme Other and also the ground of one's selfhood. On the basis of the theonomous character of faith, Paul admonished the Philippians to work out their own salvation with fear and trembling, and then added (what Kant omits) in the same breath, *for* it is

God who is at work in them, both in their willing and doing, to achieve the purposes of his own gracious will (Phil. 2:12-13).

Because of the fundamental principles of Kant's moral system, there was no way he could appropriate Paul's doctrine of a faith-righteousness bestowed by God through Jesus Christ (Rom. 3:22). On Kantian principles of moral goodness, one cannot make sense out of Paul's idea of a justification by God's grace through faith in Christ, interpreted as an unmerited gift (Rom. 3.24). The concept of forgiveness as a redemptive dynamic is always a stumbling block to the thoroughgoing rationalist. According to Kant, if goodness is authentic, man must achieve it " *by his own powers and of himself* " alone,[84] for this is what autonomy means. According to Paul, the salvation by grace through faith " is *not your own doing,* it is the gift of God — not because of works, lest any man should boast " (Eph. 2:8-9, italics added).

In short, Kant's deistic idea of God as a world-Creator and Governor, who governs at an infinite distance, could not be reconciled with the Biblical idea of Christ as an indwelling Spirit who restores a divided self to wholeness (Paul), heals the wounded will (Augustine), liberates the self from the inner hell of guilt (Luther), increases the power of the God-consciousness (Schleiermacher), or empowers one with the courage to be (Tillich). Kant lost the sense of God's immanence, his presence and power in history, in human community, in the church.

Although Kant moved out of the context of concrete historical religion to make his spiritual home in rationalism, nobody ever portrayed the moral ideal in a more demanding way as to demonstrate the concrete need of the redeeming power of revelation and grace. In his major book on religion, Kant squarely faced up to the problem of evil in the human heart. He recognized not merely human frailty, and the "mixing unmoral with moral motivating causes " that results in impurity,[85] but even the downright insidiousness of the human heart (*dolus malus*),[86] the Satanic principle incarnate in man. And he confessed the need for grace. But there he stopped! Since his rationalism was ill-equipped to support any notion

of God's real presence and action in history, Kant was unable
to develop any doctrine of grace. Having made a polite bow
in the direction of grace, he confessed that he was quite unable to adopt it into his moral maxims " either for theoretical
or practical use "; [87] and he argued that man must proceed
" as though everything depended on him; only on this condition dare he hope that higher wisdom will grant the completion of his well-intentioned endeavors." [88]

Instead of developing a doctrine of grace as an answer to
the human predicament, Kant persisted in his moralistic view.
Even after admitting the radical evil of the human heart, he
still clung to the fictitious idea that " a seed of goodness still
remains in its purity, incapable of being extinguished or corrupted." [89] What a convenient little center of the self this is,
wholly insulated from all the corruptions of mixed motives
and the perversity of self-love! We would agree that a seed of
goodness remains in the sinner, but it is psychologically impossible to hold that such a center is unaffected by man's basic
sinfulness. The apostle Paul would probably call this a rationalistic evasion of the fundamental problem. As John
Oman said, Kant would have no gospel, yet " no scheme of
morals ever stood in more need of one." [90]

Though championing a metaphysical rationalism, which
Kant abandoned, Hegel too viewed religious beliefs, in the
main, as a substandard form of rational belief. It is true that
there is ambiguity in Hegel's thought on the matter of the
relative value of religion and philosophy. Sometimes he wrote
in a way that leads one to think that religion is the original
and originating force of Spirit, while philosophy plays merely
the role of intellectual interpretation and refinement. For example, he wrote:

> Only one more word concerning the desire to teach the
> world what it ought to be. For such a purpose philosophy
> at least always comes too late. Philosophy, as the thought
> of the world, does not appear until reality has completed
> its formative process, and made itself ready. History thus
> corroborates the teaching of the conception that only in
> the maturity of reality does the ideal appear as counter-
> part to the real, apprehends the real world in its sub-

stance, and shapes it into an intellectual kingdom. When philosophy paints its grey in grey, one form of life has become old, and by means of grey it cannot be rejuvenated, but only known. The owl of Minerva takes its flight only when the shades of night are gathering.[91]

Similarly, in his *Lectures on the Philosophy of Religion,* Hegel wrote:

It is not the concern of philosophy to produce religion in any individual. Its existence is, on the contrary, presupposed as forming what is fundamental in everyone. So far as man's essential nature is concerned, nothing new is to be introduced into him. To try to do this would be as absurd as to give a dog printed writings to chew, under the idea that in this way you could put mind into it.[92]

In reading Hegel more fully, however, one repeatedly comes upon another way of assessing the relative value of religion and philosophy. For Hegel, religion is bound up with what he called picture-thinking (*Vorstellung*). The essential difference between religion and philosophy lies in the fact that " the universal spirit exists . . . in religion in the form of feeling and pictorial imaginative thinking, and in philosophy in the form of pure free thought." [93] That Hegel regarded philosophy as superior to religion is clear when he referred to Luther's principle of faith and the witness of the Spirit, and added that " the more mature mind " seeks to apprehend the essential truth of Spirit " in conception." [94] From numerous passages similar to these just cited, it is difficult to avoid the impression that " it is from philosophy rather than from religion that Hegel himself prefers to draw his own spiritual nourishment." [95] After elaborating the nature of religious faith, Hegel added, " But I have other and higher needs besides." [96] Hence, Hegel could label religious belief " ordinary thought." [97] Hence also, he could contend that " although many a great and richly endowed nature, and many a profound intelligence, has found satisfaction in religious truth, yet it is the Notion, this inherently concrete thought, which is not as yet satisfied." [98]

The inescapable impression that one receives from Hegel's writings is that he was after all a rationalist, despite the tributes he paid to historical religion and to its traditional symbols. As John Baillie says, " The light by which Hegel himself lives is not so much Christianity as Absolute Idealism." [99] Hegel gives historical religion a place of high significance; yet, to quote another interpreter, " he differs very little from the old view that religion is a kind of popular philosophy. . . . In the last issue we come upon a great formula, and when that absolute truth is found, religion is not only satisfied but surpassed." [100]

Because Hegel failed to appreciate the depth dimension of faith's relation to God as an existential ultimate, he had no hesitancy in depreciating faith, for by so doing he was able to make good his case that religious faith stands in need of revision and intellectual purification by the power of metaphysical thinking. And although he did affirm that positive revealed religion is a source of philosophical knowledge, he really concluded by subordinating religion to philosophy. This is what we mean when we say that for him, religious belief is a substandard form of philosophy. The main accent in Hegel shifts from religion to metaphysics per se. The result is a weakening of the concern for historical revelation, so that in the left wing of Hegel's followers (Strauss, Croce), religion is finally identified with mythology, with the result that to all intents and purposes, religion is dismissed from the dominating concern of the philosopher.

What the Enlightenment cherished was thus conceived as given in its fullness at all times and for all men. As Adolf Harnack aptly expressed it, " They believed that each person, from the dawn of creation, possessed in his ' reason ' a solid capital asset which enables him to pay whatever is needed for a virtuous and happy life." [101] Further, they believed that the being of man is a harmonious part of nature and needs only to unfold and develop his natural potential in order to fulfill his humanity. Such a philosophy obviously felt no vital need of history, for it conceived its own reason to be already in full possession of anything it could receive from history. History is superfluous to such rationalism. At best, a historical religion could only be a veiled or symbolic expression of true " natural religion."

Little wonder that the " once for all " revelation of God in Jesus Christ in traditional Christianity found itself in direct opposition to the " once for all " revelation of God in Universal Reason of the eighteenth century, if it is permissable to use the term " revelation " in connection with the insights of this reason. The " once for all " revelation of Christianity happened once: the decisive event called " Jesus Christ." The " once for all " revelation of rationalism happens everywhere and all the time, independent of history. In a radical way this rationalism cut the bond between religion and history.

Fifth, the fires of faith in an all-sufficient Reason gradually lost their radiance, so that the age of reason was followed by reactions of various kinds. First of all, critical reason finally turned on its own faith in reason, giving birth to the skeptical movement. This movement was most vocal in France. The main thing in the French salons of the period was to be witty and clever. According to the popular slogan: To make light of philosophy is the way to be a true philosopher.

The modern skeptical movement had two major prongs. Already in the seventeenth century, in fact, the first prong became manifest in the writings of Blaise Pascal, who used philosophical skepticism to support the claims of faith. Pascal argued that " it is a good thing to be worn out and exhausted by the unsuccessful pursuit of true good in order to hold out one's arms to the Saviour." [102] Again, " It is in vain, O men, that you seek within yourselves the cure for your miseries. All your insight only leads you to the knowledge that it is not in yourselves that you will discover the true and the good. The philosophers promised them to you, and have not been able to keep their promise. They do not know what your true good is, or what your true state is. How should they have provided you with a cure for ills which they have not even understood? " [103] Since philosophy is powerless to decide the ultimate issues of life and death, Pascal stressed the need to " wager " that there is a God. Here finally the suprarational decision of faith returns.

Throughout his writings, Pascal underscored the limits of

reason. He reminded the rationalists that it is only the part of wisdom humbly to admit that the final step of reason is " the recognition that there are an infinite number of things which are beyond it." [104] It would indeed be the height of folly for rationalism to show itself blind to this obvious fact. But Pascal went farther. He argued that one does not really know God by means of some philosophical soliloquy that fails to arrive at the dialogue of faith and worship. The philosopher merely spins out *his own theories*. The content of his knowldge is nothing but *his own ideas*. Pascal argued that it is only through the revelation of God himself in Jesus Christ that we can know God, our own selves, and the meaning of life and death. " Except in Jesus Christ, we do not know the meaning of our life or our death, or God or ourselves." [105]

The second prong of the skeptical movement received its initial expression in the stance of David Hume. Like Pascal, Hume was too critical in his insights into the weaknesses of reason to arrive at any firm rational belief in God. But he did not become an outright atheist. He remained a skeptic, that is, an agnostic, to his dying day. Though perhaps more than anything else Hume longed for a rationally defensible faith in God, he was never able to achieve such a faith. He could only give the final verdict: I do not know! One might call his position a practical sort of atheism, since it left him with no faith by which to live. Yet Hume would never *deny* that God exists, for he knew too clearly that he could not know this either.

The second prong of the skeptical movement was carried forward by men like John Stuart Mill and T. H. Huxley. Mill veered to the right of Hume's position, in cultivating belief in God, since on Hume's empirical premises, this was at least a definite possibility,[106] and since " this small and confined " human life " stands greatly in need of any wider range and greater height of aspiration " which religious imagination can generate " without running counter to the evidence of fact." [107] Theology should therefore be retained, according to Mill, for while it may not be " intellectually sustainable," it is never-theless " morally useful." [108]

T. H. Huxley stood in the same tradition of skepticism,

though he veered to the left of Hume. Huxley contended that conclusions should be accepted only when supported by adequate empirical evidence. He repudiated as "immoral" the doctrine "that there are propositions which men ought to believe without logically satisfactory evidence." [109] Huxley declared that "the foundation of morality is to have done, once and for all, with lying; to give up pretending to believe that for which there is no evidence, and repeating unintelligible propositions about things beyond the possibilities of knowledge." [110] Huxley coined the word "agnostic" to characterize the group of thinkers who shared his ultra-Humean point of view.

It should be borne in mind just here also that the deep religious hunger of the human spirit soon tired of being fed nothing but "a mess of ethical and metaphysical crumbs" (Schleiermacher). Hence, there emerged in England the great Evangelical Awakening as a reaction to rationalistic Christianity, an awakening associated with the Wesleyan movement of the eighteenth century. In Germany, however, the pietistic awakening came in the preceding century and represented a reaction to the deadness of Protestant orthodoxy. The movement of rationalism in eighteenth- and nineteenth-century Germany, which followed on the heels of the pietistic revival, assumed the form of metaphysical idealism. The subsequent reaction to this era of speculative idealism came in the form of a new and eventually profound interest in history, generated at first by Herder and by the movement of Romanticism. It was thus in Germany, more than in any other country that the discipline of historical study, as we know it today, received its initial vigorous development. As we shall see in the following section, this opened up new possibilities for the further development of Christian theology, along historical lines.

III

The Modern Development of the Idea of History

Although remnants of eighteenth-century rationalism manifest themselves even yet today, its fundamental perspective on human existence has been overcome. It has been overcome by the nineteenth- and twentieth-century development of " the historical sense," which exposed the illusory nature of the belief in a Universal Reason complete within itself. The growth of historical-mindedness exposed the superficialism and falsity of rationalism by showing how profoundly all human life and thought are enmeshed in, and determined by, historical processes and forces.

It is not our purpose in this chapter to trace in detail the development of the idea of history in the nineteenth and twentieth centuries. But we do wish to indicate some of the basic phases of this development sufficiently to show the significance of the shift from the rationalistic climate of the eighteenth century to that of the subsequent historical-mindedness. By doing this, we shall be able to see how this shift made possible a fresh development of theology, while at the same time posing new problems for it. In these developments we shall thus see another example of our thesis regarding the historical character of the Christian faith. We shall see again how the concrete expression of faith is in part determined by the intellectual climate of the age in which faith lives and seeks to fulfill itself, and how the dialogue between theology and secular thought is a fruitful one for the enrichment of theology and for its vitality in the contemporary situation.

HERDER AND ROMANTICISM

One of the earliest thinkers to break with the Enlightenment view of history was Johann Gottfried von Herder, who in 1774 published a work entitled *A Philosophy of History for the Cultivation of Mankind*. Herder's monumental four-volume work, *Ideen zur Philosophie der Geschichte der Menschheit* was published between the years 1784 and 1791.

Herder was highly skeptical toward the " space-flight " (*Luftfahrt*) of rationalistic metaphysics. It was his belief that " the action of God in Nature," or the ideas which the Eternal has " laid before us in the series of His works " are the only valid sources of our knowledge of truth. Nature is the " Holy Book " from which we may correctly learn about the divine principles of man's humanity.[1] According to Herder, the reality of man's humanity is the highest object of man's knowledge and commitment.[2] Indeed, even when we attempt to conceive of angels or deities, we are obliged to conceive of them as ideal men.[3]

On the presupposition of an organismic view of reality, Herder contended that Deity has informed Nature with the principles and laws of its being, and that henceforth Deity does not interfere with the operations of Nature. This same judgment also holds good in the case of *human* nature. Deity helps us, said Herder, only through our own understanding, through our own rational powers. Deity formed man and said to him: " You are to be my image! You are to be a god on earth! Rule and dominate the face of the earth! Whatever nobility and excellence you have the power to create out of your own nature, create it! I shall not permit you to lean on the crutch of any miracle, for I have placed your destiny in your own human hands. All my sacred, eternal laws of Nature, however, will assist you in your task." [4]

Consistent with his belief that Deity does not interfere with the processes of Nature (including human nature), Herder viewed the course of human history as a natural phenomenon, which he therefore proceeded to study in the same manner as all other natural forms of life.

As mentioned above, Herder held an organismic view of

reality. The organismic idea of reality as a totality constituted the basic frame of reference for Herder's view of the being and history of man. He viewed human life as an organic and integral part of the process of Nature. Human life emerges out of, and develops in, the matrix of Nature, and at different times and in different places finds satisfying expression and fulfills itself in a vast variety of ways. The study of history convinced Herder that Nature organized man in as great a variety of ways as possible.[5]

Herder was one of the earliest thinkers to emphasize the idea of basic differences in men. Just as in Nature no two leaves of a tree are the same, still less are any two human faces or organizations alike.[6] Human nature is indeed not uniform, but "infinitely diversified." [7] Each man is a unique world in himself, radically unique, and in his inner being different from all others.[8]

Along with the emphasis on the infinite variety in the forms of the actualization of man's humanity in the course of history, Herder still clung to the idea of progress, in general. He believed that history shows that people build their cultures and civilizations on the achievements of past generations. For this progressive movement of the human race, man is equipped with the capacity of memory.[9] This being the case, Herder held that if ancient nations so gloriously achieved the realization of a worse purpose (ein schlechteres Ziel), there is no reason why we today may not achieve a purer, nobler goal.[10] For man is the kind of being who is able to profit and learn from the mistakes of yesterday. In the general history of the human race, as in that of the individual, the folly and depravity of the human race exhaust themselves until man finally learns to live according to the laws of reason.[11] The irrationality and discord of man cannot forever block the way to progress. When reason's time comes, it will finally prevail, for reason is an "ever advancing" force in human history.[12]

While Herder thus still clung to the Enlightenment faith in reason and progress, he nevertheless repudiated the Enlightenment idealization of our modern period in two ways. First, he insisted that we must judge the historical stages of the past not on the basis of our present standards, but in relation to their own situations in history. With his eye squarely on the Enlightenment, Herder declared that only a " sense- less pride " would lead one to say that the inhabitants of all parts of the world must be " European " in order to live hap- pily and well.[13]

Each historical situation is a unique individuality. The present situation thus was not possible for the past, because everything that man achieves is conditioned by time, place, climate, circumstances, and the stream of conditions that press in upon the people involved in the situation.[14] The vast variety of historical situations is the logical outcome of the fact that the possibilities of human existence are exceedingly numerous. It is Nature's design that in the vast panorama of history all these possibilities are to be realized.

Second, Herder repudiated the Enlightenment belief in a *final period* of human perfection as the goal of history. In this regard, Herder anticipated the famous statement of Ranke, that every generation stands equidistant from eternity, and that each generation is an end in itself.

Herder contended that happiness, the goal of human life, can be realized in each and every stage of human history, be- cause happiness is an inward condition of the human mind and spirit. The measure and determination of happiness do not lie in external conditions. " Each man has within himself the measure of his happiness. " [15] Nature created a vast variety of forms of human existence, said Herder, in order to bestow upon each one his appropriate measure of satisfaction, " in his time and situation." [16]

Romanticism, which felt the influence of Herder's thought, added further strength to the historical reaction to the En- lightenment by developing a fresh, sympathetic appreciation of the different stages of human history. The outlook on history was greatly widened by Romanticism's sympathetic study of the past ages, which eighteenth-century rationalism had un- justifiably labeled as barbarous and uncivilized, or which it had simply left in total obscurity, a neglect that can only be attributed to its unwarranted self-adulation.

Now for the first time the study of history became as highly esteemed as other intellectual pursuits. This had not been the case during the Enlightenment, nor indeed during any preceding historical epoch. The new century of Romanticism even boasted of the fact that it was "the century of history," and this claim was certainly true, at least of the romantic and idealistic part of the nineteenth century. This is what marks the shift from the perspective of the eighteenth century to that of the nineteenth. The inadequate, indeed unhistorical, treatment of history by Voltaire, Hume, and others in the eighteenth century now, without argument, fell into disrepute. Those histories now seemed to be colorless, lacking any authentic feeling for history, and narrowly motivated by a propagandistic moral concern.

Romanticism picked up the principle of unique individuality that Herder had hit upon and developed it into a fundamental category of authentic existence. Schleiermacher, for example, confessed that for a long time he, too, had worshiped at the Enlightenment throne of Universal Reason, believing, like Kant and Fichte, that "there is but a single right way of acting in every situation," that true humanity calls for uniformity, and that differences between men are only skin-deep, so to speak, being due merely to differences in place and station.[17] But Schleiermacher broke with rationalism when there dawned upon him his "highest intuition," namely, the insight "that each man is meant to represent humanity *in his own way*, combining its elements uniquely."[18] By so doing, one becomes "an elect creation of the godhead." Man's essential freedom lies in this spiritual capacity "to assemble and integrate the elements of human nature to make a unique existence."[19]

Romanticism thus developed the ability to perceive intrinsic value and worth in historical situations other than its own, and thereby it greatly enlarged the sense of positive historical concern. The new taste for history was manifested in Romanticism's predominant interest in the poetry of the past, its folk songs and legends. It developed a feeling-appreciation for old national customs. It sang the old songs and dreamed the old dreams. Medieval chivalry, the drama of the Crusades, the peace and quiet of the cloister, the struggle of the Christian kings of Spain with the Arabs, England divided between the

Saxons and the Normans, the adventures of Wilhelm Tell —
all "became at this time the object of universal and national
sympathy, as did the rough, ingenuous popular literature,
poetry, and art." [20]

Freedom of self-expression and the sacrament of love were
central concerns of Romanticism. The Classicist was oriented
to the kind of social order that called upon the individual for
self-renunciation and self-restraint. Submission to the moral
law of Universal Reason was the norm. But the burning ideal
of the Romanticists was the vision of a community of free individuals conjoined in perfect union. This, said Schleiermacher, is the only reality worthy of being called a world:
"The eternal community of spiritual beings, their influence
upon each other, their mutual development, the sublime harmony of freedom." [21]

Ludwig Kahn has pointed out [22] that in the earlier phases
of the movement of Romanticism the individualistic aspect of
community was predominant, whereas in the latter state the
individualistic aspect gradually gave way to the communal, resulting in a positive appreciation even of the state, not, however, as a force that binds and suppresses the individual, but
the *ideal* state that supports the "absolute consummation"
of the individual. The earlier emphasis on individualism is
found in Tieck's *Franz Sternbalds Wanderungen* and *William
Lovell*, in Brentano's *Godwi*, and in Schlegel's *Lucinde*.
Arnim, Chamisso, and Schleiermacher tended to emphasize
the communal aspect. Said Schleiermacher, "No development
without love, and without individual development no perfection in love; each supplements the other, both increase in-
divisibly." [23]

It was the growing Romanticist interest in the communal
aspect that led to the conversion of many Romanticists to
Catholicism, for they came to see in the Catholic Church and
in the feudal state examples of the higher kind of community.
This led them to romanticize the Middle Ages. Wackenroder
and Tieck had also awakened historic interest in the Middle
Ages and in national history and art.

In the main, like Herder, the Romanticists' belief that a
past stage of history was of value *in itself*, as a unique (though,

of course, relative) expression of the human spirit, did not result in precisely the same kind of nostalgic yearning for the Golden Age of the past found in the Renaissance, though nostalgic yearning for the past was not lacking in Romanticism. Hölderlin, for example, felt that the ancient Greeks had achieved the ideal community of freedom. He therefore sang the praises of ancient Greece, as the Golden Age of freedom and harmony. Yet even Hölderlin was forward-looking, for his supreme ambition was to reawaken the spirit of ancient Greece in the Germany of his day. The new appreciation of the past was thus counterbalanced by the progressivistic belief that, after all, each stage of history takes its place in the process, leading to human expressions of still higher worth. The Romanticists looked forward to another golden age in which the controlling forces would be freedom and love, rather than law and duty.[24]

A central aspect of the historical reaction of Romanticism to the Enlightenment is thus found in the notion of *historical development,* though to be sure there were traces of this concept, here and there, during the eighteenth century. Romanticism thus provided a major increase in the modern doctrine of progress. Nor did the idea of development remain a mere academic idea; it widened and deepened into the prevailing spirit of the age. It is highly probable that the developmental aspect of the Romanticist view of history constitutes the major historic source of the central principle of Hegelian idealism. It is probably not too much to say that Hegel's system represents a metaphysical flowering of this principle of Romanticism.

Romanticism's view of the past differed from Renaissance humanism also in another respect. Humanism's admiration for the classics of Greco-Roman antiquity led it to idealize and eternalize certain elements of the past and to regard them, so to speak, as elevated above the mundane processes of human history, due to their intrinsic beauty and value. The classics were thus regarded as *permanent models* of literary excellence for all time — past, present, and future. Though Romanticism recovered a genuine taste for history, it did not thus set the classics of Greece and Rome on an eternal pedestal, but rather developed a sense of personal identity with the Greco-

Roman and other stages of man's past as a past with which they felt a deep kinship, since the same basic spirit of humanity that pulsed in their hearts also lived and moved in the ancients. There was thus in Romanticism a broader interest in the whole panorama of history than was found in humanism, and also a more authentic sense of the historical character of all human life and thought.

It is probably not too much to assert that the whole of history now became, for Romanticism, a necessary development of the world spirit, so that history per se became *Heilsgeschichte*. To be in the process of history was to be redeemed.

KANT AND THE GERMAN IDEALISTS

Immanuel Kant's brief essay " Idea for a Universal History with a Cosmopolitan Intent " marked the beginning of a long series of modern attempts to develop a " philosophy of history," especially in Germany. This movement was progressivistic in its bearings; that is, it attempted to show that history was a process of growth and development in which human life and thought reaches an ever-increasing fullness in the realization of man's spiritual, that is, rational, potential. As indicated in the preceding chapter, Kant was a true child of the Enlightenment in idealizing his own age of reason and regarding the past as "interwoven with stupidity, childish vanity, often childish viciousness and destructiveness." [25]

Further, the enormous prestige of the natural sciences led the men of the Enlightenment to assimilate the human mind to nature, to regard the human mind as an aspect of nature. This explains why they developed the (to us) somewhat strange notion of "natural" religion. Kant's view of history also reflects this naturalism, for basic to his view was the analogy between history and the teleology of nature, according to which " all natural faculties of a creature are destined to unfold completely and according to their end." [26] The natural *telos* of man is his rationality. Therefore, according to the analogy, the natural faculty of man " which aims at the use of reason shall be freely developed in the species, not in the individual." [27]

Kant thus developed the idea of a grand plan of world history. The course of history was necessary for the "gradual un-folding" of man's reason and the freedom of will which rested upon it,[28] through education and the development of a perfect constitution which would promote and protect civic freedom. Kant felt that restrictions on personal freedom were gradually being lifted during his age, and that thereby enlightenment was "gradually developing," though to be sure still with some "occasional nonsense and freakishness." [29]

But Kant's moral philosophy led him to posit here also a significant distinction between phenomena and things-in-themselves, especially when the thing-in-itself is man as a moral subject. When we view things as a spectator views them, they are phenomena. Could we view them from the inside, we would see them as an expression of mind. As man experiences his own self, thus, it is known in terms of moral freedom and responsibility. But for Kant, history is not seen from the inside, but as phenomena; that is, as nature. Kant was thus unable to escape the erroneous spectator view of history that was prevalent in his day.

Johann Gottlieb Fichte, a younger contemporary of Kant, resolved the antithesis that Kant left standing, the antithesis between phenomena and noumena. With a highly questionable arbitrariness, Fichte absorbed the world aspect of the Kantian ego-world antithesis into the ego aspect. Expressed in another way, Fichte resolved the problem of mind and matter, the ideal and the real, by interpreting the real as *nothing but* a functioning within the essential nature of the ideal.

It is not germane to our purpose here to elaborate on Fichte's idealistic metaphysics at length, but these remarks suffice to indicate why Fichte has been called the first of the great German idealists. It was Fichte who laid the basic groundwork of concepts that bore rich fruit in the magnificent system of Hegel.

Following Kant's epistemological thesis that the empirical content of knowledge must of necessity obey the laws of the a priori categories of the knowing mind, Fichte applied this basic principle to history. Like Kant also, Fichte held the view that the lines of the past converge in the present and that the whole of history "presupposes a World-plan" [30] and represents the logical unfolding of this grand plan. Among other things, the word " logical " here means " necessary," for this life of the human race, said Fichte, constitutes a development that " *must* necessarily be fulfilled, and therefore *shall* certainly be fulfilled." [31]

Each age in this logical procession of the human race represents a concrete expression of a basic Idea.[32] The successive ages of history thus form a " logical " sequence and follow upon one another according to the logical schema that tends toward the final realization of the end of the entire process. There is thus in Fichte's view a logically successive periodization of history. The end of this logical world plan is that in the life of mankind on earth all relations are to be ordered " with freedom according to Reason." [33] In terms of the *telos* of human existence thus Fichte stood in agreement with Kant. Fichte proceeded to define more exactly what he meant by the idea of a life of freedom " according to Reason " by saying that it is realized when the individual forgets himself and commits himself to the race. Selfish individualism is thus the essence of life contrary to Reason.[34]

In Fichte's analysis, there are five basic stages [35] in the logical unfolding of history. First, the primitive stage in which rational freedom is realized at the low level of unobstructed, natural instinct; here Reason acts through blind instinct and not yet through freedom of will. Second, the epoch in which Reason as instinct is changed into " an external ruling authority " by a few powerful individuals who establish the rule of authoritarian government. Though this seems to be a restriction on freedom (and indeed is), it is in reality a stage of growth and transition, for such compulsion generates its opposite — the impulse toward personal freedom, which could never emerge in the primitive stage of life according to mere natural instinct. Third, the epoch of liberation, both from external authoritarianism and from Reason as instinct. This represents the stage of revolution, a stage of " unrestrained licentiousness." [36] The progression beyond this level seems to come when democracy makes its appearance, when the distinction between those governing and the governed disappears in the democratic state, in which it is the same body of people who both govern and are governed, according to Reason.

But the dialectical development continues in regard to the relation of the individual to the "external authority" of the laws of modern science. This leads to the fourth epoch, " the Epoch of Reason as Science." Finally, rational freedom finds its highest level of fulfillment in the fifth epoch, " the Epoch of Reason as Art." At this highest level, the mind finally sees in nature not something foreign to itself, but its own counterpart. Here finally is the age in which humanity, with clarity of vision and fullness of rational freedom, " builds itself up into a fitting image and representative of Reason." [37]

At the last stage of history, we see clearly Fichte's basic understanding of reality as mind. The postulation of its own existence by the ego is the first principle of Fichte's philosophy. But for the ego to develop self-consciousness, it is necessary for it to project part of experience outside itself, for only in this fashion can self-consciousness come to being. Thus the nonego is the second principle. But all this is merely a description of the process of mind. What Fichte calls the nonego (the world) is for him nothing but a passive, negative creation of the ego, logically projected for purposes of self-realization. For Fichte, creative art is the highest expression of ego realization in freedom, for here the ego passes from a realization of simple obedience to the projected nonego to one of love and sympathy. In creative art one finds the fullest realization of freedom and blessedness, for here one's whole being " goes forth in free self-sufficient energy, in the consciousness of this activity." [38] Here one gives himself, in free and spontaneous devotion, to an objective goal that he knows to be one with his own creative spirit.

The movement toward a "philosophy of history," which began in Germany with Herder and was carried forward by Kant, Schiller, Fichte, and Schelling, reached its climax in the magnificent system of Hegel. Hegel followed Fichte in resolving the Kantian antithesis between noumena and phenomena by absolutizing the ego aspect of the antithesis, so that for him everything became a manifestation of the dynamic, self-realizing process of the absolute ego.

Hegel began his book on The Philosophy of History by

making clear what he meant by a "philosophy" of history.[39] He distinguished between original, reflective, and philosophical history. In the works of Heroditus and Thucydides we have examples of original history. Here the author describes what he himself has seen, heard, and shared in his own experience. The author thus translated external happenings into conceptual presentations, using, of course, not only what he himself observed but also reports and narrations of others as well. But his data have to do only with contemporaneous events, deeds, and situations.[40]

Reflective history is that history whose presentation refers, not to the contemporary situation, but to a historical epoch of the past. This task calls for the exercise of the historian's critical powers and insights on the materials supplied wholly by others, in order to set forth a representation of the entire history of a people, or a country, or even perhaps the entire world.

Philosophical history is distinguished from the former two in that what is here attempted is an exposition (*Erläuterung*) or justification (*Rechtfertigung*) of historic process.[41] In history, thought is subordinate to facts and events and is guided by the historically given. But philosophy comes to the material of history with an a priori. It is not content to leave the events of history *wie sie ist*, but rather it determines to *organize* history according to thought, to *regulate* it by an a priori. For "the Spirit knows that Nature and the World must also have reason in them since God has created them according to Reason."[42] As Hegel saw it, the only idea that philosophy rightly brings to history as an a priori is the simple idea of Reason, the idea that Reason presides and reigns over history, and that therefore world history develops according to the rule of Reason.[43] The task of the philosophy of history is thus to unfold the development of Reason (*Weltgeist*) in the historical course of its life. Its task is to show that history is "the rational, necessary development of the World-spirit, which is the substance of history, the one Spirit (Mind) whose nature is always one and the same, and which expresses and explains its own nature in the being of the world."[44]

Like Fichte, thus Hegel began with a logical a priori. But

unlike Fichte, it was not for Hegel a *purely* a priori approach.
Hegel avoided the nonempirical rationalism of Fichte and the
Enlightenment on the one hand, and the historical empiricism
of the positivists on the other. Hegel took his cue here from
Kant's *Critique of Pure Reason*, in which a priori *and* empiri-
cal elements are welded into a unity in the cognitive act.
Hegel's philosophy of history represents a colossal effort to
bind the logical and the empirical together in a similar way.

It is precisely this twofold basis of Hegel's approach to the
study of history that generates some difficulties. Kant encountered no difficulty in making empirical sense data con-
form to the a priori forms of the mind in the act of knowledge. But he did encounter a certain recalcitrance in the data
when, by the same schema, he developed his moral philosophy.
Hegel's system runs into a similar difficulty, because the empirical data of historical knowledge are events the inside of
which are human beings, with their instincts, passions, and
irrational drives. Hegel wrestled valiantly with this difficulty.
The reason with which he was concerned is not the abstract
Reason of the Enlightenment, but concrete human reason, the
totality of finite minds. Hegel was only interested in viewing
the Spirit — in Universal History — " in its concrete reality." [45]
The *Weltgeist* (Reason) includes everything that has interested man and which now interests him. Whatever *man*
does — it is this in which this Spirit is active. "The realm of
Spirit is that which *man* has brought forth." [46]

What now of the conflict between human reason and human
passion? Hegel's answer is that Reason is a wiser, broader
force which, *in the final analysis,* includes and controls man's
passions and freedoms. Here we come upon Hegel's famous
" cunning of reason " (*List der Vernunft*) ,[47] which operates
in such fashion that though human passions and freedoms are
genuine in their subjectivity, they are yet made to serve the
ends of Reason. A wise, overruling Reason (Providence?) ex-
ercises a beneficent " cunning " in order to lead the passions
and irrational forces to more worthy ends than those at which
they immediately aim. In this way, Reason so to speak tricks
passion into fulfilling (unconsciously of course) the former's
ends. By following the call of caprice and arbitrary humor,

man thus finds that there is a logic in the nature of things which causes his acts to turn out something quite different from what he himself had willed. Schopenhauer gave a popular expression to this " cunning " of Reason in what he called the illusions of love, by means of which the propagation of the human species is carried forward. This is a "tricky" way for Reason to accomplish this end, but effective nonetheless.

The " cunning of reason " brings us to an ambiguity in Hegel's concept of Reason or Spirit. Presumably the conflict is not between God conceived as transcendent Reason (Providence) and human passion, but between *human* reason and *human* passion. For the most part, Hegel consistently avoided the idea of a transcendent Providence in his idea of God, and held to a resolute immanentism. Though Hegel has been interpreted as a theist, a pantheist, and even an atheist, one is perhaps not far from the center if he regards Hegel's system to be a metaphysic of pantheistic monism or logical evolutionism.[48] Hegel's Absolute Mind is not to be construed as a transcendent reality, either in the Greek sense or in the sense of the Biblical Creator Lord. Absolute Mind is, rather, for Hegel, the essence of all finite minds. He wrote: " History is the development of the finite worldly mind (*Weltgeist*) in its totality as it unfolds itself and becomes conscious of itself in its temporal development." [49]

Yet the " cunning of reason " nevertheless sounds very much as if he were speaking of some reality that transcends the finite realm, something that works, through human passion, to achieve an end that strictly speaking is Reason's end, but not that of these human beings. " A divine Will reigns powerfully in the world," said Hegel, " and is not so powerless that it cannot determine the vast content of the world." [50] Universal Reason remains in the background, " uninjured " by the play of human passions. Hegel explicitly stated that it is the *phenomenal* world which Reason treats in this fashion; which would seem to imply that this " cunning of reason " is transphenomenal.[51] Many critics [52] feel that Hegel here slipped into a non-Hegelian mode of thought. He seems to have fallen back upon the theological idea of Providence, or perhaps on the secularized version of Providence found in the Enlightenment and in

Kant, where the scheme of history is carried out not by man but by Nature.

A second weakness in Hegel's logicoempirical approach to history is the difficulty encountered by all a priori approaches to history. The empirical facts are not permitted to stand in their own integrity, but are molded to fit the a priori schema. Hegel's philosophy of history is not entirely free from this weakness. His critics at this point are numerous. Robert Flint argued that Hegel was thus led unnaturally to separate the major developments of history, and unnaturally to exclude some of the most important history from the province assigned to the philosophy of history,[53] namely, art, religion, and philosophy.

The latter criticism just cited is not too weighty. It does correctly point up a schematic weakness in Hegel's system. His system is divided into three great divisions: the Logic, the Philosophy of Nature, and the Philosophy of Spirit. Each of these has three subdivisions, and each subdivision divides again into three parts. Hegel was extremely fond of the threesome analysis — the familiar old Hegelian friend, the triad of thesis, antithesis, and synthesis. The Philosophy of Spirit is divided into subjective, objective, and absolute mind. Subjective mind includes anthropology, phenomenology, and psychology. Objective mind includes legal right, morality, and ethical obedience. Absolute mind is divided into art, religion, and philosophy. The philosophy of history is thus, according to Hegel's system, that part of the Philosophy of Spirit which deals with the evolution of Reason in the state; that is, it belongs to the province of objective mind. Logically, the philosophy of history does not deal with art, religion, and philosophy, for these belong to the province of absolute mind.

But the weakness here is purely schematic, for Hegel's contribution to historical method is found, in good measure, not merely in his book *The Philosophy of History*, but also in eight volumes under the titles *Aesthetics, Philosophy of Religion*, and *History of Philosophy*.

It is not easy, however, to alleviate the former criticism, namely, that Hegel's a priori led to an unnatural handling of the facts of history. He dealt with Oriental history only " very summarily," since it offered little that would fit his logical categories.[54] He was able to demonstrate a world progress only by ignoring historical regressions into barbarism and by ignoring also "a contemporary plurality of civilization." [55] This illustrates how Hegel's a priori approach did violence to the facts, for according to his logic of historical process only one nation at a time can represent Absolute Spirit, which made it necessary for Hegel to "rule out all others from history." [56] Hegel's scant treatment of American history was the result of the classic tradition "which identified the history of certain parts of Europe with the history of the world, to the utter neglect of the rest of humanity." [57] Cohen contends that Hegel both grossly neglected the facts and also did violence to them,[58] as a result of his mistaken notion that the historical order of particular events is necessarily identical with the logical order of his grasp of the categories of reason.[59]

Further, although Hegel was aware of "estrangement," "unhappy consciousness," nonbeing, and similar existential concepts, and took them into his system,[60] he nevertheless held that these are overcome and that man is reconciled to, and realizes his final unity with, the Absolute or Divine:

> God only to behold, and know, and feel,
> Till, by exclusive consciousness of God,
> All self annihilated, it shall make
> God its identity.[61]

Hegel argued that God's love for man and man's for God *is* the eternal life "in which one's temporal nothingness is both annihilated and affirmed," and that we should banish all illusions which resolve the triumph of essential over existential being into a futuristic "beyond," separated from the present.[62] "History both *is* and *overcomes* its own inadequacies." [63]

Kierkegaard and the existentialists reply that Hegel was in error in permitting his essentialism to swallow up the concrete fact of man's estrangement from the Ultimate. "Existence," says Paul Tillich, "is estrangement and not reconciliation; it is dehumanization and not the experience of essential humanity." [64] Hegel's system hides from our eyes the real truth about man's historical predicament. Instead of being a self-manifestation of Absolute Spirit, history is existence in *real* conflict, "threatening man with self-destruction." Therefore Hegel's central doctrine of essentialism is dead wrong.[65]

It is important to remember that for Hegel, history is only one phase of the life of Absolute Spirit, construed always as dynamic process. The totality of things, for Hegel, assumed the form of the Infinite (*Weltgeist*) rising to consciousness in the finite and realizing its own essential nature in and through the finite process which we call the world. The Absolute Idea " is itself in its pure essence when it is enclosed in its Notion in simple identity and has not yet entered into the state of *showing* in any form-determinateness." [66] But in the process of the self-realization of this Absolute Idea everything is but a passing *moment* of the Absolute and accordingly *can only appear* as it does and when it does. All is determined by the necessity of the inner logic of the Notion.

In the course of its self-realization the Notion passes through three distinct stages. First, it moves through the realm of the universals, which underlie both nature and the finite mind; the science of logic deals with this stage. Second, the Notion moves to particularize itself — the realm of nature, physics, and organics; the Philosophy of Nature deals with this phase. Third, the Spirit frees itself from nature, and returns to itself, now as absolutely free Spirit and fully self-conscious Reason. But this final, perfect freedom and self-knowledge can only be accomplished by thus realizing itself in the multitude of external forms of being. We can say thus of world history that it is " the manifestation of the Spirit, the manner in which it attains to the knowledge of itself as it is in itself." [67] In another passage Hegel said that " Absolute Spirit is the living and actual identity of the eternal being which *is what it is in itself,* but which also is its own eternal self-differentiation, eternally reabsorbed by itself. As this absolute knowledge, absolute spirit is this process *for itself.*" [68]

For Hegel, though man is regarded as finite spirit, he is ultimately identical with the Absolute Spirit, for only in the development of finite mind does the Infinite Spirit (God) first rise to the level of self-consciousness. As a finite individual, I am thus a fleeting but real *moment* in the life process of Absolute

Spirit. In a number of passages scattered throughout his writings, Hegel expressed the idea that "Man knows God only in so far as God Himself knows Himself in Man." [69] The self-knowledge of Spirit that emerges in the process of its self-realization is the Spirit's self-consciousness in man, or the knowledge which man has of God. The ontological identity between man and God was expressed boldly by Hegel when he wrote that "the Spirit of Man, whereby he knows God, is simply the Spirit of God Himself." [70] If this last statement doesn't completely obliterate the Biblical boundary line between man the creature and God the Creator Lord, no conception of the absolute identity of God and man could do so. Gone for Hegel is the over-againstness of God the Holy One, in relation to man as sinner.

Whatever be the errors in Hegel's idealism, he is to be praised for avoiding the pitfall into which so many thinkers of the latter nineteenth century fell by approaching history via the analogy of nature. It is true that Hegel was pre-Darwinian in his view that the life of nature "describes only a recurrent circular movement." [71] This traditional error was later corrected by the theory of evolution. But Hegel was correct in distinguishing the process of nature as nonhistorical and in viewing history as the process of mind or thought. In the life of man as spirit, said Hegel, there exists a real capacity for change and indeed "for the better. . . . a propensity of perfectibility." [72]

History, then, for Hegel is the history of *thought*. The Spirit is the *thinking* One who is creative in itself. "As such we find it in world-history." [73] History is part and parcel of the eternal and universal process of Absolute Spirit or Idea. The entire life of human mind or spirit is a history of some aspect of the life process of Spirit, as it moves toward the fullness and perfection of knowledge.

Hegel thus preserved the idea of the unity of history, not under the traditional idea of Providence, but as the unity of Absolute Spirit realizing itself in the dialectic of history. In this way Hegel overcame the static view of Being in traditional metaphysics, which regarded the Cosmic Ultimate as a timeless, motionless Absolute, beyond and outside the realm of history. In his analysis of the determination of Spirit, the very first thing that Hegel said was that Spirit is *not an abstraction* from human nature. Rather, the Spirit is "individual active, and absolutely living." [74] The essence of Spirit's being is to have itself as its object of consciousness. The Spirit is therefore characterized by thought. Thinking is Spirit's inner essence, and this thinking is a thinking that has its own actuality and intelligible structure for its object.

Hegel was correct at least to the extent that in order to understand history it is necessary to get beyond the objectivistic view that merely sees the *outside* of human events and happenings. True historical understanding must penetrate to the *inside* of these events, for the meaning of these happenings lies in the thought of the people who executed them and who gave concrete expression to their ideas in these external actions.

What now about the direction of the movement of history? Does Hegel interpret world history in a teleological sense? The answer is yes, but the end of history, for Hegel, was not eschatological, in the sense of a futuristic fulfillment. He complained against the kind of teleology that is connected with the idea of " an extra-mundane " understanding, for it is removed from the true investigation of nature that attempts to understand the actualities of nature " not as extraneous but as immanent determinateness." [75] For Hegel, the end or goal of history is *the historical process itself,* which as such is the self-realization of Absolute Spirit as rational freedom.

It was Hegel's view that the history of the world is " the progress of the consciousness of freedom." [76] His analysis of the historical " progress " of freedom distinguished three stages.[77] First, the Orientals failed to realize that the Spirit of man *as such* is free. At this first stage the Spirit slumbers, so to speak, in ignorance of its freedom and therefore in passive submission to civil and spiritual despotism. They knew only that *one* is free, and because of this the freedom of the one (Maharajah, for example) was an arbitrary, wild licentiousness. Second, the Greeks developed the idea of the freedom of many, but still had no idea that man *as such* is free. The institution of slavery still placed severe restrictions on the idea of freedom among the Greeks, and their freedom was only an uncertain, imperfect, and circumscribed freedom. Third, the full consciousness that man *as such* is free was the product of religion, especially the Christian religion. But here, too, it underwent a long process of development until, as Hegel believed, it had finally reached its ripest expression in the Germanic or modern epoch.

In view of subsequent historical developments, Hegel's belief in the glorious modern triumph of rational freedom is placed in serious question by the brutal historical facts that contradict the thesis. To put it another way, Hegel paid too much attention to the logic of his own system of dialectics and too little attention to the actual facts of history.

Hegel thus viewed world history in terms of stages of development of the basic teleological principle whose inner content is the consciousness of freedom.[78] His version of the doctrine of progress is metaphysical, but the metaphysics of immanentism. The Absolute is not a static Being outside world process. Hence, Hegel's idealism represents a reinterpretation of Platonism in the light of the historical consciousness of his age.[79]

But although Hegel's analysis of history set forth a doctrine of the development of human freedom and even stated that the essence of the goal of the World Spirit is reached " through the freedom of each individual," [80] we cannot forget that for him the individual is, in the last analysis, unreal. The individual is but a passing *moment* in the self-realization of the Absolute. Only the Absolute Spirit abides, and only the Absolute is absolutely free, that is, in the sense of being determined by nothing outside itself.

Reinhold Niebuhr's criticism of Hegel is well taken when he claims that Hegel's error was that he misunderstood the nature of the evil in history to be overcome. Hegel held that the task of theodicy is to comprehend the ills found in the world so that " the thinking Spirit may be reconciled to the negativities of existence." [81] The evil to be reconciled with the thinking Spirit is the conflict between the inner life of the person and the actual world. This, says Niebuhr, is to misunderstand the real drama of history. The real drama lies not in the discord between man as free spirit and the hard facts of nature, but rather in "the evil which men bring upon themselves and each other in their freedom." [82]

The Historiography of Positivism

Subsequent to Hegel, there was another major movement in the nineteenth century that came increasingly to reject all "philosophies of history" as worthless speculation. This was the movement known as "positivism," a movement that Collingwood aptly describes as "philosophy acting in the service of natural science, as in the Middle Ages philosophy acted in the service of theology." [83] Approaching the study of history with the method used in the natural sciences, positivistic historiography conceived of its task as twofold: first, discover the facts; second, formulate general laws. Others had searched for the *end* of history; the positivists would quest for *causes*. Others developed a *dynamic* of history; they would set forth a *mechanic* of history, a "social physics."

Historians now set to work to develop critical methods of ascertaining the facts of history. Since historical knowledge opens upon a vista into what Jacob Burckhardt called "an infinity of established facts," [84] it is not difficult to see why this first part of the program of positivistic historiography went on and on, while the second part — formulating general laws — was indefinitely postponed. Understandable also is the growing complaint both from the common people and from the philosophers. The former complained that the multitude of bare facts, compiled in catalogue fashion, is dry as dust and without significance to us in the living of our lives, while the philosophers objected that so long as the historians remained at the level of mere fact-finding, they were not yet fully "scientific" in their methodology.

Although such mere fact-finding and tabulation are indeed dry as dust and seemingly pointless, since the question of significance was not even raised, positivistic historiography did nevertheless result in a massive compilation of detail of this kind of encyclopedic information: compilations of historic inscriptions, the technical apparatus for archaeological research, new editions of historical texts, etc.

The spirit of the new historiography thus generated a whole school of highly trained philological technicians, who developed an exaggerated opinion of the superior "scientific" character of their "documentary history." This kind of history flourished more in Germany than elsewhere. The techniques and methods of research into chronicles and documents were developed to the nth degree. And as Benedetto Croce says, "Every mean little copier of a text, or collector of variants, or examiner of the relations of texts and conjecture as to the genuine text, raised himself to the level of a scientific man and critic, and not only dared to look upon himself as the equal of such men as Schelling, Hegel, Herder, and Schlegel, but did so with disdain and contempt, calling them 'anti-methodical.' " [85]

One of the most impressive results of positivistic historiography is to be found in Theodor Mommsen's massive, six-volume *History of Rome,* in which the author was concerned to present an extremely detailed "narration of the events." [86] Yet even Mommsen was unable to keep his narration wholly free from subjective value judgments. Indeed, it must be said that some of his value judgments possess an ethically negative significance, as for example when he manifestly shared in, and even glorified, the romantic, irrational love of war in his narration of the life of Caesar, "the entire and perfect man," [87] and defended the principle of Caesarism.[88]

Meanwhile, Darwin's *Origin of Species* was published, in 1859, representing a new development in science. It was really not new in setting forth the thesis that new species come into existence in the course of temporal process; this belief had already replaced the other static view which held that all species had been formed and finalized at creation. The novel element in Darwin's theory was the notion of "natural selection, or the survival of the fittest."

To use Darwin's own illustration, a wolf attacks various animals, capturing its prey sometimes by craft, sometimes by its superior strength, or possibly by its superior fleetness. Assuming that the wolf finds itself in a situation in which the fleetest deer were plentious and all other prey scarce, it seems obvious that nature would, in this instance, "select" the slimmest, swiftest wolves to survive, "providing they retained strength to master their prey." The theory of "natural selection," said Darwin, seems most reasonably to account for the difference between the greyhoundlike wolf that preys on deer, and the bulkier type of wolf that preys on sheep.[89]

Given a survival situation comparable to that of the wolf just cited, over a period of time, Darwin held, a variation in the wolf species would likely occur. "If the variation were of a beneficial nature, the original form would be supplanted by the modified form, through the survival of the fittest." [90] Natural selection thus operates "by the preservation and accumulation of beneficial variations." [91]

Darwin brought his famous treatise to a close with a note of optimism regarding the future of man. He praised Spencer's psychology which had already laid a solid foundation, "that of the necessary acquirement of each mental power and capacity by gradation." [92] The view that sees all beings not as special creations, but as lineal descendants in an evolutionary line of development is, said Darwin, an enobling view. He concluded:

> Judging from the past, we may safely infer that not one living species will transmit its unaltered likeness to a distant futurity, and very few will transmit progeny of any kind. But we may feel certain that the succession by generation has never once been broken since long before the Cambrian epoch, and that no cataclysm has desolated the whole world. Hence we may look with some confidence to a secure future of great length. And as natural selection works solely by and for the good of each being, all corporeal and mental endowments will tend to progress toward perfection.[93]

The popular mind was unable to distinguish between the idea of the emergence of new species in the temporal process and Darwin's concept of natural selection. Hence, Darwin gained the reputation of having invented the idea of evolution. The result was that history and science were now bound more closely together. The antithesis of the idea of history as a progressive development and the notion of science as the study of something static was now resolved. As Collingwood says, " The scientific point of view capitulated to the historical, and both now agreed in conceiving their subject-matter as progressive." [94] The word " evolution " now became the magic word in both disciplines, with the result that while in positivistic historiography there was a tendency to reduce history to nature, this tendency was now in part counterbalanced by the opposite tendency to reduce nature to history.

Despite the positivistic emphasis on fact-finding, the idea of development inherited from Romanticism and from German idealism had never been wholly forgotten. It now received a new impetus due to the growing popularity of Darwin's theory of evolution. The new thrust of this notion, combined with the idea that if history is to be " scientific " it must reach the second stage of formulating general laws, gave Auguste Comte the idea for his *philosophie positiv*. Comte addressed himself to the growing complaint that mere fact-finding in historical study is insufficient, and that for historical study to become significant something more meaningful must be done with the bare facts beyond merely ascertaining what they are. Comte proceeded to develop a new science, following the application of the method in natural science to the study of human history. It was to be a science of sociology, or " social physics." [95]

The evolutionary schema that Comte imposed upon the facts (discovered in them, he would argue) was what he regarded as " a great fundamental law " to which the development of human intelligence is " necessarily subject." [96] The logic of this development is characterized by three stages: the Theological (fictitious), the Metaphysical (abstract), and the Scientific (positive). These three stages of history represent respectively the intellectual childhood, adolescence, and maturity of mankind. [97]

It is not difficult to see how the emergence of metaphysics among the ancient Greeks represents a " development " of theology, since metaphysics does represent a modification, or more rationalistic version, of their theology. The supernatural beings (ultimate causes) of religion were rationalized into abstract ontological forces by the power of metaphysical think-

ing. But in holding to the same law of "development" in the
transition from metaphysics to science, Comte was a bit more
arbitrary in his logic, for the scientism for which he was plead-
ing represents an abandonment of the ancient quest for causes.

Comte therefore wished to eliminate the use of the word
"cause" in his positive philosophy, due to its inherited con-
notations of the ultimate origin and final purpose of the
world, both of which he felt to be utterly beyond the ken of
scientific thought. Instead, he proposed to study social phenomena exactly as the natural scientist studies the phenomena of nature. This meant that in his view, nature and history
are in principle identical. Social physics is to apply itself to
the study of the laws (scientific generalizations) of social
phenomena, that is, "their invariable relations of succession
and resemblance." [98]

According to Comte's philosophy, the sociologist would be
a superior kind of historian, for he transforms history into a
real science and thus treats scientifically the empirical data
that most positivists were content to treat purely factually.
With Francis Bacon and the empiricists, Comte agreed that
all valid scientific theories must be based on observed facts,
but he added: "It is equally true that facts cannot be observed without the guidance of some theory," for without the
latter mere facts would be "desultory and fruitless." [99]

The intellectual labors of Comte show that the danger
present in the new category of evolution was that it might
have blocked the further development of the discipline of history by generating the idea that historical development depends on the same basic law as does natural development, and
that the methods used in the study of natural science are therefore wholly adequate to the discipline of the study of history.
But this danger was averted by the fact that by the middle
of the nineteenth century the methods of critical-historical
research, in dealing with literary and archaeological sources,
were already developed to such a high degree that the growth
of history as an autonomous discipline could not, in this way,
be arrested. Especially in Germany, this critical-historical
method had become firmly entrenched.

The critical historians therefore ignored Comte and his

new "social physics"; they resolved to stick to their own fact-finding methodology and refused to move on, after the manner of natural science, to develop any so-called "general laws." Thus the idea of history as an intellectual pursuit that deals with individual facts was gradually shaping itself into an autonomous intellectual discipline, and clearly distinguishing itself from science as an intellectual pursuit that deals with general laws.

A dominant element in the new historiography was its emphasis on objectivity. Not only was the concept of individuality a ruling principle in historical method (in contrast to the general laws of science), but also it was held that the historian must avoid all subjective value judgments. It is not his business to pass judgment on the data of his study, but merely to ascertain and state the facts. History, that is, was regarded as a purely descriptive and nonevaluative discipline.

Leopold Ranke is usually recognized by historians of historiography as the most impressive exponent of positivistic historiography. Its general spirit is given clear and emphatic expression in the introduction that Ranke wrote to his book *Geschichten der romanischen und germanischen Völker,* published in 1824. Ranke began by warning the reader not to expect to find in his monograph the entire histories of these nations, but only a small part of such: " *nur Geschichten, nicht die Geschichte.*" [100] This was typical of Ranke's entire career as a historian, whose results assumed the form of independent monographs, which resolutely avoid any universal constructions. Further, Ranke frankly parted company with the idealistic presupposition of the Romanticists, namely, humanity in its factuality, unity, and fullness. He confessed that he was far removed from this approach to history. As he saw it, the object of historical knowledge is mankind as it is (*wie sie ist*), explicable or inexplicable: " the life of the individual, the race, the people." [101]

Prior to Ranke, and even yet in his day, it was held that it was the task of the historian to *judge* the past and to *instruct* the present, and thereby to serve a useful educational function for the present as it moves into the future. But Ranke contended that a higher kind of historiography will

renounce such moralistic aims and simply describe the past
as it really happened *(wie es eigentlich gewesen)* .[102] The
highest law for the historian is to give a stern and forthright
presentation of the facts, however qualified and unlovely they
may be.[103]

Ranke clung to the method of this positivistic historiography throughout his entire academic career. It enabled him
to write an objective history of the popes of the Counterrefor-
mation (though he remained a Lutheran) that was warmly
received by Roman Catholics, and a history of France that
met with the pleasant approval of the French.

Twentieth-century historiography, of course, recognizes
definite values in the nineteenth-century emphasis on objectivity. It certainly led historians to pay close attention to historical details and made it possible to see the past *wie es
eigentlich gewesen*. It was thus a definite step forward in overcoming the tendency to " modernize " the past. And it taught
historians the lesson that *all facts are facts,* and should not
therefore be quietly forgotten, despite the inevitable limitations involved in the *selection* of a particular group of facts
for study by any one historian.

But along with this element of truth in the emphasis on
objectivity there were elements of error also, for the method
was not, indeed could not be, as objective as it represented
itself to be. Far more than these historians realized, subjectivity
was at work in their method, both in the matter of deciding
what data to select for study, and in the schema of classifica-
tion of the data. In large measure, the personal interest of
the historian determined the former, and his own rationality
determined the latter. As Hegel reminded us, even the ordinary recorder of history, who insists that he is doing nothing
but objectively cataloging the facts, as they present themselves to him, brings his rational categories along with him
and views these " facts " through and by means of these categories.[104]

Further, there was really no way in which these historians
could hold to the idea of development, as they actually did,
apart from an answer to such a question, for example, as to
why this or that period represented an " advance " in religion

or in politics. Their concept of objectivity also made it impossible for them to appropriate *critically* the judgments that the people of the past themselves made about their contemporary situations and happenings. This meant that this historical method prevented the historians from appropriating the fullness of the life of the past. This method could only end in a kind of history which studies the external side of events, and not the inner thoughts of historical figures which generated these events. Hence, this study of history resulted in a lopsided externalization of real history. It thus becomes clear why these historians were so preoccupied with political history to the point of identifying it with history per se, and why they ignored religious history and the history of art. Their externalizing method ill equipped them for a study of the latter kinds of history.

The refusal to evaluate facts led to a further difficulty that proved the undoing of such objectivistic methodology. When, for example, such a historian came upon the record of a miracle, what was he to do? Put it down as a " fact "? Obviously the *documentary* evidence for the miracle's happening was just as clear and certain as was that for any other kind of event, for wars, peace treaties, etc. The only possible way out of this difficulty for the naturalistic historian was to appeal to *thought* and to deny the happenings of what (by his own naturalistic philosophy) was impossible because it was unthinkable. At this point a philosophical value judgment entered into positivistic historiography with a vengeance. And this clearly shows the bankruptcy of its method.

There was also a serious weakness in the emphasis on individuality and the neglect of wholes, for this meant that history must limit itself to microscopic units of human life; thereby the whole of history was dissected into an infinite number of minute segments, each of which had to be treated independently of the others. Such a method generated the illusion that history was made up of isolated, fragmentary bits. The method thus proved itself incapable of grasping the organic togetherness of historical human existence — which itself was indeed a *fact* to be reckoned with.

In England the spirit of positivism remained dominant

throughout the latter part of the nineteenth century. The historians of this movement were motivated by a strongly negative attitude toward philosophy in general, and toward any philosophy of history in particular. They were, of course, guilty of a sort of blindness to their own philosophical presuppositions, which led them to hold a particular philosophy, whether they were or were not conscious of it. This was the empirical philosophy which said that the only valid knowledge of which man is capable is that which is attained by the method of natural science, the empirical method. This view is, of course, not science but philosophy. Whether the positivist admits it or not, he does have a *Weltanschauung*.

THE FINAL STAGE OF THE IDEA OF PROGRESS

In the late nineteenth century the idea of progress had entered the final stage of its development in the modern period. Bury points out [105] that the *first* stage, up to the French Revolution, was one in which the concept had been taken for granted, with little critical thought about it. One sees this in the breezy faith in progress during the period of the Enlightenment. The *second* stage is marked by a search for a general law in terms of which the idea of progress could be buttressed by an adequate rationale. The *third* stage, says Bury, was inaugurated by Darwin's *Origin of Species*.

The heliocentric astronomy had administered a severe shock to man's pride. The geocentric perspective of Ptolemaic astronomy had permitted man to develop a cozy, sheltered feeling in the cosmos. It flattered man's sense of dignity by placing him at the geographical center of the cosmos. It represented the earth as the center of the universe, and man as occupying the place of central importance on the earth. But with the Copernican revolution, the being of man was greatly dwarfed. Modern Copernican man acquired the status of a displaced person in the universe. No longer could man flatter his sense of dignity by regarding his solar system as a " heating and lighting plant constructed for his special convenience." [106]

The impact of Darwin's theory dealt the second great shock to modern man's dignity. " Evolution, shearing him of his glory as a rational being specially created to be the lord of the earth, traces a humble pedigree for him." [107] The theory of evolution provided the idea for the further development of the notion of progress.

Herbert Spencer, for example, extended the idea of evolution to sociology and ethics, and was himself a leading exponent in the optimistic interpretation of the new doctrine. Indeed, Spencer had already developed his evolutionary concept prior to Darwin. Nine years before the publication of Darwin's *Origin of Species,* Spencer had already given expression to this idea in his work *Social Statics.*[108] He argued that the " essential principle of life " is the adaptation of an organism to its environment,[109] and that " all evil results from the non-adaptation of constitution to conditions." [110]

In his work *First Principles of a New System of Philosophy,* published in 1865, Spencer worked out a full and concise definition of the concept of evolution. After a long examination of a multitude of evidence, he concluded that " evolution is a change from an indefinite incoherent homogeneity, to a definite, coherent heterogeneity; through continuous differentiations and integrations." [111] This law of evolution is applicable equally to the earth, the growth of living organisms, the development of human society, government, language, and art.[112] Man " exhibits the same adaptability " that is the law of the entire natural process.[113] Nature is infinitely complex in its continuous growth to new developments. Human nature too obeys the same basic law, the law of indefinite variation.

With this evolutionary law of all phenomena, Spencer provided a new rationale for the belief in progress. The belief in human perfectibility, he argued, " merely amounts to the belief that, in virtue of this process, man will eventually become completely suited to his mode of life." [114] Indeed, Spencer contended, progress is not an accident, but " a necessity." [115] He insisted that

> as surely as the tree becomes bulky when it stands alone, and slender if one of a group; as surely as a blacksmith's arm grows large and the skin of a laborer's hand thick

. . . as surely as passion grows by indulgence and dimin-
ishes when restrained . . . so surely must the human
faculty be moulded into complete fitness for the social
state; so surely must evil and immorality disappear; so
surely must man become perfect.[116]

Spencer was so thoroughly persuaded of the validity of his
extension of the scientific category of evolution to human civilization that he not only regarded human perfectibility to be
within the realm of possibility, but indeed inevitable. The
" seeds " of civilization among primitive man had been dis-
tributed across the entire earth. In the course of time it was
inevitable that they " fall here and there into circumstances fit
for their development." [117] Therefore, Spencer believed that
" in spite of all blightings and uprootings," these germinal
seeds were destined " ultimately to originate a civilization
which should outlive all disasters." [118] In virtue of " the law
of adaptation," man's advance must be toward a state in which
" the entire satisfaction of every desire, or perfect fulfillment
of individual life, becomes possible." [119]

The latter nineteenth-century historians labored under the
dominant influence of this idea of progress, despite the fact
that, as Collingwood says, it was " a piece of sheer metaphysics
derived from evolutionary naturalism and foisted upon history
by the temper of the age." [120] Mommsen, for example, intro-
duces his *History of Rome* by pointing out that though a
particular civilization has its orbit and completes its course,
" not so the human race, to which, just when it seems to have
reached its goal, the old task is ever set anew with a wider
range and with a deeper meaning." [121]

REALISTIC PROTESTS AGAINST THE IDEA OF PROGRESS

Spencer's gigantic evolutionary philosophy was widely ac-
claimed due in part to the supporting influence that it received from Darwin's work, which was greatly strengthened
also by the growing science of paleontology. But some critical
minds were aware of its unrealistic features. For every civilization of the past advanced to a high point of development, sub-

sequently declined, and passed out of existence. How did Spencer's thesis square with this historical fact? Did Spencer's hope that the present civilization would grow into a veritable millennium rest on a solid basis?

Even in the latter part of the nineteenth century, skeptical voices began to be heard. T. H. Huxley was, in general, an ardent advocate of Darwinian evolution. But in his famous Romanes Lecture of 1893, Huxley felt obliged to expose the fallacy of the Spencerian extension of the principle of evolution to ethics. Huxley argued that the law of nature (evolution) is one thing, the principles of ethics quite another. It was his view that social progress by no means has the momentum of evolution on its side. On the contrary, " social progress means a checking of the cosmic process at every step and the substitution for it of another . . . the ethical process, the end of which is not the survival of those who may happen to be the fittest, . . . but of those who are ethically the best." [122]

Huxley sharply criticized the Spencerian doctrine that the theory of evolution encourages millennial anticipations,[123] for as he saw the matter, the development of social life does *not* obey the general law of evolution that is operative in the realm of nature. " Once and for all," he wrote, let us understand " that the ethical progress of society depends, not on imitating the cosmic process, still less in running away from it, but in combating it." [124] The development of what is ethically best runs squarely contrary to the evolutionary struggle for existence.[125]

Though advocating the ethic that " might makes right," an ethic different from that of either Spencer or Huxley, Nietzsche also raised his voice against evolution. In nature the struggle for existence is one of adaptation, that is, of *submission* to the organism's environment — so said Darwin. Said Nietzsche, it is the exact reverse: The struggle for existence is one of nonadaptation, to struggle *against* environment, a struggle to master one's environment and make it subservient to one's own desires and aims. Indeed, not only in his ethics but also in his interpretation of " all active force unequivocally " Nietzsche argued that its essence lies in " Will to Power," and in nothing

else.[126] He felt that the teachings of " respectable but mediocre
Englishmen " such as Darwin, Mill, and Spencer possess
" charms and seductive power " only for " mediocre Spirits." [127]
Instead of Spencer's doctrine that evil lies in nonadaptation to
environmental conditions, Nietzsche contended that every system of morals is, in the very nature of things, " a sort of tyranny
against ' nature ' and also against ' reason.' " [128] In Nietzsche's
philosophy one sees the ethics of the Superman, the Superrace
(German, of course!) : the roots of the totalitarian idea of the
state, exemplified by Adolf Hitler.

Yet another protest against the nineteenth-century gospel
of progress was raised by Jacob Burckhardt, the influential
Swiss historian. Burckhardt was an original thinker, and it is
hardly possible to classify his view of history in any of the
dominant ideas of history during the nineteenth century.

Burckhardt raised a powerful protest against the possibility
of any valid " philosophy of history " in general, and against
the popular doctrine of progress in particular. For him, the
philosophy of history is a " centaur, a contradiction in
terms." [129] He opposed Hegel's bold philosophy of a history of
the whole world. All such philosophical world plans are
" colored by preconceived ideas." [130] Burckhardt felt that the
imposition of a logical schema upon the multifarious forms
and facts of history by such a philosophy is much too arbitrary
a procedure. Hegel's idealism of the Absolute Spirit, Spencer's
evolutionary progressivism, and the modern expression of the
ancient Greek cyclical view of history by Vico, Schelling, and
Lesaulx (and later by Spengler's famous *Decline of the West,*
published in 1919) — all tend to distort the actual shape of
historical events and reshape them into a mold that does not
do full justice to all the historical realities involved. One is
reminded of Voltaire's *Candide,* in which he mercilessly exposed the incongruency between the actual facts of human experience and Professor Pangloss' Leibnizian a priori axiom
that " all is for the best in this best of all possible worlds." In
studying history, therefore, says Burckhardt, we have no use
for Hegel's concept of Absolute Spirit working itself out in
the dialectic of historic process, for " we are not privy to the
purposes of eternal wisdom: they are beyond our ken." [131]

It is true, of course, that external historical events and sources must be studied in relation to the inner mental forces and ideas that shaped them and gave them their original meaning. Historic sources and events must be studied in such a way that one learns how historical figures felt, thought, and believed.[132] It is also true that mind is "immortal"; yet it is subject to change,[133] and that not in any inevitably progressive direction. The essence of historical life and thought is change, not the change of evolutionary progressivism, but repetitious, constant trends, and recurrent types of human situations.[134] For basically, man everywhere remains the same. His mind was complete "early in time," [135] and "neither the spirit nor the brain of man has visibly developed in historical times." [136]

Modern man must therefore dispossess himself of " the fuzzy baggage of public opinions " called progress, for it is a deadly enemy of " true historical insight." [137] What colossal egotism this doctrine of progress reflects! As if the world and its history had existed "merely for our sakes! " [138] Is there then no moral progress in the course of history? In the life of the individual, yes; but not in historical epochs! For example, the fact that in ancient times men gave their lives for one another clearly shows that "we have not progressed since." [139] The current sentiment that identifies the "present" with historic progress is simply the result of "the most ridiculous vanity, as if the world were marching toward a perfection of mind or even morality." [140] The difficulty lies in the fact that everyone regards the historic past as prologomena, as a past that reaches fulfillment in our present, enlightened age; whereas a sounder *historical thinking* will lead one to see his own age "as one of many passing waves " [141] in the total ocean of historical humanity.

While Burckhardt totally repudiated any Hegelian or Augustinian theodicy of history, insisting on a purely human, that is, secular, approach to the study of history, he broke with the dominant trend in the latter nineteenth century which, following the dictates of natural science, attempted to eliminate the element of subjectivity in historical study and reduce it to a purely objective narration of bare facts. Indeed, Burckhardt was one of the earliest of modern historians to recognize not only that subjectivity is inescapable but indeed desirable in the study of history. It was his thesis that history is the record of that which one age *finds significant and worthy* in another. An essential qualification of a good historian is therefore that he be possessed by the belief that every dustheap of history contains "jewels of knowledge, whether of general value or of personal value to us." [142] And though the works of Thucydides may have been exploited a thousand times, there still may be in Thucydides "a fact of capital importance which somebody will note in a hundred years' time."[143] Not only so, but by the touch of life a dead and forgotten past may come to life in the present. As Croce says, the Romans and the Greeks simply lay in their sepulchers, unthought and unremembered by generations "until awakened at the Renaissance by the new maturity of the European spirit." [144] The thing that makes the study of history such an exciting and rewarding adventure is the fact that historic sources are inexhaustible and are thus able to speak to a vast variety of interests.

The two basic facets of Burckhardt's view of history are: First, he begins with the one point accessible to all — "the one eternal center of all things — man, suffering, striving, doing, as he is and was and ever shall be." [145] Second, he treats the historical character of human existence which provides a "spiritual continuum" as our spiritual heritage. The values of the present generation are thus not only generated by the past, but increasingly enriched and ennobled by a growing knowledge of the past. And the present generation will also bequeath to the future its added store of this fund of cultural values. The only people who renounce this high privilege of historical existence are barbarians, who without intellectual reflection merely accept "the cake of custom" as preordained and never break through it.[146]

Burckhardt's most significant contribution is perhaps that he greatly augmented the growth of the historical sense and the awareness of the importance of historical understanding of human existence. He correctly drove home the point that only by appropriating our spiritual and moral heritage from the past through adequate methods of historical study can our present survive the dreadful threat of militarism and move ahead toward a realization of the good and the true, subject of course to the conditions of our time.

To Nietzsche and Burckhardt one could add the similarly critical voices of Kierkegaard, Dostoevsky, and Tolstoy, who, in terms of different interests, were all similarly critical. The developments of the twentieth century have added further dimensions to the basis for protest against the liberal doctrine of progress and the perfectibility of man. The staggering social tragedies of our century, the horrors of two world wars, the stubborn persistence of man's barbarous inhumanity to man — all have punctuated the liberal belief in progress with a decisive question mark. Erich Frank voices the feeling of a growing number among us when he says that it is hardly possible any longer to cling to this liberal belief. He writes:

It is the strange irony of our time that all progress in science and civilization, nay, in moral and social consciousness, is turned eventually into a means for war and destruction. Even those peoples who do their utmost to prevent such a tragic reversal are forced to submit to the necessity of history. To the extent to which man, through his reason, has learned to control nature, he has fallen victim to the catastrophes of history. Thus his dream that he may be entirely free to shape his future according to the ideals of his own reason is frustrated by history. Man is thwarted by himself, by his own nature.[147]

IV

Recent Developments in Historiography

In the preceding chapter we have surveyed the major movements and tendencies in the development of the idea of history during the eighteenth and nineteenth centuries. We must now extend our survey into the twentieth century. We cannot, in this small volume, present an exhaustive analysis of all the historiographical currents and developments during recent decades. We shall, rather, limit ourselves to descriptive statements about the historiographies of three thinkers whose influence has been pervasive and profound: Benedetto Croce, Arnold J. Toynbee, and R. G. Collingwood.

BENEDETTO CROCE

Perhaps the most significant aspect of Croce's view of history is that he got completely free from the positivistic position that was dominant in the latter half of the nineteenth century, a position that sucked history into the orbit of naturalism. For Croce, history bears much greater similarity to art than to science. In his early essay *History Subsumed Under the Concept of Art* (1893) he contended that whereas science is a knowledge of general laws of phenomena, history does *not* so understand its object. Rather, like art, history contemplates individuality. He even argued that history is "identical" with art, a view which he later modified by showing that philosophical thinking, involving the concepts of the individual and the universal, is necessary in historical knowledge. Yet basically, the clear distinction between history and science remained.

The naturalistic view of history says: First assemble the facts, then connect them by general laws under the principle of causality. But Croce showed that fruitful historical method does not proceed in this fashion. The data of historical study are no bare, objective facts, but rather facts " in relation to the new action and the new life which is created " by historical thinking itself.[1] The " facts " of history are, so to speak, the stuff of the human spirit. We must start from the principle, said Croce, that " the spirit itself is history, maker of history at every moment of its existence, and also the result of all anterior history." [2] Hence, " the spirit bears with it all its history, which coincides with itself." [3] History is not the work of nature, but of spirit or mind coming " to understand itself." [4] It is clear, then, that the " facts " of history are of a kind different from those of natural science, and that the attitude of an objective observer (spectator) is inappropriate in the study of history, for in the latter we have to do with the vital, life unity of the human spirit itself. In history a past fact answers to a present interest " in so far as it is unified with an interest of the present life." [5]

The unique character of history, in Croce's view, becomes clearer still in his oft-repeated thesis that history consists in a " contemporizing " of the past. It is his thesis that all history is contemporary, not in the sense of the word " contemporary " when, for example, we speak of the contemporary situation in contrast to the past but, rather, in the more profound sense that all history, whether of the preceding five minutes or five hundred years (the time differential is purely relative), is what takes place in the present mind of the historian who rethinks the actions of the past.

Not everything that has happened is history. Much has happened that has been totally forgotten. Much is now entirely undiscoverable and unrecoverable. This is not history. History has to do only with the past for which there is evidence: documents, inscriptions, artifacts, archaeological remains, etc. But even such evidence is, as such, not yet history. A mere document as such is not history, but at best only a chronicle. It was history, of course, at one time, but it became

chronicle when it was no longer thought, " but only recorded
in abstract words, which were once upon a time concrete and
expressive." [6] And now, today, all such chronicles and documents *become* history only when the deed of which the history
is told vibrates " in the soul of the historian." [7] Since, then, real
history is only " the history that one thinks in the act of thinking," [8] the meaning of Croce's statement becomes clear, that
" every true history is contemporary history," [9] for in rethinking the Hellenic life of the past, for example, that life becomes
present in and for the one engaging in historical thinking.

The appropriation of the past is, of course, not a harmless
pastime to keep historians out of michief, but a necessary condition to responsible action in the present, for the shaping of
the future. But the idealistic character of this historical act of
appropriation, as Croce understood it, should be noted. For
him, man's humanity consists in his rationality.[10] It is mind or
reason that constructs history.[11] Thus whereas for a historian
like Dilthey, history is viewed as an act of *experience,* for
Croce it is an act of *knowledge.* For Dilthey, the past is appropriated by means of psychical empathy through the power
of psychological imagination. For Croce, the revitalizing of
the past " in the soul of the historian " is achieved by thinking. The past confronts us with problems to be resolved by
reason, just as we are confronted by problems in our business
and other affairs of daily life. The task is to solve these problems by means of critical thought.[12]

With this dynamic, idealistic view of history, Croce struck
out a position midway between the right wing of a Hegelian
" philosophy of history " and the left wing of scientific naturalism or what he labels " historical determinism." [13] It was
Croce's view that both of these positions " leave the *reality of
history* behind them." [14] What did he mean by this criticism?

Croce found several things wrong with the naturalistic view
of history which first posits objective, disconnected, brute
facts, and then proceeds to ferret out their causes. This view
holds that such facts are brute, dense, and lacking in meaning,
until an intelligible character is *imposed upon them* by the
search for and discovery of their causes. Such a search, however, at once discloses its inadequacy because it logically

leads to infinite regression. An attempt to resolve this difficulty is then found in the notion of " proximate " causes. But, said Croce, this idea is a mere " fig leaf " used to cover the embarrassing aspect of a method of which the historian, as a critical thinker, is not altogether proud.[15] Besides, who can say what is and is not a " proximate " cause? To possess this ability, one would have to know already the " ultimate " cause, for the former concept has meaning only in relation to the latter. Naturalism thus inevitably ends in some philosophy of the Whole, some notion of the Ultimate. Hence, the search for causes finally ends (unless terminated in an arbitrary and fanciful manner) in the search for the transcendental end — which is precisely a " philosophy of history." [16]

The naturalistic method has gone astray because it failed to begin at the proper place. Croce asked: Whence come these brute, disconnected facts as data for such historical method? This kind of history has indeed *manufactured* them by its own fallacious method, for the " facts " of history are, to begin with, *not* given in any such fashion. They are, rather, given as " acts of the spirit, conscious in the spirit that thinks them," and not as external brute facts.[17] That is, the true point of departure for historical method is not the " facts already disorganized and naturalized," but " the mind that thinks and constructs the fact." [18] If we but " raise up the debased countenances of the calumniated ' brute facts,' . . . we shall see the light of thought resplendent upon their foreheads." [19]

The primary error of those who follow the lead of Hegel, on the other hand, and develop a " philosophy of history " is, said Croce, basically the same as that of naturalistic determinism, namely, starting with brute facts. But in this case the process of intelligizing these facts is executed, not by way of finding links in the chain of causes, but rather by way of conferring on these brute facts a meaning, thereby representing them as partial aspects of a " transcendental process " defined in terms of a transcendent *telos*.[20] This end or " general plan " for the whole of history is construed in various ways; there are many " philosophies of history." The most popular one in the nineteenth century was the plan that read the whole course of history as leading to the (eschatological)

kingdom of human liberty, a (millennial) time when all men
would finally one day be free. The dialectical materialism of
the Marxian "plan" moves from the golden age of primitive
Communism, through the Middle Ages of capitalistic slavery,
and finally to the restoration of pure Communism — the Marxist version of the Hegelian triad: thesis, antithesis, and synthesis. It was Croce's view that, although these philosophies of
history have served a useful function in counterbalancing
naturalistic determinism, they are nevertheless to be frankly
recognized for what they in truth are: "cosmological ro-
mances." [21] But they have served to point up gaps in historical
method in the past; and with their false provisional solutions
they "have heralded the correct solutions" of the historical
problem.[22]

The correct solution can only be found when we clear
away the shadows of the vain attempt to employ "the ce-
ment of causality" on the one hand, and to wave "the magic
wand of finality" on the other.[23] The search for scientific
causes and for final ends have both led us astray, for in different ways both approaches left the reality of history behind
at the very outset of their methods. If, as we have already
pointed out, history is the spirit itself, if the spirit is the
maker of history at every moment of its existence, and the historian thus "makes live again in imagination individuals and
events" and "thinks what is within them," history is already
achieved! What more of history can be desired than this?
Croce believed that if one approaches history with this understanding of what it is, there remains nothing more to seek.
Why, pray tell, should we proceed to break up this life unity
of historical humanity, slay the *living* fact, separate its abstract
elements, and then set out on a quest for "causes"? In history, "the fact historically thought has no cause and no end
outside itself, but only in itself, coincident with its real qualities and with its qualitative reality." [24] Idealist though he was,
Croce consistently resisted the metaphysical temptation to
understand history in the light of a teleological or eschatological presupposition. He wished to remain *in* history.

It should now be clear why Croce felt that the writing of
any "universal history" is impossible. It is impossible for the

simple reason that the historian's mind is thoroughly embedded in the historical process, and is thus limited and determined by its own finitude. It is incapable of forming any valid picture of all that has happened to the human race from its origin to the very end of the world. Take any of the " universal " histories that have been written — if one but scratch the surface of any one of them, he quickly perceives that it is, instead, a " particular " history.

Polybius' universal history, Augustine's City of God, Hegel's philosophy of history — each bears marks of the finite and the particular. Polybius dealt only with those peoples who were related to Rome. Augustine, too, had his ax to grind: the conflict between Christianity and paganism — hardly universal, since there were whole civilizations before Christianity came into being. Hegel's philosophical world history eliminated prehistory from the philosophy of history and " considered Oriental history very summarily, since it did not offer much of interest to the prosecution of his design." [25]

Croce recognized an element of validity in the tendency in historical knowledge toward universality. Such a tendency was at work, for example, in the birth of the new interest in antiquity during the Renaissance. Such a tendency is a therapeutic corrective for the illness of parochialism. But in the strict sense of the word, " universal history " inevitably " disappears in the world of illusions, together with similar Utopias, such, for instance, as the art that should serve as a model for all times, or universal justice valid for all time." [26]

With all his tirades against a " philosophy of history," Croce, the idealistic philosopher, nevertheless champions one himself. His view too is teleological, for he held that the process of history is one of development and growth. History is not just " one damn thing after another "; it does add up to something significant, and indeed something *ethically* significant. The true understanding of progress, said Croce, is " the passage from the good to the better." [27] But the mistake of the nineteenth century was twofold at this point. First, it defined the " better " too narrowly, in terms of physical comfort and well-being; and second, it mistakenly located progress in a particular epoch and a particular society, " thereby materializing and arresting eternal spiritual progress." [28] True progress, Croce argued, never terminates in any finally realized millennium of liberty, but is instead "the perpetual growth of its own spirituality." [29]

There is, then, an end of history, in Croce's view; but the relation of this end to historic process is wrongly conceived when it is construed as *extrinsic* to process. When so construed, it is thought that it can one day be fully achieved (*progressus ad finitum*), or that it can be infinitely approximated (*progressus ad infinitum*). Croce held that the correct interpretation sees the end " as *internal* — that is to say, all one with development itself." [30]

Croce thus gives us what he believed is a much needed correction of the teleological views of history that have dominated the history of Western thought. He of course rejected the traditional, otherworldly teleology of Christianity, for it is suprahistorical. And he found that Hegel, Marx, and the nineteenth-century liberals are all guilty of the same basic error in principle. They read history in terms of a birth of liberty, then its growth, and finally its maturity and "its stable permanence in a definite era in which it is incapable of further development." [31] This accounts for Hegel's error in absolutizing the Prussian State, which subsequent history has now transcended. It accounts for the illusion of finality in Russian Communism and its failure. The failure to realize the communistic dream and the need for continually projecting it into the future have become the source of such embarrassment to the ideology of Communism that in contemporary Russia all verbs have to be conjugated in the future tense. Croce wanted to correct the " illusion of finality " in all these philosophies of progress, and he did this by absolutizing historic development itself. He wished to overcome the relativism of history by radicalizing it.[32] Instead of defining progress as a movement toward some actual terminus of beatitude, it was his view that it should be construed as " the idea of infinite progress of the infinite spirit, which perpetually generates new contrasts, and perpetually rises superior to them." [33]

ARNOLD J. TOYNBEE

In contrast to Croce, who got wholly free from the naturalistic historical method of positivism, Toynbee's *Study of History,* which is mammoth in its detail and enormously impressive in its erudition, represents a modified version of the positivistic approach, combined with certain elements derived from the Biblical-Augstinian view of history.

The positivistic (naturalistic) doctrine that the basic unit of study in history is an individual " fact " receives a unique expression in Toynbee's system. He begins his magnum opus by clarifying what, as he sees it, is the proper unit of historical study. The traditional, positivist definition had almost habitually made the nation its unit of study. Toynbee rejects the validity of this definition of the " intelligible unit " of historical study, for no single nation has a history that is sufficiently complete in itself to the extent that it can be self-explanatory. He rejects also the impossible idea that the unit of historical study should be mankind as a whole. He develops his definition of the basic unit as " a certain grouping of humanity " which he calls a " Society " or " Civilization." And he distinguishes between civilized and primitive societies. Toynbee finds twenty-six such " civilizations," sixteen of which have run their cycle and passed out of existence. Five are still living: Western Christendom, Eastern Christendom, Islamic Society, Hindu Society, and the Far Eastern Society.[34]

The basic purpose of Toynbee's monumental study is to determine how and why such societies come into existence, how they grow and develop, and how and why they decline and finally disintegrate, terminating their histories.

The explicit methodology of Toynbee's study of history is: (1) to ascertain and record the " facts "; (2) to elucidate, through a comparative study of the facts, certain " general laws." [35] He adds that the historian also finds himself obliged, at times, to have recourse to the artistic recreation of the facts in the form of fiction.

The two basic phases of this historical method constitute the method used in the study of the natural sciences. There is thus a substantial measure of truth in Collingwood's criticism that Toynbee's conception of history is "ultimately naturalistic." [36] It can hardly be denied that in terms of method, at any rate, Toynbee's study of history falls into the naturalism of positivistic historiography, which derived its methodological principles from natural science.

Not only in his method, but also in his new definition of the unit of historical study, Toynbee remains basically true to the spirit of positivism, which defined the unit in terms of the naturalistic principle of individuality. Like a unit in nature, a stone or any physical body, a civilization is comparably viewed as self-sufficient and cut off from everything else. As the natural scientist deals with "brute facts," so also does the historian. At the outset thus Toynbee's view of history seems to be basically pluralistic. Collingwood felt, therefore, that Toynbee's method betrays a mistaken understanding of history, for in history, said Collingwood, we have to do with the world of mind, "where individuality consists not of separateness from environment but of the power to absorb environment into itself." [37] Toynbee's method consequently leads to the mistaken idea that Western civilization is related to Hellenic civilization in an "utterly external way." On the contrary, "Western civilization expresses, and indeed achieves, its individuality not by distinguishing itself from Hellenic civilization but by identifying itself therewith." [38] Toynbee's lines are drawn too sharply "into mutually exclusive parts." He thereby misses what is the fundamental nature of history, namely, "the continuity of the process in virtue of which every part overlaps and interpenetrates others." [39]

It cannot be denied that in terms of Toynbee's explicit method, Collingwood's criticisms are sound. But Collingwood might have recognized more forthrightly that Toynbee nevertheless proceeds to qualify his view of history in significant ways, even though in doing so he may not be wholly consistent with his method. First, in his treatment of these civilizations, Toynbee himself sees considerable overlapping and cross-fertilization. Many of them, says Toynbee, are connected by "apparentation and affiliation." Indeed, fifteen of them are "affiliated to predecessors of the same species." [40] And Toynbee frankly admits that in a few instances the affiliation is so close that a legitimate question can be raised about his thesis that they are "separate individualities." [41] A complete breakdown in these separate individualities of course would nullify the basic scheme of Toynbee's method, so that, in the main, Collingwood's criticism is justified.

Second, Toynbee verbally parts company with the naturalistic method. He warns that the historian must be on guard against the error of applying to *historical* thought "a scientific method devised for the study of inanimate nature." [42] Throughout his writings Toynbee preserves the awareness that there is an unpredictable element in history which is due to the factor of man's freedom, a freedom not possessed by natural objects. The clear recognition of this unique element in history leads Toynbee to reject Spengler's cyclical view of history, even though Toynbee's study of the birth, growth, and decay of civilizations leads him, at the same time, to recognize elements of truth in Spengler's interpretation.[43]

Third, it is true that as one reads Toynbee's vast network of pigeonholes in which a veritable multitude of facts are neatly tucked away, he can scarcely avoid the impression that Toynbee has indeed adopted the spectator (scientific) point of view in observing and cataloging the great mass of material. For the most part, all these phenomena are presented externally; they are not experienced from the inside of the events recorded and cataloged. There is some truth in Bultmann's criticism that because Toynbee proposes to stand over against history as a disinterested spectator, as the scientific observer observes his data, from the outside, Toynbee "seems not to be conscious that the historian himself stands within history." [44]

Nevertheless, at several points Toynbee breaks with the spectator approach. Even two years prior to the Gifford Lectures of 1955 in which Bultmann made the above-mentioned criticism, Toynbee had already modified the spectator view, which does stand out fairly boldly in his major work, *A Study of History*. In Toynbee's Gifford Lectures of 1952–1954, he began his first lecture by underscoring the point that the historian, like all human observers, is limited by his own historical situation. Hence, the historian's view "will inevitably be partial and subjective." [45] Toynbee adds that the study of history is, however, or can and should be, a therapeutic corrective that helps to overcome a narrow self-centeredness and provincialism; for fruitful historical study " makes the life of other people in other generations and at other places revive in the historian's imagination so vividly that he will be able to recognize that this alien life has had the same objective reality, and the same moral claims, as the life of the historian and his contemporaries has here and now." [46]

Toynbee here recognizes not only that the historian qua historian is himself historically conditioned, but the spectator approach is modified in the additional sense that not only does the historian recognize an earlier generation's integrity in its own right, but he also " enters sympathetically into his predecessors' feeling." [47] Statements like this tend to qualify the spectator approach to history, even if they do not radically alter Toynbee's basic spectator method.

We need not here elaborate at length the well-known law or " positive factor " [48] in the birth and growth of civilizations which Toynbee finds by comparing the various units of his study, the general law of " Challenge-and-Response." Every society, at its birth and throughout the course of its life, is brought face-to-face with challenges of various types, which serve as stimuli. After the Ice Age, for example, the Afrasian area was characterized by a profound physical change in the direction of desiccation. This placed the primitive inhabitants of this area in a crisis of survival. Some of them refused to change either their traditional way of life or their habitat, and as a result became extinct. But other communities met the challenge both by changing their habitat and by altering their mode of life. It was this dynamic response to the challenge, says Toynbee, " which created the Egyptiac and Sumeric civilizations of some of the primitive societies of the vanishing Afrasian grasslands." [49]

Another example is found in the birth and growth of the United States in North America. Everything considered, says Toynbee, soil, climate, transportation facilities, and the rest — " the original home of the New Englanders was the hardest country of all." The present nation of the United States serves as a dramatic example of what happens when men set their hearts and heads, responding with vigor to taming the wilderness and winning the West.

Other challenges operating in the emergence and growth of civilizations, Toynbee finds in severe blows by an enemy, or internal conflicts in the society itself, or subjugation by a foreign power. But the challenge must not be so great that it totally crushes the people, nor so light that its stimulus is ineffective. What happens when the challenge strikes a people is unpredictable. It all depends on the kinds of response given to it, and in general, Toynbee always leaves the door open at this point, thus avoiding any doctrine of natural necessity in the movement of history.

Toynbee's reading of historic process is thus not deterministic. He analyzes the various deterministic theories and rejects them all with the verdict: Not proved by the historical evidence! Spengler's interpretation of history by the analogy of the biological life span is an a priori dogma that Spengler arbitrarily imposed on the facts of history, which do not confirm the validity of the metaphor.[50] The metaphor is misleading, for societies are not living organisms; they are communities of human beings whose movements are in part determined by freedom. Against Spengler, Toynbee contends that there is no a priori reason why a succession of challenges might not be met by "a succession of victorious responses ad infinitum."[51]

For the same basic reason, Toynbee rejects the interpretation of the breakdown of civilizations as being due to the "running down" of the "clockwork" of the universe (another naturalistic view), or to the deterioration of the quality of individuals (racial degeneration). The ancient Platonic cyclical view similarly runs against the historical evidence. The presence of "periodic repetitive movements" in the course of civilizations does not prove the truth of the cyclical theory. In view of the evidence, what must be inferred from the periodicity of civilization's movements is that "the major movement which they bear along is not recurrent but progressive. Humanity is not an Ixion bound forever to his wheel nor a Sisyphus forever rolling his stone to the summit of the same mountain and helplessly watching it roll down again."[52]

Toynbee feels that all the deterministic philosophies of history represent a moral failure of nerve by which man seeks to shuffle off his own responsibility upon the shoulders of God or nature. But the real hinge of history lies in man, in his limited but genuine freedom, in his capacity to shape history, thereby sharing in the creativity of the divine. " The divine spark of creative power is still alive in us, and, if we have the grace to kindle it into flame, then the stars in their courses cannot defeat our efforts to attain the goal of human endeavour." [53] Man himself must shoulder the burdens of history — " it is up to us." [54]

Civilizations, therefore, do not wane and perish due to the law of natural necessity, to failure in industrial techniques, nor to assaults from a foreign adversary.[55] The breakdown is, rather, due to three things: (1) a failure in the creative use of freedom by the " creative minority"; (2) a resulting withdrawal of allegiance and mimesis on the part of the majority; and (3) the consequent loss of unity in the society as a whole.[56] At the heart of the decline and decay stands the twofold sin of pride and idolatry, in one form or another: the idolization of an ephemeral self (Judaism and ancient Athens), an ephemeral institution (the Hellenic city-state and the Eastern Roman Empire), an ephemeral technique, or the *hybris* of militarism.[57] There is a clear, ringing Biblical note in Toynbee's analysis of the breakdown and decay of civilizations.

The full picture of Toynbee's view of history is not seen until we address ourselves to the problem of teleology and the unity of universal history. Toynbee is not a humanist; he is a firm believer in a suprahuman divine reality. He does have a teleology of history, but it must be seen in the light of his religious belief in God. It is not altogether clear how the conception of the unity of universal history, teleologically interpreted, logically coheres with the frankly pluralistic view implicit in Toynbee's historical method. His *method* and his teleological *interpretation* of history do not seem to " hang together " in a coherent system of meaning. One reads his writings to get the impression that he begins his study of history along positivistic lines and ends up by superimposing insights drawn from religious faith upon the general laws discovered.

Our human views of the whole panorama of history, says Toynbee, bear the marks of our finitude and the limitations of our historical situation.[58] " God alone knows the true picture." [59] Hegel's " cunning of reason " is retranslated into Providence by Toynbee. For example, one of the unforeseen results of the modern technological development of Western civilization has been to lay the basis for the contemporary unification of the world. Thus " through the providence of God " we have unwittingly done something, not merely for ourselves, but for the whole of mankind, " something so big that our own parochial history is going to be swallowed up by the results of it." [60] Man has been *ruling* in developing his scientific mastery of nature; but Providence has all the while been *overruling* for the realization of a purpose larger than man was able to envisage.

Toynbee holds that there is an ultimate spiritual *telos* at work in the whole process of history. The movement of history, he feels, is " towards some higher kind of spiritual life," [61] a movement that is centered in the progress of the religions of mankind. The possibilities for progress in increasing spiritual opportunity for individuals are inexhaustible.[62] While there is truth in the view that the movement of civilizations is cyclic and recurrent, the movement of religon may be one of a continually ascending line. And " if religion is a chariot, it looks as if the wheel on which it mounts to Heaven may be the periodic downfalls of civilizations on Earth." [63]

At this point one finds in Toynbee an expression of the modern doctrine of progress. One is tempted to say, however, that Toynbee's ascending line of religious progress is derived more from his religious faith and hope than from his empirical marshaling of the facts of history. Does the process of history actually disclose any such steady progress of religious sensitivity and insight? Reinhold Niebuhr seems to me to be more empirically correct when he says that it is not possible to prove historical catastrophes to be instruments of such religious development.[64] Toynbee encounters difficulty in fitting our Western post-Christian secular civilization into his theological pattern of religious progress, for here there seems to emerge instead " a pernicious back-sliding from the path of spiritual progress "; and the Leviathan — the self-worship of the tribe — in greater or lesser degree claims the allegiance of all of us.[65]

Toynbee is an ardent advocate of greater unity among the living religions of the world, in the face of the common threat of the modern idolatry of collective human power and of secularism. But he still feels that a worldwide Christian church "may be left as the social heir of all the other churches and all the civilizations." [66] He recognizes that the Kingdom of God will always transcend the church as an institution, necessary though the latter will always be, for the ultimate meaning of the soul's experience lies neither wholly in history nor wholly beyond it.[67] The essence of religion lies finally in the relation of transcendence that the soul sustains to God. The true purpose of religion is to afford the individual opportunity for personal progress in his spiritual life. Yet the effective expression of Christlike love cannot fail to result in " an immeasurable improvement in the conditions of human social life on Earth," [68] even though this is not the ultimate aim of religion. In terms of social patterns of human existence, thus, the progress of religion, which gives spiritual significance to history, means "a cumulative increase in the means of Grace at the disposal for each soul in this world." [69]

Toynbee thus wishes to avoid an otherworldly view of religion that takes all religious significance out of history, and at the same time he is resolved to steer clear of the modern secularization of eschatology. History can and should be a " province " of the Kingdom of God.[70] The end of human existence lies in man's relation to the transcendent God; yet history can and should be so structured as to make possible real progress toward the fulfillment of this end in history.

R. G. COLLINGWOOD

The phrase "philosophy of history" has more than one meaning. Because of the widespread influence of Kant, Hegel, Vico, Arnold J. Toynbee, and others, the phrase is often used to mean universal or world history. Collingwood agreed with Croce that any such endeavor to describe the unified structure of world history in terms of one all-embracing law or meta-physical principle must be regarded as "cosmological romance," though such philosophies of history do possess amusement value, and even emotional value for propaganda purposes, as in Marxist philosophy.[71]

Voltaire, who it appears coined the phrase "philosophy of history," meant by it something less pretentious than the meaning indicated above. Voltaire meant merely critical, scientific thinking on the problem of history, while the positivists of the nineteenth century used this phrase to mean the discovery of general laws that determine the course of historical events.

Collingwood used the phrase "philosophy of history" to mean something a bit different from any of the meanings stated above. He used it to mean philosophical thinking about the new problems of knowledge generated by the recent development of historical study and research.

Collingwood observed that the particular problems which hold the attention of philosophy vary in the changing historic stages of critical thought. The ancient Greeks dealt with epistemology by way of focusing on mathematical knowledge. The philosophy of the medieval period focused on its central theological concern. From the sixteenth to the nineteenth centuries philosophical endeavors concentrated on the problem of knowledge as it focused in the urgent need for laying adequate foundations for the enterprise of natural science. During the past one hundred and fifty years a new set of problems has appeared, problems related to the steady growth of interest in, and critical thought about, the historical dimension of human life and thought.

Collingwood was deeply concerned to demonstrate the irrelevance and inadequacy of traditional theories of knowledge for fruitful philosophical reflection on the unique problems related to historical thinking and historical knowledge. To what he felt to be one of the most urgent needs of our age, the need for adequate philosophical understanding of historical knowledge, he addressed himself in his book, *The Idea of History*.

Like Croce, Collingwood drew a sharp distinction between

natural science and the science of history. This basic methodological distinction between the two sciences runs like an unbroken thread throughout Collingwood's works. He felt that only recently, in the twentieth century, have we come to stand on the threshhold of a new era in the understanding of man, for only now have we begun to get free from the fallacious tradition stemming from the influence of John Locke and David Hume, a tradition in which inquiry into an understanding of the mind was conducted by an epistemological method analogous to that used in the natural sciences. This attempt, together with the sciences of sociology and psychology which grew out of it, was admirable and valuable in many ways. Yet it ended in failure to provide the human mind with true self-understanding. It was one of Collingwood's major convictions that this "science of human nature" failed because it operated on a false presupposition, namely, that the methodology which had proven so fruitful in the pursuit of knowledge in the natural sciences would, if applied with persistence and critical care, prove equally fruitful in the mind's self-understanding. The presupposition is fallacious because the subject matter to be known in natural science is *not* analagous to the reality to be known in the study of man.

Since the age of Locke a significant change has come over the intellectual climate of our age, a change brought about by the rise of historical consciousness, or " a new habit of thinking historically." [72] The science of history has only in recent years gained its rightful autonomy; its rich possibilities have therefore not yet been fully explored. Collingwood believed that it is only by an adequate historical method than an understanding of the human mind can be achieved, for the mind is a historical, not a natural, reality. The method used to attain understanding of the mind must be structured in ways dictated by the nature of the subject matter, not in ways that ape the method used in the study of natural events.

One fundamental difference between a natural event and a historical event is that in understanding the latter, critical attention must be given to what Collingwood called the distinction between the outside and inside of the event, whereas this distinction is irrelevant to a knowledge of the former. This is what he meant by calling the object of knowledge in natural science a " mere " event; [73] it is an event that has an outside but no inside. Scientific method does not terminate, of course, with the simple observation of mere events. The scientist proceeds to compare these events with other events, works out a correlation of likenesses and differences, develops a concept of logical classes of things, etc.

Like the scientist, the historian, too, begins with the outside of events: documents that record the action of people, artifacts and inscriptions that have given empirical expression to ideas and aspirations of the past, etc. But from this beginning point forward the historian moves in a different direction from that followed in scientific method; for the events in historical study are " actions," and an action is " the unity of the outside and inside of an event." [74] The historian is confronted by the documented event of Caesar's crossing the Rubicon. To understand this event historically one must ask: Why? To what purpose? What was Caesar's intention in performing this act? By such questions the historian puts history to the torture until she gives him truthful answers. He probes to the inside of the event in order to discern the thought of its agent. Raymond Aron has similarly said [75] that history is the reconstruction of " the life " of the past.

To say that history is the study of actions is another way of saying that the substance of historical study is mind or thought. Accordingly, the historian's task is to rethink the thought of the past. When he has done so, said Collingwood, he has arrived at historical understanding and needs to go no farther. It is a false historical method that seeks to emulate the natural scientist by searching for causes or laws of historical events. Scientific understanding of natural events is achieved only when one understands their causes. But historical understanding is perfected not by searching for extraneous causes but rather by penetrating to the thought of the agent who performed the act. To discover the thought is already " to understand " the historical event.

One could express the difference between historical method and scientific method by saying that the concept of causality *is* used in both disciplines, but in different ways. At the heart of the idea of causality is the notion of relatedness. The relatedness relative to the study of historical events is a *kind* of relatedness *different* from that which characterizes natural events. In historical events the concern must be with the relation of happenings to the thought that produced them and which found concrete expression in them. In science the relatedness has to do with the spacio-temporal connections with other events, or as Hume put it, the next-to-next structure of things, or the relation of antecedent and consequent in the temporal series of events.

It is an oversimplification, however, to distinguish between scientific knowledge and historical knowledge by saying that the content of the former is universal, of the latter the individual. There is, of course, a measure of truth in this distinction, but it is a misleading oversimplification to say that history is the knowledge of the individual. This way of putting the distinction, said Collingwood, affirms too much and too little. Too much, because the totality of the individuality, either of a person or event of the past, includes much that falls beyond the scope of historical knowledge. The emotional quality of the immediacy of experience, for example, is a nonsharable aspect of the individual's life. It does not have the ability " to revive itself in the historian's mind." Only that element of the individual's experience which possesses this ability, namely, thought, can correctly be regarded as the object of historical knowledge. But to say that history is knowledge of the individual at the same time says too little, for it leaves unaffirmed the universal character of the aspect of the individual that forms the content of historical knowledge. It is the universal character of the experience or event in question that gives it the power to be the object of historical knowledge, for universality here means that the inside of historical events is the kind of ideational reality which, transcending the individual and particular, is shareable by all minds.[76]

From the fact that historical study deals with the unity of the inside and outside of historical events, another significant difference between history and natural science comes to light. In history, the past is contemporized (to use Croce's term). The past of history therefore constitutes a kind of past different from the past of natural events, which is to say that historical time and the time of natural events are different kinds of time. In the process of nature the past is superseded and dead. In history, the past is far from dead. It becomes a determinative force in the life of the historical present. The "historical present" is a meaningful phrase because the historian's process of thinking is itself an integral part of historic process. Unlike the past in natural process, Collingwood pointed out that the past in historical process is a living past, a past kept continually alive by the power of historical thinking. That man is a historical being thus means that through the power of memory he possesses the ability to appropriate, in a critical way, the heritage of the past. This historical heritage is not transmitted in any natural way. Nor is it transmitted merely by memory, that is, by an objective recitation of what happened in the past, or by what Collingwood called "a passive surrender to the spell of another's mind." [77] It is transmitted by historical thinking, that is, by critical, existential encounter with the thought of the past. In reenacting past thought the historian criticizes it, evaluates it, corrects errors that he discerns in it.[78]

If the historian fails critically to assess his evidence, he is a pseudohistorian following what Collingwood called the "scissors-and-paste" method of historical study, which belongs to the oxcart period of the growth of historical science. Pseudohistory, or what Croce called "philological history," was "tied by the leg" to its authorities.[79] The pseudohistorian's method led him to swallow his historical authorities whole. He proceeded on the belief that what the historian should do is merely to repeat statements about what happened in the past, statements that are found ready-made by the historian's authorities.[80] Such a study of history would indeed merit the famous quip of Hegel, that the only thing one can learn from history is that nobody ever learns anything from history. No reputable contemporary historian, however, is so gullible in his attitude toward his authorities. Rather, he recognizes it to be his own responsibility to decide whether his "authority" is stating a fact, or perhaps thought that he was doing so but was unconsciously deceived for some reason or another, or perhaps misstated the facts with deliberate intent.

For example, the author of a series of writings that appeared toward the close of the fifth century A.D. claimed to be Dionysius the Areopagite, referred to in the New Testament book of The Acts. Not until relatively modern times did historial thinking become sufficiently critical to call into question the veracity of the self-identification of the author of these works on grounds of literary evidence. Once historical thinking became critical in the treatment of its evidence, the historian took it upon himself to decide whether the author of this series of works was who he claimed to be. Such responsibility is now everywhere recognized as an essential and vital part of the historian's task. At this point, the historian's autonomy is most clearly manifested, for he possesses the rightful power to repudiate something explicitly told him by his evidence and to assert that something else really happened. In this sense, historical method embraces a rigorous principle of objectivity, for the historian must aim to reconstruct the facts, making use of the most effective techniques available to achieve this end.

Historical knowledge, however, would be impossible to achieve if the element of objectivity in historical method is distorted into the kind of objectivity in which the historian's attitude toward his data becomes that of a mere spectator. The subjective factor is too determinative in historical understanding for this. The object of historical knowledge is not objective in the sense taught, for example, by the school of philosophical realists, so vigorously opposed by Collingwood. Central for these realists was the slogan: "The known is independent of, and unaffected by, the knowing it." [81] This Cartesian type of subject-object relation between the knowing ego and the object known was correctly abandoned by Collingwood as inadequate to describe historical reality. Collingwood called for a more Heideggerian concept of historical reality. The object in historical knowledge is no mere object, that is, "something outside the mind which knows it." [82] The object of historical knowledge is at bottom mind, that is, thought. And thought can be known only if the knower reenacts it and is aware that he is doing so. The historian does not observe his object of study in the spirit of scientific detachment. Rather, he participates in it experientially, grasps it as it grasps him, incarnates it in his own mind. The activity of the object becomes the knower's own activity, as he relives, rethinks it.

It does not nullify the judgment, that in radically opposing the historiography of positivism Collingwood developed the idea of history along fruitful and essentially valid lines, to point out the distortion, as some critics have done,[83] that Collingwood perhaps restricted the notion of reliving the past a bit too exclusively to rethinking it. It is true that his characteristic way of defining historical process was to describe it as "the process of thought,"[84] or "the life of mind itself."[85] Yet he was not unaware of the fact that human life is more than mere thinking. One's immediate experience consists not only of thought but also of feelings, sensations, etc. Nevertheless, the thought that studies this complex of another's experience cannot, according to Collingwood, reenact its volitional and emotional qualities. It can only rethink them. At the same time, Collingwood clearly recognized that historical acts have intention and purpose behind them. To understand an act of the past one must therefore grasp the volitional impulse that prompted the act. That human thinking is much broader than mere reason is evident when Collingwood wrote that the thinking of the historian himself " must spring from the organic unity of his total experience, and be a function of his entire personality with its practical as well as its theoretical interests."[86] Further, Collingwood recognized the need for the historian to rethink the past by way of entering the experience of others with sympathy and imagination.

There is, nevertheless, an experiential sense in which every historical event is unrepeatable, a sense in which Socrates' experience of drinking the hemlock cannot be relived by the historical knowledge of it. One can only reenact the event of Socrates' death by rethinking it, of course, "with sympathy and imagination." Indeed, there is a sense in which even thought cannot be rethought. The ambivalent word "thought" is both a verb and a noun. It may mean an activity or the content of an activity; the act of thinking or *what* is thought. In its immediacy, as an act of a thinking subject, thought is unique and nonrepeatable. But *what* is thought is not so limited. Collingwood underscored his conviction that when the historian rethinks the thought of the past, it must be " the very same thought, not another like it." [87] I may this moment think the thought that the square formed on the hypotenuse of a right-angled triangle is equal to the sum of the squares formed on the other two sides, being aware that I am rethinking what Pythagoras thought long ago. It is clear, said Collingwood, that what we have here is two acts of thinking the same thought, at different times, the latter thinker being aware of the fact that he is reenacting past thought. The difference is one of context [88] or " complex of activities." [89]

According to Collingwood, for Pythagaros, this thought was a " present thought "; for me, it would be a past thought living in the present, " but incapsulated, not free." [90] By this he meant that rethinking the past forms a secondary dimension of the present life of mind. The idea present in the process of rethinking is " living," to be sure, but " forms no part of the question-answer complex which constitutes what people call the ' real ' life . . . of the mind in question." [91]

Although there is painfully obvious truth in Collingwood's idea of different life situations and in his notion of different levels of the mind as it realizes its life in the matrix of history, it would seem that there are further distinctions in the appropriation of the past that Collingwood might have more clearly recognized. Some thoughts of persons of the past obviously do not enter directly into the primary life of the present self, due to differences in historicocultural contexts. Yet is it not perhaps true that other thoughts do? Assuming for the sake of argument that the New Testament idea of grace is true, and if so, equally relevant for all men, the deepest level of my understanding of the apostle Paul's idea of grace would be reached when I not only rethink Paul's idea of God's forgiveness, but when I share this experience existentially, when I reexperience this divine gift. When I do so, it does enter directly into the *primary* level of the present life of my self.

Take another example toward which Collingwood might have been more favorably disposed. We have every reason to believe that Plato's representation of Socrates' thought was true when in the crisis of Socrates' trial and execution, Socrates thought, and said to Crito, "We are never intentionally to do wrong." Is not the most significant level of historical knowledge achieved not when my rethinking this thought of Socrates remains only a part of my " secondary " life, but when it becomes a basically determinative factor in my " primary " selfhood? When it becomes such, Socrates and I are united in the community of humanity at its highest and best.

Nevertheless, Collingwood's concept of historical knowledge is, it seems to me, basically sound. One does not know the meaning of past happenings unless and until he rethinks the thought expressed in them. The objection that this view of historical knowledge reduces historical reality to subjectivity is not wholly sound. This objection says that in the process of reenactment, the thought in question becomes my very own thought (as Collingwood repeatedly insists), and that therefore historical knowledge is reduced to a form of self-knowledge. According to this reasoning, the reality of historical knowledge is merely a factor of the knowing ego's total experience, of which he becomes aware. At best, an objective referent could only function as a sort of catalytic agent to stimulate this self-awareness or to cause it to vibrate in the historian's mind. By becoming subjective, it is argued, thought has ceased to be objective. By becoming present it has ceased to be past, and this stands in contradiction to Collingwood's thesis that it is the thought of the past which forms the content of historical knowledge.

Now, to be sure, subjectivity in historical knowledge, there indubitably is. Kant exposed the fallacy of Locke's *tabula rasa* notion of the knowing mind and showed that knowledge of any sort would scarcely be possible apart from the active involvement of the knowing ego in the cognitive act. And when thought is the object of knowledge, it becomes obvious that it can never be mere object, for thought can be known only by thinking it. The objection that this view of historical knowledge reduces historical reality to pure subjectivity, however, is based on a false interpretation of the disjunction: subjectivity or objectivity. The proposition " historical knowledge is either subjective or objective " is, of course, a true proposition. But not all disjunctive propositions necessarily exclude one or the other of the alternatives. We often use such a proposition merely to affirm that *at least one* of the alternatives is true, and possibly both, as, for example, when one says, " Either Smith committed the crime himself or he is implicated in it." This proposition merely affirms that *at least one* of the alternatives is true. It does not imply that both alternatives cannot be true. In the cognitive act it is erroneous to state the disjunction in an exclusive way — it is either subjective or objective — as if the object of knowledge must be *reduced* wholly to subjectivity or to objectivity. A moment's reflection makes it clear that historical knowledge is both subjective and objective. It is objective, for *something* is known; it is subjective, for something *is known*.

In Collingwood's idea of historical knowledge, the object of knowledge is subjective, for this object is rethought by the historian; it is objective, because it is the past thought of another mind that is known in this way. It is also objective in a further sense. Merely to perform an act of thought that another's mind has performed does not, in itself, constitute historical knowledge. One must at the same time be aware that he is reenacting the thought of another. One is not thinking historically unless he is aware of what he is doing.

Collingwood's concept of historical knowledge is possible only if acts of thought in some way transcend the transiency of time. It was his conviction that they do. He challenged the beliefs that acts of thought are like feelings and sensations whose reality can be possessed only in immediacy, that thought exists " in the flow of consciousness, whose being is simply its occurrence in that flow," and that once the thought has occurred, the flow of consciousness carries it into the irrecoverable past.[92]

The yawning chasm between past and present is bridged in Collingwood's hermeneutics by knowledge, for knowledge has within it something that is universal in character. It is, therefore, an error to construe the process of knowledge as the mere flow of consciousness, for thought is the kind of activity by which the flow of consciousness is arrested and which in some sense "stands outside that flow." [93] The general structure of historical knowledge is therefore something in which "the past is not dead and gone, but can be envisaged together with the present and compared with it." [94]

If an act of thought were nothing more than an element in the flow of consciousness, then, of course, the historian's act of thought would be reduced to pure subjectivity. In that case the present (act of thought) could not be organically united with the past (act of thought), and the yawning abyss between past and present would remain forever unbridged, whether the gap is between the present and what happened one minute ago or one thousand years ago — the time differential is in principle wholly relative. Such misunderstanding is exposed for what it is by the simple fact of memory and by historical knowledge, in which the present thought *is* the thought of the past. The gap is bridged by the power of historical thinking to reenact the thought of the past and " by the power of past thought to reawaken itself in the present." [95]

Collingwood was careful, however, to avoid the error of much historiography prior to the twentieth century, which was misled by a distorted notion of objectivity in historical method. This error manifested itself in the reduction of the object of historical knowledge to the practical actions performed by men of the past. Even if the element of purpose was taken into account it was possible to argue that only the act performed was what was executed " on purpose." Hence, there could be no history of thought, since thought is the theoretical activity that lies *behind* the act. Collingwood correctly pointed out that any such sharp distinction between the theoretical and the practical aspects of action does not hold good, for the act performed and the intention behind it are organically interrelated parts of a whole. The intention, indeed, must be regarded as the initial stage of the act.[96] We can reconstruct and rethink the history of politics, war, ethics, and religion, only if the deeds performed were performed on purpose and only if we have the power of imagination and insight to fathom what the purpose was and how accordingly the person or persons whose purpose it was sought to execute what was purposed.

Collingwood added that even if a man's thought is said to be purely theoretical, as, for example, in a particular piece of scientific inquiry, the element of purpose is not lacking. Scientific inquiry is a form of reflective thinking, which means that the scientist is consciously confronted by a problem and is endeavoring to discover its solution. Perhaps he is seeking for the cause of a particular disease, and his purpose is to discover what this cause is. In this sense, therefore, there can be a history of science, just as certainly as there can be a history of war and politics.

Collingwood's emphasis on the volitional element of purpose in historical method can be expressed by saying that a primary task of the historian is to identify the problem, for all reflective thinking consists of answering questions or solving problems. And it is because the thinker of the past addressed himself to his contemporaries, who knew what the problem was, that the thinker often felt it to be unnecessary to lay down an explicit statement of the problem. The historian must therefore bring to light the influences in the process of history which generated the problem confronting the thinker whose thought he attempts to rethink. The influence of Socrates on Plato, for example, must be grasped, in the history of philosophy. The historian must gain an understanding of " the way in which the conclusions reached by one thinker give rise to problems for the next." [97]

If now we ask, What is historical reality, as Collingwood saw it? the answer is a complex one. It is not a group of brute facts to be known, remembered, and cataloged. It is not a set of happenings to be reflected in the historian's imagination by an uncritical framing of the story, as presented by the evidence. Like the novelist, the historian constructs a picture that is a narration of events, a portrayal of situations and motivations, and an analysis of personalities. But unlike the novelist, the historian aims " to construct a picture of things as they really were and of events as they really happened." [98]

Does historical reality then consist in an encounter between the historian and the persons of the past whose thought the historian endeavors to rethink? In a sense, yes. The concept of encounter points in the direction of Collingwood's idea of historical reality. But it is a particular kind of encounter. The encounter concentrates finally on the thought, for *what* in the past the historian can participate in is the reflective thought that lies at its inner core.

On the surface Collingwood appears to have been not wholly consistent at this point. He argued that " science lives in a world of abstract universals," while the reality on which the historian's mind works is "not abstract but concrete, not universal but individual." [99] Yet in another context he modified the statement that historical knowledge deals with the individual, because this would exclude universality, " and it is just the universality of an event or character that makes it a proper and possible object of historical study." [100] It is because the thought of the past possesses the power to reawaken itself in the mind of the present that historical knowledge is possible. The realm of thought must therefore be something universal, something which, so to speak, can find concrete expression repeatedly, in the ongoing process of historical existence, something that therefore transcends the transiency of time.

According to Collingwood, the difference between the universals of scientific knowledge and the universals of historical knowledge would seem to be that the former are *abstract* universals, while the latter are *concrete* universals. The historian is concerned to use his power of imagination to reconstruct life situations and portray the ways in which these determine subsequent life situations, and thereby to show how the past lives in the present.

It would thus be an oversimplification to represent Collingwood's idea of historical reality as a kind of Platonic temporal reflection of the realm of eternal ideas. At times in the past [101] Platonic realism has led to the notion that since the universal alone is real, in the utlimate sense, the difference between individuals is only skin-deep, so to speak. All individuals comprehended under the universal are *fundamentally* the same, differing only in accidental modifications of their common essence. It would be a misunderstanding of Collingwood's idea of the universals of historical knowledge to construe their relation to individuals in such an ultra-Platonic way. The process of historical life is too dynamic and too vastly complex to be viewed as a *mere repetition* of finite expressions of eternally fixed ideas. Such a view of the reality of history would miss the organic way in which each present has its own unique past, a past to be grasped by the power of imaginative historical reconstruction. Further, each historian is himself enmeshed in the relative process of history; hence, no achievement of historical knowledge can ever be regarded as final, in the absolute sense. History, too, has its history. The historian, together with his complex and vast body of evidence, is an organic part of the life process that he studies. The historian's perspective is one that has its place *in* the process. He cannot stand outside the process and see it *sub specie aeternitatis* but only from the perspective that is possible for him in his historical situation.

As a historian, Collingwood had little to say regarding the knotty problem of meaning in history. The meaning of the word " meaning " in the question of the meaning of history is somewhat ambiguous. If by this question one means, Is there an all-embracing rational structure into the logical pattern of which the whole development of human history neatly fits? Collingwood (at least as a historian) replied in the negative. The temper and attitude of Collingwood the historian is much closer to the attitude of contemporary physicists who, it appears, are backing away from any metaphysics. As a historian, Collingwood had little use for what Isaiah Berlin called "metahistory." Collingwood felt that it is not the task of the historian, qua historian, to discover an overall pattern or to ferret out a general law of the whole of history. He believed that it is more legitimate, in the study of history, to have done with any attempt to annex history to theological or metaphysical speculations and to restrict oneself to a critical study of the individualities of history. On this question, Alan Bullock has aptly said that it is a pertinent question to raise: " Who sees the more — the airman who flies continually across several countries five thousand feet up, from where he can see the land for miles and miles, or the countryman who has lived in one place all his life but knows the valleys, the woods and lanes of his own countryside, like the back of his hand? " [102]

Another dimension of meaning has to do with the question

of teleology. Is there any *telos* of the whole historic process? any eschatological or transcendent goal toward which history strains forward? Again, Collingwood the historian replied in the negative. No legitimate study of history can discover any such eschatological meaning in history.

In yet another sense, however, Collingwood did find meaning in history. There is room in his system for the notion of historic progress. Such progress is related to his answer to the question: What is history (that is, historical knowledge) for? He replied that it is for human self-knowledge.[103] The value of history is " that it teaches us what man has done and thus what man is." [104]

The progress possible in history must not be confused with the idea of natural evolution, in which new forms of species emerge in natural process. A mere change from an agrarian to an urban way of life does not necessarily represent progress, for the adoption of the urban way of life may entail a loss of basic social and moral values preserved and sustained by the agrarian mode of existence. The only valid meaning that Collingwood allowed to the word " progress " is one associated with the purpose of historical knowledge as the achievement of self-understanding. If and when one possesses the ability for historical understanding and can thus sympathetically reconstruct or relive (through the power of imagination) a former historical period, he fulfills the one essential condition that is the possibility of progress. If he does this, he is in a position to compare his present historical period with a past one, critically but sympathetically. He is thus able to see whether or not the present form of existence resolves problems left unresolved by the past, yet at the same time preserves all the positive values of the past.

Collingwood observed that the clearest example of progress is perhaps found in the development of scientific theory. The only legitimate reason for permitting a new scientific theory to supersede a former one is that the new theory takes into full account all the valid resolutions of the past theory, and at the same time explains problems left unexplained by the superseded theory, problems that the old theory should but did not solve.

According to Collingwood, this interpretation of the notion of progress holds good also in other areas, such as philosophy, religion, and morality. There is progress in the history of philosophy only insofar as "one stage of its development solves the problems which defeated it in the last, without losing its hold on the solutions already achieved." [105] The same principle holds good in the development of religion and morality, whose social institutions determine, negatively and positively, the realization of moral values.

It thus becomes clear that for Collingwood, historical knowledge is the basic condition for the possibility of progress in any area of human endeavor, for only through historical knowledge is self-knowledge achieved.

In his understanding of the historicity of human existence, Collingwood escaped the perils of historical relativism construed in a deterministic way. The past, of course, determines the present; but the meaning of this determinedness must be clearly grasped. If by "determine" one means a rigid doctrine of causality that leaves no room for freedom in man's response to his past, then Collingwood would contend that the present is *not* determined by the past. But if by "determine" one means that the past provides the condition for the possibility of present action, Collingwood would agree. The present's past (and historical knowledge of it) is not only the condition but the indispensable condition for responsible action in the present.

That man is free does not mean that he is always able to do what he pleases, or even what he chooses, for man's rational activity and decisions are not performed in a vacuum. They occur in a given situation or context of existence and stand, therefore, under the compulsion of facing the facts of the situation. The more rational action is, the more radically it faces and accepts this compulsion. The measure of success of one's action is directly correlated with the extent to which he correctly grasps the character of the situation within which his action occurs. Said Collingwood, freedom means, in part, that this compulsion is imposed on man's rational thought by nothing else but itself.[106]

But freedom also means something more than voluntarily

facing up to the hard facts of the situation as given. As we have already seen, in reenacting past thought, the historian criticizes it, compares it with his own thought, " forms his own judgment of its value, corrects whatever errors he can discern in it." [107] This critical quality of historical thinking points up its autonomous character, " its power to solve its own problems for itself by its own methods." [108] With this awareness of the autonomy of historical thinking comes also the awareness of the freedom of man as a historical agent, his freedom from the domination of nature. Over against man's natural existence, which he shares with all forms of life, stands man the historical agent, who possesses the ability to build his world of human affairs at his own bidding and in his own way. [109]

Collingwood escaped the nihilism implicit in the doctrine of radical historical determinism. For him, every present is full of potential meaning. It has within itself its own unique meaning, or at least the possibility of such meaning. Part of the heritage of the past consists in a bundle of problems left unsolved. Rational activity wrestles with these problems to find more adequate solutions than was possible at a past stage of the development of thought, yet in such a way as to preserve the solutions to other problems correctly discovered by the past.

Collingwood thus pointed to man's responsibility. He argued that historical knowledge is useful as a " guide to action." [110] The crucially important thing about historical knowledge is that it is useful in resolving the problems of the present. What history brings to moral and political life is " a trained eye for the situation in which one has to act." [111] It brings the insight needed " in diagnosing our moral and political problems." [112] Collingwood opposed the positivistic view of history and agreed with the essential notion of Nietzsche's *Unseasonable Reflexions,* namely, that history is to be studied not as an end in itself but as a means for the improvement of life and thought in the present. As Aron aptly puts it, because history is inspired by a present interest, " it has a present purpose." [113]

In the matter of self-knowledge, Collingwood moved a significant step beyond Croce, who limited the mind to reason. As we have seen, for Collingwood, the thought which is the object of historical study is *reflective* thought, that is, " the effort to do something of which we have a conception before we do it." [114] As pointed out above, Collingwood stressed the element of intention or purpose (the will) behind the events of history. The essence of historical existence, according to Collingwood, would thus seem to consist in rational decisions. At the core of human existence, man is what he wills to do and to be. The "thought " that Collingwood stressed would therefore be misrepresented if it is construed as a mere rational act; it is, rather, an act of the whole man, whose whole being is brought to focus in the moment of decision.

A question arises regarding the place of the future in Collingwood's view of historical existence. With eloquence and cogency he has shown beyond doubt that only by means of historical knowledge can man arrive at self-knowledge.[115] This is true because of the life unity which binds man's historical past with his present. Question: In his analysis of self-knowledge, should not Collingwood have more explicitly included the consciousness of responsibility as the self faces the future?

Collingwood would probably reply to the above question by saying that the question points beyond history, which is the present appropriating the past. " The historian," he wrote " has no gift of prophecy." Historical study " can neither foretell the future developments of human thought nor legislate for them," though we can say that the future must grow out of the present.[116] There is here in Collingwood's outlook on human existence a definite openness toward the future. But he failed to develop the implications of this openness. If thought includes the element of intention or purpose, as he repeatedly insisted, thought is not merely theoretical but also an act of decision. Recognition of this element of decision at the core of selfhood would seem to suggest something more positive in man's openness toward the future. One can neither " foretell " the future nor " legislate " for it. Agreed. Yet if at its center the self consists of an act of decision, must it not be said that, within limitations of course, man is responsible for future developments? If so, the full historicity of human existence calls for a more adequate consideration of this living in responsibility toward the future than Collingwood has presented. Such consideration, however, would not contradict any of Collingwood's theses regarding the nature of history. It would be a supplement, but a vitally important supplement that one wishes Collingwood had not overlooked in his analysis of self-knowledge.

Like Croce, Collingwood believed that the writing of universal history is impossible. Each universal or world history bears the marks of the particular intellectual climate out of which it emerged and has, therefore, at best only a relative, partial truth. The writing of world history, Collingwood observed, is mainly a nineteenth-century phenomenon, which subsequent developments have shown to be " the offspring of caprice." [117] He argued that the development of the " philosophy of history " movement resulted from the inadequacy of scissors-and-paste history. Historians rightly became disgusted with the task of merely copying the statements of their authorities. In a commendable, though fallacious, effort to use their own brains, they proceeded to invent a system of pigeonholes in which they could schematize the products of their learning. This, said Collingwood, is the origin of Vico's philosophy of historical cycles, Kant's universal history, Hegel's philosophy of history as the progressive realization of reason, Comte's philosophy of progress, and others such as Karl Marx, Flinders Petrie, Oswald Spengler, and Arnold J. Toynbee.

Why now did these philosophies of history possess a measure of cogency? The reason, said Collingwood, lies in the fact that each such philosophy rested on the metaphysical presuppositions of the intellectual climate in which it was written. The system was impressive, not because it appeared to be scientifically cogent, but because it had become " the orthodoxy of what is in fact, though not necessarily in name, a religious community." [118]

History cannot produce a final, philosophical schema valid for all times and in all cultures for the simple reason that no view of the whole of history possesses any such universal acceptance and significance. This is to say that all such views of the whole of history are themselves enmeshed in and limited and determined by changing stages in the historical process of human thought. As Charles A. Beard has aptly put it, " The pallor of waning time, if not of death, rests upon the latest volume of history, fresh from the roaring press." [119] Each philosophy of history, like each philosophical system, is merely what Collingwood called " an interim report " [120] on the progress of thought to date. It is an interim report because " the doors of the future are always open." [121]

Dealing more generally with philosophical systems per se, Collingwood sought to transcend the radicality of relativism by means of the concept of a scale of forms. The philosopher who thinks systematically (as every philosopher worthy of the name must do) has his place in an ascending scale of systems " whose structure is such that every term in it sums up the whole scale to that point." [122] This summary, however, represents only a relative end. By no amount of philosophizing can one reach an absolute end of the series, for every new horizon brings with it a bundle of new problems to which subsequent thinkers must address themselves. It is, however, a relative end, for this particular summary can only be made once; in this sense the system is final. Viewed from one perspective, a system of philosophy is individual: it is but one in a series of such systems. All past systems must be so regarded by the present. From another perspective, however, a present system, by appropriating and reinterpreting past systems, summarizes the entire series to date. In one sense the system is thus individual; in another it is universal.[123]

V

Implications of the Modern Idea of History for Theology

Theology fulfills its unique responsibility only if it is profoundly involved in the cultural situation within which it carries on its work. Faith becomes impoverished when theology seeks to preserve and protect its life and thought in such a way that they are " hermetically sealed off " [1] from the intellectual climate of its age.

To be sure, like every " science," theology is an autonomous intellectual discipline. Its unique nature and peculiar task derive from its own essential and definitive ground, namely, the gospel of God in Jesus the Christ. Theology would forfeit its *raison d'être* if it permitted the shifting, ideological waves of cultural change to sweep it from its primary base. Only if the church retains this fundamental conviction and holds it with clarity of understanding and firmness of purpose can it fulfill its prophetic mission in the world. For the ground of this mission lies not in the church itself, but in the gospel that generated the church and continuously fashions it anew out of the life of the world. Christian faith is thus forever determined by a given criterion in relation to which all cultural and all theological idols stand under judgment.

In this regard, contemporary theology owes a substantial debt to Karl Barth's corrective of " old-fashioned " liberalism, which stood in serious need of prophetic reform. Barth has rendered the theological enterprise a noteworthy service by destroying the idolatrous claims of the goddess of modernity, and by rescuing theology from the tragic plight of overculturization. Barth called the church back from the worship of false deities to the revelatory source of its inner integrity and life. He showed that theology must be radically determined " by the impetus which it receives from within its own domain and from its own *object*. Its object — the philanthropic God himself — is the law that must be the continual starting point of theology." [2]

A number of us,[3] however, feel that Barth's corrective has become an overcorrective. The grave danger confronting Barthianism is that it may cause the Christian gospel once again to be frozen into a fixed confessional form and thereby lose its redemptive vitality and contemporaneity. Only if theology does its work and takes its shape out of its dialogue with other intellectual disciplines can it possess the cultural integrity essential to its vitality and genuine contemporaneity. To whatever extent theology permits its confessional concern to become isolated from the intellectual life of culture, to this extent it becomes sterile and fails to serve the purposes of God for our day. The life of culture offers not only problems but also resources for meaningful articulation of the Christian message.

The demand for dialogue, however, between theology and the intellectual disciplines of culture is not merely a demand for " conversation " between the two. Barth himself staunchly insists that theology " to some extent " must thus be open to the life of the world, that "retreats behind Chinese Walls never served theology well." [4] Included in theology's dialogue with culture (and here Barth parts company with us) is theology's need to take its form and shape from its involvement in the situation in which it seeks to give meaningful expression to the gospel. As Tillich correctly says,[5] the situation cannot be neglected in theology without the dangerous consequence of sliding back into orthodox attitudes, a consequence that he feels Barth has not consistently avoided.

The issue pertains not to the inner content of the gospel, but rather to the forms of expression, which in any theology that possesses cultural integrity must in part be dictated by the situation. While theology brings the prophetic criticism of the gospel to bear on all human ideals and philosophies, including theology, at the same time it must manifest an openness to all truth that comes from the scientific and philosophical disciplines of modern thought. Theology must take seriously the quest for truth in all areas of human endeavor, as directly relevant to its own work.

For example, there is no legitimate reason to demand of modern scientific man that in responding affirmatively to the call of God in Jesus Christ he must accept literally the mythological forms of expression in terms of which the primitive church responded. That would be absolutizing the historically relative — the sin of sins. The forms of faith's expression correctly vary from age to age, and from situation to situation. They take their shape as faith reawakens in the minds of persons whose beings are, in general, structured by the situation in which they have their existence.

The above comments must suffice to indicate the methodological presupposition with which we now confront the question regarding the impact of the modern idea of history on theology.

Beyond Orthodoxy

The character of the theology of seventeenth-century Protestant orthodoxy is most dramatically symbolized by the famous creeds, such as: The Formula of Concord in German Lutheranism; The Canons of the Synod of Dort precipitated in the Netherlands in the Reformed wing of Protestantism; The Westminster Confession of Scottish Presbyterianism; and the Thirty-nine Articles of Anglicanism. These creeds became binding, external authorities, together with the Bible; they were used as rigid norms to determine membership in the various Protestant bodies.

Twentieth-century fundamentalism in America represents a comparatively mild, anachronistic residue of seventeenth-century orthodoxy, which was one of the major chapters in the development of Protestantism. European Protestant orthodoxy was a vastly greater and more widespread movement than American fundamentalism has ever been.

Othodoxy represented the crystallized stage, after the dynamic phase of classical Protestantism had spent itself. It represented the doctrinal consolidation of germinal seeds in the classical period. It would, therefore, be erroneous to classify Luther, Calvin, and Zwingli as belonging to orthodox Protestantism. They belonged to the dynamic phase when theology was alive, growing, and effecting numerous reforms in the church " in head and members." That was a time when the experience of the gospel bulked large in theological perspective. As his controlling hermeneutical principle, " justification by faith," shows, Luther attempted to keep the norm of *sola scriptura* correlated with *sola fide*. During the classical period, the Bible had not yet been distorted into an external, objective authority.

It is, of course, true that because Luther failed adequately to clarify the precise relation between "the Word of God" and the words of Scripture, this ambiguity eventually led to the orthodox identification of the two.[6] One searches Luther's writings in vain, however, for an expression of the conception of verbal infallibility. He could scarcely have held such an idea and treated the writings of Scripture with such " royal freedom," [7] calling The Letter of James an " Epistle of straw," [8] repudiating the apostolicity of the book of The Revelation,[9] arguing that Jude was in large measure taken from II Peter,[10] and placing higher normative value on the Gospel and first letter of John, the letters of Paul, and II Peter than on other parts of the New Testament.[11]

For Luther and Calvin, the authority of the Bible was established by " the inner testimony of the Holy Spirit," that is, by the experience of faith. Orthodoxy, however, rejected the correlation of Biblical authority with the Holy Spirit's operation in faith as dangerous subjectivism. To be sure, orthodoxy retained the concept of the present working of the Holy Spirit, but to a different end. Luther and Calvin were close to the apostle Paul's understanding of the function of the Spirit. For Paul, the Spirit bears witness, confirming our consciences " that we are children of God " (Rom. 8:16) ; for orthodoxy, the Spirit bears witness " that the doctrines of Scripture are verbally inspired and therefore infallibly true." In principle, faith was thereby wrenched free from the person-to-person relationship and distorted into an objective, legalistic affair. Lost now was the blessedness of communion with the Eternal " in the Spirit," as Paul put it. This represents a tragic misunderstanding of the nature of faith, which orthodoxy generated and bequeathed to its children. It is the fallacy of heteronomous objectivism.

The intellectual demands of orthodox Biblicism, however, were mammoth and beyond the ability of the average church member. How could the butcher, baker, and candlestick maker learn and understand the multitude of infallible truths of the Bible? Even if they had had the time for such a task, many lacked the ability, for they could not read. Orthodoxy's answer to this problem was to distinguish between the essentials and the nonessentials. The creed was developed to inform people what the essentials were; creed and Scripture were therefore inseparably bound together.

The beginnings of the collapse of orthodoxy are to be found in the Netherlands and Germany with the emergence of the movement of Pietism. Due to external (the Thirty Years' War, for one thing) and internal reasons, orthodoxy was shortly found wanting in the inwardness of Christian devotion. Its life became barren, stoggy, and religiously unfruitful. Its worship became fixed and formal. Its people became " God's frozen people." Pietism emphasized anew the subjectivity and inwardness of faith. It put Christian living before Christian doctrine. It was a reaction, on the subjective side of faith, to the objectivism of orthodoxy. The subjective side had been frozen out, so to speak, by external formalism and by the dominating belief that religious truth consists of a body of objective and infallible doctrines. Not that the subjective side of faith was totally ignored by orthodoxy, but for it the subjective side did not mean very much. Orthodoxy lives on the objectivity of doctrinal and ecclesiastical systems.

The movement of Pietism, however, finally spent itself. It represented an attempt to put new religious wine in old theological wine flasks. It too naïvely thought that theology meant the system of orthodoxy; it therefore failed adequately to understand the essential wrongness of its enemy. Hence, the pietistic distaste for theology, which lives on to this very day.

Although Pietism made a substantial contribution in its demand for greater inwardness in religion, it was too theologically dim-sighted to see that the system of orthodoxy could not and would not support the sort of experiential interests that the Pietists had in mind. Pietism failed adequately to perceive that by absolutizing its creedal expressions, as if they were irreformable, orthodoxy hindered the continued performance of critical theological work to which the creeds owed their birth. By such creedalism, religion lost its creative vitality and was buried in the formalism of the dead letter.

The second blow against orthodoxy was more powerful and effective. It came from the rationalism of the Enlightenment. Rationalistic Christianity emerged partly due to the inadequacy of orthodoxy to adapt itself to the spirit of the modern age, born of the Renaissance. The Enlightenment emphasis on intellectual freedom, rational integrity, and individual responsibility for one's beliefs, and its enthusiastic devotion to the new enterprise of science were powerful weapons, used with decisive effect against the depressing yoke of creedalism, Biblicism, and ecclesiastical dogmatism. Whatever the weakness of Enlightenment rationalism (and we have already seen that it was considerable), these admirable qualities and concerns represented a valid and greatly needed protest to the theological posture of orthodoxy.

The final blow against orthodoxy, which has in the main destroyed it as an intellectual system worthy of theological support, came from the historical movement, about which we are mainly concerned in this volume. In the light of the new historical understanding of human life and thought, both orthodoxy and the absolutist rationalism of the Enlightenment have given way to a new, profound awareness that all human thinking is enmeshed in, and determined by, the relative forces of historic process. All thinking is shaped by one's point of view, as we say, which takes its posture from the time, place, and situation in which the individual realizes his being and thought.[12] This historical relativity characterizes theological thinking as certainly as all other human thinking.

This new insight of historical consciousness provided a weapon in the struggle for freedom from the idols of orthodoxy against which the latter had no valid defense. By the power of this new historical outlook, traditionalism collapsed, the creed lost its idolatrous hold on the Christian mind, and Biblicism was exposed for what it is, namely, an irrational fabrication born out of ignorance. In this sense, the historical movement has wrought a noteworthy reform in theology, whenever and wherever the implications of this movement have been taken with intellectual seriousness and honesty. No longer tenable is the view that the gospel message recorded in Scripture constitutes a cozy deposit of absolute truth; for the Biblical writings are genuinely historical writings and must be so regarded. Theology can no longer view the New Testament as a compendium of religious truth, an objective datum insulated against, and unaffected by, the relative forces of history. No longer can the Bible per se be identified with " the Word of God," nor can the creeds per se be regarded as an absolute deposit of formal truth.

Out of the new historical understanding, there has come the whole historicocritical movement of Biblical studies. Indeed, the new historical movement was initiated not merely by outside sources, but by Christian scholars themselves. This was to be expected because Christianity, by its very nature, has a solid stake in the historical question, as the church's early successful struggle against Docetism shows. The Christian faith is anchored to its basic belief that the historical Jesus is the one whom God made Lord and Christ, and to the historic process of tradition, by which the original message is handed down, generation to generation.

The historicocritical school of Biblical studies, however, reached its flowering period in the nineteenth and twentieth centuries. It is today a matter of common knowledge that this new " historical method " has given to the church a rich historical knowledge of the Biblical writings of which the church through seventeen centuries had very meager awareness. This school of Biblical study has demonstrated, beyond all intelligent doubt, the historically conditioned forms of the messages of the Bible. It proved that the forms of these messages were determined by the language and mythological concepts of the cultural milieu of Biblical times. It is no longer a point of debate among thoughtful students of the Bible as to whether or not the formal concepts of the Biblical message were conditioned by the relative forces of history.

As the new historical interpretation of the Bible steadily increased, the orthodox view of the Bible gradually waned. The historicocritical school compelled theology to face the historical facts about the Bible, even the historical fact that the faith perspective of its authors qualified the historical reliability of their witness in such a manner that they were able to describe historical facts in unhistorical (mythological) ways and even maintain something to be a historical fact that perhaps actually did not happen, as, for example, some of the sayings attributed to Jesus.

The historical movement, however, did more than destroy the Bibliolatry of orthodoxy. To a large degree, to it goes the credit for compelling theology to rethink its belief in the authority of the Biblical message in the light of the findings of the new historical approach. Historical criticism disclosed the fact that neither the text, nor the concepts, nor the translations of Scripture are infallible. Christianity thus owes a sizable debt to the historical movement for delivering it from false beliefs about the Bible, thereby setting theology free to quest for a truer understanding of the nature of Biblical authority.

The *theological* significance of the new historical approach to the study of the Bible lies in the fact that in a new way the question is now raised: What does this *historical* book mean to us today? But here again modern historiography is of positive benefit to the work of theology, for the conviction is much alive in contemporary historiography that there is an *inner* truth in history beyond mere external fact (Collingwood's unity of the outside and inside of historical events), an inner truth which is not accessible to the neutral, detached observer, but which is accessible only to one who participates in historical study existentially. Hence, there is a new interest today in the *theological* as well as the *historical* understanding (in the nineteenth-century sense) of the Biblical message.

BEYOND RATIONALISM

The modern historical movement has not only been a major influence in liberating theology from the idols of orthodoxy.

It has also been equally powerful in liberating the faith from the rationalism into which theology was drawn by the pervasive impulse of the Enlightenment.

Although remnants of eighteenth-century rationalism manifest themselves today, the "natural" religion of rationalism has been rendered obsolete. As we have seen, the nineteenth-century movement of Romanticism reacted against the rationalistic idea of the universal, and glorified instead the variety and uniqueness of individuality. Instead of cold formal reason, Romanticism emphasized the aesthetic dimension in human experience.

The lack of historical realism in the somewhat fantastic notion of "natural religion" was exposed by Schleiermacher, who showed that in so-called natural religion the real, historical flesh and blood of religion is "so much refined away" that little of the peculiar character of religion remains.[13] If we remove our rationalistic spectacles, said Schleiermacher, and look at historic fact, it becomes obvious that natural religion is "only a vague, sorry, poor thought that corresponds to no reality," and that religion *as it actually is* appears only in historically individualized expressions.[14] The idea of universal (natural) religion is therefore wrong, for if everyone has the same religion no one will have "his own true and right religion." [15]

Through the influence of the Romanticists, Schleiermacher, and other exponents of the modern historical movement, the grand eighteenth-century delusion of a Universal Reason complete within itself was overcome. These men exposed the superficiality of rationalism by showing how profoundly all human life and thought are enmeshed in, and determined by, historical processes and forces.

The historical sense generated a new basic category for understanding the whole of human existence, which has sometimes borne the label "historical relativism." This represents the historicosociological dimension of the modern doctrine of relativity, a particular expression of which Einstein popularized in physics and astronomy.

The modern sciences of history and sociology have taught us that the historical conditionedness of all life and thought

means that we are beings whose concepts inevitably fall short
of Universal Reason. The fallacy of the eighteenth century
lies partly in the fact that its exponents failed to distinguish
between ontological Reason and reason as it actually is under
the sociohistorical conditions of man's finitude. We mortals
simply do not hold in our possession a Universal Reason common to all men. It is, rather, a reason filtered through the
medium of finite mind and modified by a sociohistorical
heritage; it is a historically conditioned reason.

The law of historical relativity holds true in all of man's
intellectual life, in ethics [16] as well as politics, in metaphysics [17]
as well as in theology and ecclesiology.[18] The classic British
empirical philosophers — John Locke and his followers — were
keenly aware that concrete empirical experience places a limit
on the powers of human reason, as was the great Immanuel
Kant. They all perceived with clarity that in the matter of
epistemology it is not permissible to transgress the bounds of
human experience. As Kant put it, it is only from experience
of the phenomenal world that the constitutive elements of the
cognitive act are derived. The subsequent development of
awareness of the historical character of human existence demands that we move beyond these early empiricists and recognize that the *subject* of knowledge also stands under the law
of relativity. The reason that operates in the field of experience
is itself further limited by historical and social conditions.
The limitations of time not only circumscribe man's existence;
they run through it. Furthermore, as H. Richard Niebuhr reminds us, this time that is in man " is not abstract but particular and concrete; it is not a general category of time but rather
the time of a definite society with distinct language, economic
and political relations, religious faith and social organization." [19]

The recent technological acceleration of global intercom-
munication and interrelation has driven home the truth of
historical relativity beyond all equivocation. Different peoples
operate with different cultural *Gestalts,* different languages,
different intellectual frames of reference. Language is always a
dynamic, changing, relative quantity. To understand what a
person from another cultural frame of reference is saying, one

must somehow adopt his point of view. Words have meaning only in a particular frame of reference. The word "Nirvana" has no meaning in the context of American, activistic, this-worldly culture. But it does possess a meaning, a powerful meaning, for minds that exist in another intellectual frame-work. Every human community thus possesses its own unique structure, which has been fashioned out of its own history. It is a unique, historically determined entity.

It should be borne in mind, of course, that this law of the relative, historical character of all thought does not mean that there is no valid knowledge of truth or perception of good. Though man is incapable of possessing a universal knowledge, he still may arrive at a valid knowledge of the universal. He possesses no absolute knowledge, but he may possess knowledge of the absolute. By the grace of God he is able to possess the "heavenly treasure," but only in "earthen vessels."

With the nineteenth and twentieth centuries' development of the historic outlook, a new appreciation of Christianity as a historical phenomenon came into being. It was now realized that it is through history that we receive what we have. It was realized that the present has grown out of the past, and that whatever truth or value comes to us for our existence today comes through the medium of history. Paul Tillich has under-scored this historical source of meaning in present existence by pointing out that historical groups are the "bearers of his-tory," [20] though, of course, *precisely how* the past lives on in and determines the present is dependent on the way in which the individual responds to his heritage, out of his transcendent freedom.

The new appreciation of Christianity as a historical con-tinuum made itself felt in Christian theology and decisively affected it in all of its branches. It gave to modern theology a fresh impetus toward the historical study of the Christian faith. It inspired theology to seek greater self-understanding through the study of its own historic sources, rather than by means of a metaphysic that was derived elsewhere. Perhaps the most dramatic example of the new appreciation of Chris-tianity as a historical phenomenon lies in the realm of Biblical studies which, as pointed out above, proceeded to develop an understanding of the Bible itself in its historically conditioned character.

The historical dimension of the theological renaissance of the past few decades has also been a major factor in the heartening emergence and growth of ecumenical Christianity. It is, indeed, not possible to understand the ecumenical movement unless one sees it, in large part at any rate, as the product of the impact of modern historical-mindedness on the theological enterprise. Members of different church groups have been able to break out of their isolation from the total Christian tradition and shatter the bonds of their sectarianism because they have finally arrived at historical self-understanding.

The historical movement has thus enabled us to overcome a blind spot in much of the Protestant attitude toward tradition. The Reformation doctrine of " the Bible alone," coupled with the conviction that much of the Christian tradition represents a corruption of Christianity by the papacy, misled Protestants to develop a warped view of Christian history as consisting mainly of Scripture, plus the traditions of their own confessional group. Traditional Protestantism thus tended to set tradition too sharply over against the Bible, and mistakenly fancied itself to be determined solely by the Bible, and free from the "shackles" of tradition. The development of an ecumenical outlook in theology has disclosed the fact that such Protestants have not infrequently been the most tradition-bound of all.

The new historical understanding of Christianity has fostered the development of interest in, and appreciation of, other traditions than our own. To use historical imagination and project oneself into the personal crisis of Luther's situation at the Diet of Worms in 1521, to feel the tension and heartthrob of Luther as he stood fast by his loyalty to the Word of God and refused to recant in spite of the joint demand of pope and Emperor that he do so, even though he felt that this steadfastness of faith would probably mean his own death; or to share John Wesley's conversion experience, when he returned from Georgia to Great Britain and attended a Moravian meeting to hear the reading of the preface of Luther's Commentary on Romans; or to share Thomas Campbell's deposition from "the holy ministry and from the sealing ordinances," which he received from the Senate in Philadelphia and from the Presbytery of Chartiers in Southwestern Pennsylvania, because he made the Lord's Supper an inclusive fellowship — thus to rethink and through the power of historical imagination to reexperience what such stalwart exponents of the faith thought and experienced is to enrich and deepen one's own experience of faith. By such historical knowledge one does indeed arrive at self-understanding; he overcomes the tragic impoverishment of the isolated ego (which could not be an ego if absolutely isolated) and joins with others in sharing the diversified meanings in the mutual experience of the Christ. Only thus has the spirit of ecumenicity been born, and only thus has it grown: by developing sensitivity to meaning and value in the personal relationships of community.

The historical study of the mind of the church through the centuries has convicted sectarian Christianity of the sinfulness of ecclesiastical segregation. It has generated a new vision of the universal scope of the community of God's making, and has enabled the church to rediscover and to recover the idea of the church " as a corporate historical social fact." [21]

The impact of the historical movement on theology, however, has not only broken the bonds of sectarian isolation; it also helped greatly to rescue the faith from the superficialism of Christian provincialism. As James Moffatt has aptly said, " Once men and women are content to become isolated from the deep influences of yesterday . . . they are in danger of being reduced to the level of the artificial and the superficial." [22] To appropriate the fullness of our historic heritage and the vitality of the total Christian tradition is to rise above the superficialism of a provincial faith. A knowledge of the past helps us to reach more elevated heights, from which we may gain a deeper grasp and clearer vision of the relations of God and man.

Because of the rich variety of ways in which theology has been influenced by the modern historical movement, it is hardly too much to say that in our day theology has become historical in its basic character, in a profound way. Instead of

the seventeenth-century theology of *dogma* (orthodoxy) or the
eighteenth-century theology of *reason* (rationalistic theism),
theology now became *historical* in its bearings. Ernst Troeltsch
scarcely overstated the case when he said that " the meaning
of history for faith has . . . become the central problem in
modern theology." [23]

Beginning with Schleiermacher, who was one of the first to
bring the new historical sense to bear on the task of theology,
the new historical theology recognized that if theology was to
be really fruitful it must take as its point of beginning the
religious identification with the historic Christian community.
That is, theology must be a faith-theology. This is the significance of the title of Schleiermacher's major work in theology:
Glaubenslehre (faith-doctrine). Taking as his point of beginning, faith's identification with the Christian church,
Schleiermacher argued that theology must " entirely disclaim
the task of establishing on a foundation of general principles
a Doctrine of God, or an Anthropology, or Eschatology either,
which should be used in the Christian Church, though it did
not really originate there, or which should prove the propositions of the Christian truth to be consonant with reason." [24]

There is truth in the oft-repeated criticism that Schleiermacher's theological method was too subjective. The task of
systematic theology, he felt, is to explicate the corporate, religious self-consciousness of the Christian community, the unique
feature of which is found in the fact that everything in it is related to " the redemption accomplished by Jesus of Nazareth." [25] Such a definition of the datum of theology tends to reduce theology to the psychology of religion. Instead of making
the religious self-consciousness the datum, Schleiermacher
should have more adequately recognized that theology's datum
is the religious relationship between God and man, a relation
that objectively is Jesus Christ, and subjectively man's response
in faith.

While recognizing the subjective distortion in Schleiermacher's method, in developing a historical approach to theology Schleiermacher's method is to be evaluated positively,
even though a serious question remains regarding his perhaps
too uncritical use of philosophical presuppositions as prolegom-

ena to his historical method. As a theologian, Schleiermacher had no sense whatever of beginning *de novo*. His theological impulse inspired him to study earlier stages in the development of the mind of the church, by which study he gained clearer self-understanding and found a multitude of connections that he compared and contrasted with his own individual ideas.

One basic function of theology, Schleiermacher argued, has to do with its responsibility for the guidance of the church. Such guidance demands a knowledge of the whole that is to be guided, viewed in its present condition. This whole, however, has a " historical character." It can therefore be understood only when it is viewed as " a product of the past." The present cannot be rightly dealt with as the germ of a future which may correspond more nearly to the essential truth of the gospel unless theology perceives how this present itself has been developed out of the past.[26]

Albrecht Ritschl, Wilhelm Herrmann, and Adolf Harnack carried forward, each in his own way, this new historical approach. Karl Barth in our day stands basically in the same tradition, though, of course, with significant modifications which we shall point out later. The very opening words of Barth's *Church Dogmatics* are: " As a theological discipline, dogmatics is the scientific test to which the Christian Church puts herself regarding the language about God which is peculiar to her." [27] And the late H. Richard Niebuhr similarly argued that although Protestantism has long endeavored to say what revelation means by pointing to Scripture, " we have found that we cannot do so save as we interpret them in a community in which men listen for the word of God in the reading of the Scriptures, or in which men participate in the same spiritual history out of which the record came." [28]

Christian theology must begin with the concrete faith of the historic Christian community for the simple reason that no other stance is possible for it. In this sense it must be a church-theology. The historical character of all religious faith and thought about God makes it inevitable that theology begin with and carry on its work within and as a part of a definite, historical, religious group. There is no other place for any theologian to begin. No purely neutral standpoint is possible. One cannot somehow extricate himself from the nexus of history, stand towering above it, and view it *sub specie aeternitatis*. At least, one who is a *historical* being cannot do so. Angels may perhaps do so, if such there be, but not man. Furthermore, the character of religious faith is such that its existential dimension makes it not only impossible but undesirable to attempt the herculean feat of extricating oneself from the historical involvement of religious commitment. Theology, therefore, must be viewed as a function of the church, that historical religious community which finds its point of historic origin in the event summed up in the phrase " Jesus Christ."

Beyond Historicism

Delineated above are some of the more significant benefits that the historical movement of the nineteenth century bestowed upon theology, whenever and wherever theologians were sensitive and alive to its theological implications. As theology pursues its work in the contemporary situation it will suffer serious reversals if it fails to learn and remember these lessons taught by the modern development of the idea of history.

Karl Barth has spearheaded the movement in contemporary theology that attempts to break through the historicism of nineteenth-century historical Christianity by developing (or recovering) the radicality of the idea of God's self-revelation in Jesus Christ. Yet Barth pays tribute to the historico-critical theology for the " valuable stimulation, illumination, and guidance it offered with regard to the Bible and Church History." [29] In reply to those who accuse him of being an enemy of historical Biblical criticism, Barth affirms that he has " nothing whatever " to say against it. He recognizes it to be " both necessary and justified." [30] Indeed, no perceptive student of Barth's theology can fail to see that his breakthrough on the idea of revelation could scarcely have been possible had Barth not been taught lessons of nineteenth-century theology.

While theology must thus cherish the development of the

historical movement, and with it the positive achievements of the nineteenth-century theology that it generated, it must also recognize that each new historical development brings with it a set of new problems. Barth correctly reminds us that the critical weakness of nineteenth-century historical Christianity is found in the basic questions that it "triumphantly by-passed." [31] Its baneful but historically understandable tend-ency was to study the Bible purely historically (in the nine-teenth-century sense), accompanied by no vital concern for the authority of the revelation of God mediated through Scrip-ture. As G. Ernest Wright puts it, "The science of biblical study became a neutral science, largely separated from any responsible feeling for the on-going life of the churches." [32]

These new insights into the theological weakness of histori-cal Christianity resulted in the recent development of the new Biblical theology. Men like Wright, Barth, Rudolf Bultmann, Walter J. Harrelson, Floyd V. Filson, Millar Burrows, Wil-liam R. Baird, and others, while not abandoning the historical approach, began to realize that historical study (in the nine-teenth-century sense) can lead only to a knowledge of histori-cal facts; and that a knowledge of religious truth, in the deeper existential sense, cannot be attained by scientific objectivity. Hence, the feeling arose that there is an *inner* truth of histori-cal events, which lies beyond the realm of mere historical fact, an inner truth that is not accessible to the detached observer, but is accessible only to one who participates in it personally. It is interesting to note that this theological tendency cor-responds roughly to the new developments in recent historiog-raphy, as pointed out in the preceding chapter.

Barth pointed to the need of the *theological* dimension of interpretation in the preface to the first edition of his famous Commentary on Romans (1918). While recognizing the legiti-macy and usefulness of the historicocritical method, he wrote: "My whole energy of interpreting has been expended in an endeavor to see through and beyond history into the spirit of the Bible, which is the Eternal Spirit. . . . If we rightly un-derstand ourselves, our problems are the problems of Paul; and if we be enlightened by the brightness of his answers, those answers must be ours." [33]

The fact is well known that Barth (at the time Professor of Systematic Theology at the University of Bonn), was the leading spokesman at the famous Barmen Synod of January 3, 1934, which organized the protest of the Confessional Church against Hitler's attempt to Nazify the German Church.[34] The first of the six Barmen Theses disclosed the fact that the struggle of the German Church with the Third Reich in principle resolved itself into the question whether the church's confession would be for or against Jesus Christ. This thesis reads:

> Jesus Christ, as witnessed to us in sacred Scripture, is the one Word of God, which we must hear and whom we must trust and obey in life and in death. We reject the false doctrine which says that the church can and must recognize other events and powers, structures and truths as the revelation of God and therefore the source of its proclamation.[35]

In a widely circulated (30,000 copies sold in six months) essay that followed, Barth summed up the doctrine of the new German Christianity and responded with a resounding " No," which reverberated throughout the Western world. Barth saw clearly that the only way effectively to resist the threat to the religious integrity of the church's life posed by Hitler's Third Reich was for Christians to hold fast to their one and only true authority: the Word of God in Jesus Christ, according to the witness of Holy Scripture.[36] It is high time, said Barth, " for the church to become self-controlled again," sober to the recognition that it has *only one* Führer: Jesus Christ, the Word of God.[37]

Because the nineteenth-century historical school of Biblical study " triumphantly bypassed " the crucial theological question, the twentieth-century development of Biblical theology has found itself compelled to make it clear that what it is doing is *not* to restore the notion of the authority of the Bible operative in Protestant orthodoxy. In a new way, therefore, it is obliged to break the hold of orthodoxy, which held Scripture in bondage to a fixed set of dogmas, and to establish a new understanding of the nature of Biblical authority in terms of historical interpretation and historical knowledge.

To understand the work being done in the Biblical theology of our day, it must be clearly perceived that its new theological concern does *not* mean that there is a shortcut around the historicocritical approach. The new Biblical theology builds upon the achievements of the historical school. The careful, critical work of historical Biblical scholarship thus continues unabated. As William R. Baird has finely said, since the New Testament is a historical witness to God's self-revelation in history, and is itself a historical phenomenon, it " must be interpreted by the best methods of historical research. This indicates that the modern approach of scientific historical criticism is essential to a valid understanding of the New Testament." [38]

What is new in Biblical interpretation is the widespread recognition that man does not live by the bread of objective historical fact alone, but by the *living* truth of the gospel, and that, therefore, the question of the ultimate meaning or truth by which we live life today and to which we are to commit ourselves with absolute religious devotion — this question of *theological* interpretation begins where *historical* study (in the nineteenth-century sense) ends. Or perhaps it might be more accurate to say that both concerns should be interlaced and move forward together.

In a discerning and helpful essay,[39] Robert W. Funk deals with the vital hermeneutical problem of *how* historical criticism functions with respect to the text of Scripture, which faith holds to be the medium of revelation. Funk shows that the obedience of faith is possible only if one approaches the text of Scripture with a method that makes possible access " to what the text intends to bring to understanding." [40] Hence, fruitful historical study of the Bible is achieved only if it removes " obstacles that impede the heremeneutical function of the text." [41]

The question that stands at the center of contemporary theological inquiry is: What is the basic intention or abiding meaning in the historically conditioned message of the gospel? What is there in this ancient message that transcends the very forms in which it was originally proclaimed, indeed transcends all historical forms, and is equally valid for religious living today? In contemporary theology, the conviction is dominant that the ultimate outcome of Biblical study is, or should be, the fulfillment of God's act of revelation in the participating subject.

In a way, philosophical developments in twentieth-century historiography have augmented the growth of theological concern in the disciplines of historical theology and New Testament studies. Both Croce and Collingwood developed a method in historical knowledge that probes to the inside of the historical event, attempts to rethink the thought which was expressed in the event, and points beyond the determinism of historicism. As we have seen, Collingwood stressed the element of intention or purpose at the core of the event. Contemporary theological interpretation of the New Testament is similarly speaking of the basic intention of the text that is embedded in its cultural form of expression, an intention that it is the task of historical interpretation to clarify. Obedient response to the call and claim of the word of revelation is possible only if historical criticism can fulfill its work in such a way that " what the text intends " is brought to understanding. Only when this intention of the text is disclosed can the power of the gospel be liberated from its outmoded ancient forms and bring to bear on life in the present its probing judgment, its illuminating light, and its claim for obedient response.

Several things need to be said regarding the problematic issue of the relation of faith to culture, which is bound up with the present appropriation of the word of revelation of the church's past. We have already affirmed both the general validity and importance of the Barthian breakthrough, which pointed up the primacy of this Word in the work of theology. In this regard, the affirmation of the Barmen theses must be evaluated positively. Over and above, or in contrast to, all other " authorities " that impinge upon our being in the present situation, faith's primary loyalty is oriented to the God who reveals himself in Jesus Christ.

We must not again lose sight of the prophetic insight of Barmen, namely, that the supreme revelation of God in Jesus Christ is the substance and criterion for theological statements in answer to man's situation in existence. The solemn warning of Barmen against the corruption of the gospel by cultural forces must be taken seriously, as Hitler's German Christianity, eighteenth-century Deism, and second-century Christian Gnosticism eloquently show.

Barmen is also significant, however, for what it fails to say. Although theology must not place *alongside* the revelation in Christ other events and powers, structures and truths, as " sources " of revelation, are not these to be regarded as legitimate " resources " of faith? The question is: Do not these cultural factors have a much more positive significance in the appropriation of faith than the Barmen posture recognizes? The word of revelation and man's response do not constitute an event that occurs in an acultural vacuum. The tendency in Barth's theology, and even in the existentialist theology of the Bultmann school, is to construe the event of revelation in terms of an eschatological " moment," too unrelated to the historicocultural dimension of the responding subject. Unless one takes seriously the positive function that the cultural situation performs in the reawakening and fulfillment of faith, the " Word of God " theology tends to slip back into patterns of Biblicism and conservative restorationism. It is because of this tendency that Amos Wilder criticizes the new hermeneutic now being developed by such men as Ernst Fuchs and Gerhard Ebeling, for this hermeneutic seems to rest on " a violent a-cultural and anti-cultural impulse and sees both the divine word and the human response in a kind of cultural vacuum "; [42] and it also concentrates too narrowly on the volitional element of decision, to the neglect of the noetic aspect of faith. While faith is certainly a matter of response and commitment to the claim that awareness of the divine Presence lays upon the subject, it is at the same time a matter of cognitive apprehension.

This emphasis on the need for the word of revelation to be acclimated to the situation is not to be construed to mean that this divine word does not speak " against " culture. The word of revelation is indeed a probing word; in calling up man's being it also places it in question. This vital aspect of the appropriation of the word in the event of faith is, of course, underscored by Bultmann. He writes that real understanding of the text of Scripture means " paying heed to the question posed in the work interpreted, to the claim which confronts one in the work." [43] The revelatory event of faith thus brings the fulfillment of salvation. That is, by it one is " called forth " out of his incomplete self, out of a self corrupted by idolatrous attachments to substitutes for life's Ultimate. In this way, the response of faith opens up life to its rich, spiritual possibilities.[44]

But now when all this has been said about faith, have we still said enough about the life context or the sociohistorical situation within which the faith event occurs? Does not the movement of the self that thus comes to faith, in different times and different historical contexts, involve and include sociological and psychological factors, and cultural patterns of thinking and feeling, apart from which faith could hardly be regarded as reawakening in the life of the present? As Wilder correctly argues these are not " accidental and gratuitous and interchangeable accompaniments but essential in the action of God in time and place." [45]

Indeed, kerygmatic theologians themselves are obliged to make use of the conceptual tools of modern culture in order to render meaningful the content of the gospel message. The original message was not spoken in a cultural vacuum, nor can it be appropriated by a contemporary mind in any such vacuum. Paul Tillich has well said that "since language is the basic and all-pervasive expression of every situation, theology cannot escape the problem of the situation." [46]

To be sure, theology must not distort the cultural situation into the *criterion* of faith. To do this would be to revert to the stance of nineteenth-century theology. The place of culture in the reawakening of faith is rather a structural one; its function is instrumental rather than normative. In fact, every preacher is aware of the homiletical need to make positive use of the life situation of his hearers; he therefore places in the service of preaching countless illustrations and analogies drawn from the concrete daily patterns of life and thought, even as Jesus did in his parables.

As we have already indicated, the message of faith is not

merely added to the prefideistic structure of the self, as a kind of adornment or supplement. This view of faith and culture smacks too much of the Thomistic two-story relation of grace and nature. According to the Thomistic view, there are *two equally valid levels* of religious knowledge: natural theology and revealed theology. Some truths about God, man, and the world are within the reach of man's "natural" cognitive powers, through the *via immanenz.* Yet there is also the second level of "revealed" theology. Revelation is necessary for an extension or expansion of our knowledge of God. Revelation is a supplement or an addition to knowledge gained at the lower level.

Several things are wrong with the Thomistic two-story synthesis of nature and grace. For one thing, the modern historical movement has disclosed the historically relational character of all human thinking, including theological thinking. Therefore, there is no "revealed theology." There is, theology affirms, revelation *through* words and concepts, but no "revealed doctrine," no infallible dogmas. The notion of "revealed theology" is the major idol of orthodoxy, which the historical movement has shown to be fictitious and erroneous.

In terms of method, it must be said that the Thomistic view stands in need of the "corrective spice" of the Barthian plea. Barth, of course, will have no positive bond whatever between revelation and the rational structure of man's existence. For him, salvation is a complete re-creation, from the ground up. Although Paul Tillich is not so radical as Barth, in this regard, he nevertheless recognizes the need of the corrective principle of Barth's thesis. In Tillich's method of "correlation" the most that can be derived from the substructure of philosophical reason is a disclosure of the basic *questions* of existence. Prefideistic reason can only expose the contradictions of being, in its transition from essence to existence; revelation alone provides the answers. Therefore, the two-level theory of Aquinas is inadequate, for it holds the erroneous belief that it can seek and anticipate a part of the answer in a framework of reference where only the questions can be disclosed.

Whatever be the weakness of both Barth and Tillich, they correctly point up the fact that in the faith event the Holy

Spirit effects radical changes in the basic orientation and ontological structure of the self. Correlated with these changes is the fact that significant things happen also to the cultural elements of which the Holy Spirit makes use in the revelatory event. One cannot read the Bible and fail to see that in almost every theological statement, analogical use is made of concepts and relationships drawn from the cultural situation. Its language about God is symbolic and analogical in character. God is Shepherd, Father, Refuge and Strength, King, and Lord — all symbols drawn from the general intellectual milieu of the culture of Biblical times. These cultural elements played a positive role in the awakening of faith and in liberating the saving dynamic of revelation in the subject of faith. Yet these elements are not taken up into faith unaltered. By the power of the Spirit they undergo a transsignification, when used in the service of faith. New Testament writers for example appropriated the Messias myth from Jewish culture, and the *Sōtēr* myth from Hellenic culture. Yet powerful new meanings were injected into these concepts by faith's identification of Jesus as Christ and Savior. The revelatory impact of Jesus transformed these concepts; they were demythologized by being baptized into Christ, so to speak. There is, therefore, a significant difference between the Christian belief that Jesus is " Lord," and the belief in religious " Lords " in the Greek mystery religions.

Emil Brunner correctly urges [47] that philosophical concepts of culture can and should be used in the work of theology, but not uncritically. By baptizing them into Christ, they can do fruitful conceptual service in theology. They help to illuminate faith's vision but are at the same time corrected by being subordinated to the commitment of faith to the claim of the gospel.

The historicity of the word of revelation, whether in its original moment or in its contemporaneous expression, is even more radical than we have thus far indicated. While theology must never lose its hold on the transcendence of the reality experienced in revelation, it must recognize that faith never experiences the *naked absolute*. Faith is not oriented to a God who dwells in the solitude and silence of some suprahistorical, timeless realm. It is bound to the God who is the "Lord of history." While in his eternality God transcends time and history, he makes himself known to us in and through history. It is in and through concrete historical events that he acts to generate the vision and commitment of faith.

This historicity of revelation means that while it is imperative that we distinguish between the abiding, transcendent aspect of the word of revelation and its transient forms of expression from age to age and situation to situation, we cannot isolate the "essence" of the gospel from its form, and then proceed to translate this clearly defined "essence" into categories that are relevant to the modern mind. This was the methodological error of old liberalism. The relation of the inner reality of the word to its concrete forms of expression is not analogous to the relation of peas to the pod. John Dillenberger correctly warns [48] that the program of demythologizing and the new hermeneutic cannot "lay bare the center" of the gospel. Any attempt to do this shows that one has not yet taken the historicity of the word of revelation as seriously as it must be taken.

These historical limitations of theology have been a source of perennial embarrassment. As the history of Christian thought shows, theology would like to break through all such limitations and possess its object, finally and absolutely. It would like to define the "essence" of revelation unambiguously and with semantic clarity. Were it able to do so, however, faith would no longer be faith. For faith lives in relation to a reality that in the strict sense of the word is not an "object," but is nonobjectifiable. Hence, the relation of faith to ultimate reality is not a "relation" in the usual sense of the term, in which "relation" signifies "correlation" of subject and object. The essential mystery out of which faith lives fades in man's vision whenever the reality toward which faith is oriented is erroneously conceived as mere "object." Such an impoverished faith may, of course, become conceptually certain and definite in regard to its "object"; that is, it may be reduced to knowledge. Genuinely religious faith assumes a humbler role, for it is willing to let God be God.

Part of the conceptual difficulty in faith's appropriation and interpretation of the word of revelation lies in the impossibility of capturing the ineffable fullness of the believer's person-to-person relation with its object, in conceptual categories that only symbolically express the life of faith. However, one must not permit this Pauline recognition that "now we see in a mirror dimly . . . [and] know in part " (I Cor. 13:12) to glide into a radical relativism that ends in skepticism. The miracle of revelation does occur; faith does hear the claim that life's Ultimate lays upon it. And as H. Richard Niebuhr says: " If we cannot say anything adequately, we can say some things inadequately. If we cannot point to the heart and essence of this Christ, we can at least point to some of the phenomena in which his essence appears. Though every description is an interpretation, it can be an interpretation of the objective reality." [49]

While, therefore, the historicity of the life and thought of the man of faith means that there is no escape from historical relativity, relativism and historicism are overcome. They are overcome, in the existential sense, by the freedom of man in relation to his past, a freedom that by critically appropriating the past determines the character of one's response. In this sense, historical knowledge is achieved in order that one may act with cultural responsibility in the present and therefore with reference to the future. This is what Ernst Troeltsch had in mind in his oft-quoted saying that we must " overcome history by history." By exercising his responsible freedom, man achieves authentic being in creative freedom and escapes the evil of being a mere object of the forces of history.

In the ethical and theological sense, relativism and historicism are overcome in the commitment of faith. To say that faith's understanding must be formulated in language characterized by historical relativity and articulated in terminology dictated by perennially changing conditions does not mean that faith must abandon its posture of absolute loyalty to the divine claim laid upon it. Nor must faith relinquish its belief in the universal relevance of the Christ event. For faith's claim to absoluteness rests upon the ultimate character of its object, decisive insight into which, theology maintains, is given in the Christ event. From the very beginning, Christian theology has centered about the profound conviction that the eternal Word became manifest in the flesh, enabling faith to behold his glory, a glory " full of grace and truth."

At three vital points, then, the absolute element appears within the relativities of faith. First, one stands under absolute obligation to follow the light of truth, as it is given to him to see it. To be willing to do anything less than this is to be morally culpable at the deepest level of being. Nor is the highest good of one's religious vision any less valid *for him* merely because others see the issue from another point of view.

Second, the absolute element is manifest in the ethical expression of faith. For Christian faith finds its ethical motivation in Christlike love (*agapē*). Such love seeks the good of its neighbor unconditionally. The formulations and maxims in terms of which *agapē* finds concrete expression will vary from situation to situation and culture to culture, if love responsibly faces the situation. Ethical formulations bear the marks of their time, place, and societal condition. Though an individual would be a fool if he ignored the great moral codes of human history, he would equally fail to fulfill the responsibilities of Christian love if he manifested an inability to face the situation radically and to make his decision as to what Christlike love requires of him in terms of his own situational involvement. Yet within the relativities of moral wisdom, concrete decisions, and specific actions, love acts without losing its unconditional character. As John A. T. Robinson has finely said, the ethic of Christian love is the only ethic " which offers a point of constancy in a world of flux and yet remains absolutely free for, and free over, the changing situation." [50]

Third, Christian faith can believe nothing less than the universal relevance of the Christ reality experienced in the event of faith. The fact that all theological and ethical expressions of faith must inevitably be formulated in relative terminology demanded by changing conditions in historic process does not nullify the basic belief in the universal relevance of the revelation in Christ. All theological attempts to describe the Christ reality will be partial and incomplete, and all confessions of faith will be relative to time and place. But a finite apprehension of this infinite reality is not an apprehension of an essentially finite reality. And a historically relative description of the Christ reality is not a description of a similarly relative reality. That man is incapable of attaining to absolute knowledge does not mean that he cannot know the absolute.

The logic of the relation between the absolute and relative in the experience of faith is applicable not only to this experience. It appears in practically all of man's knowledge. That the physicist disclaims any absolute knowledge of the reality labeled " atomic energy " does not nullify the validity of scientific knowledge of this reality. Partial and incomplete though such scientific knowledge is, it is accompanied by an awareness that the reality thus cognitively grasped transcends the finite grasp of it. This dimension of mystery has been constantly operative in the scientific pursuit of truth.

The finite mode of knowing in the experience of faith then falls short of total comprehension of its object. Yet it embraces the fullness of conviction in the absolute goodness and faithfulness of its object. As John Baillie aptly put it, " The pulse of certainty beats throughout the whole of our Christian knowledge, but we can never quite capture it for our particular formulations." [51] Furthermore, that no one formulation or group of formulations is wholly adequate to capture the essence of its object is no more occasion for distress in theology than in science. On the contrary, it is itself part of Christian doxology, which praises God precisely because he infinitely transcends our highest thought of him. The very heart of worship lies in the humility of faith, which praises God precisely because his thoughts and ways are higher than man's thoughts and ways " as the heavens are higher than the earth " (Isa. 55:9). The certitude of faith thus rests not in possessing its object, but in joyful willingness to be possessed by its object.

The understanding of faith that we have been advocating breaks through the prison of historicism by laying hold on the transcendent God. But this transcendence is to be distinguished from the traditional notion of transcendence which, due to metaphysical influences, was otherworldly in its orientation. The demand for recognizing the radical historicity of faith calls for a this-worldly transcendence. Dietrich Bonhoeffer pointed us in the right direction in his quest for a form of faith that is *in* the world and *for* it, even as the God Incarnate in Christ was in and for the world. The transcendence of God, said Bonhoeffer, is in the very midst of this present life. " The Church stands not where human powers give out, on the borders, but in the centre of the village." [52]

Christian faith thus fulfills its life by means of a dialectical relationship. It maintains both " identity with " and " distinction from " the life of the world. When either pole of this dialectic is overemphasized or distorted, the success of the church's mission is to this extent placed in jeopardy. Whenever faith attempts to *secure itself* in its identity with the world and interprets this identity in a way that forfeits its hold on the Lord of life and history, it loses its spiritual birthright and is sucked into the ethos of the world. But whenever faith seeks to preserve its distinction from the world in a way that forfeits its genuine historicity or its identity with the world, it falls prey to the irrelevancy of otherworldliness.

By the redemptive power of the God-relationship out of which faith lives, the church performs its task of prophetic criticism of human life and society. But in doing so, the church must at the same time fulfill its mission by identifying itself with the life of the world, even as Christ fulfilled his mission by identifying himself with sinful man, indeed by taking upon himself the entire burden and guilt of man's estrangement and bearing the full weight of it in his body on the cross. The church must identify itself with the life of the world in this Christlike, cross-marked way. Only when faith is reawakened in this way can the Christian tradition be rescued from the museum of yesterday's relics and come alive in the traffic of human living in today's world.

VI

Christological Problems Posed by the Modern Historical Understanding of Human Existence

The modern development of historical-mindedness brought a new dimension to our understanding of the basic character of all human life and thought. In this present chapter we shall address ourselves to some basic theological problems which are posed for the church's Christology as a result of the deepened awareness of faith's organic relation to historical forces.

Three basic problems, in particular, have emerged in the encounter of faith with the new historical understanding. To these we now turn our attention.

First, history is a process, a process of the intertwining and interdependence of infinite momenta. Everything is determined by the historical influences that are brought to bear upon it — individuals, communities, ideas, philosophies, religions, and civilizations. Nothing can be conceived to be genuinely historical if it stands insulated from the floodtide of historical forces. We can no longer even conceive of human existence, human ideas, and human cultures except as enmeshed in and determined by the processes of history. As a historical religion, Christianity too is subject to this same law of historical relativity. Presumably, therefore, it is but one phase of the whole of history, with its endless ebb and flow. And by the same law the Christian belief in the absolute uniqueness of its founder becomes a *skandalon*.

Second, even if theology can make good its plea for the uniqueness of Jesus, he still lived and died over nineteen centuries ago. He belongs to the past. How therefore is it possible for Jesus to be the source of spiritual life and power for a vital and vibrant faith today? Perhaps his teachings, perhaps the ideal of life for which he lived and died can be a source of life for faith today; but not Jesus *as a person,* for he belongs to the past.

Third, the attachment of faith to Jesus as the Christ has been rendered highly problematical by the results of historical criticism of the gospel sources. This criticism has exposed the arbitrary and fallacious character of the so-called "lives of Jesus." The difficulty in arriving at any certain knowledge of the historical Jesus lies in the fact that we have no way of getting at him save through the eyes of the church's faith. It is now clear that the faith perspective of the gospel writers was a determinative and formative influence in the portraits of Jesus which are drawn in their different witnesses. It seems clear, for example, that they were thus led to put sayings in the mouth of Jesus which in all probability he did not utter. They attributed deeds to him which in all probability he did not perform. Some critics go so far as to say that the actual, historical Jesus remains a total enigma to us. In any event, it would seem to be the case that our knowledge of particular historical facts about the life of Jesus can never be so certain that a victorious religious faith can be based upon them.

THE SKANDALON OF PARTICULARITY

What is theology's answer to these formidable objections to the Christological focus of the Christian faith? What is the answer, first, to the *skandalon* of particularity? Since history is a process in which everything is related to, and determined by, other historical influences and forces, the uniqueness of one event would seem, by definition, to be no different in principle from the uniqueness of any other event. Moses, Gautama, Socrates, and Jesus — each is a unique historical figure. Every historic event is, of course, unique in the sense that it is unrepeatable. But how, in this *historical* understanding of human existence, is it possible, so to speak, to raise one event out of the ongoing process and view it as singularly unique, as *the central focus* for the understanding of the whole of life and history? For obviously, this one event, the figure of Jesus, is itself immersed in the relative flow of history and determined by it, like all other figures.

The first answer is the reply of simple fact. It is a simple fact that Christians are led to make infinitely more of this pivotal historical event in the Christian religion than is made of other events. What is there, we ask, about the nature of the flow of history that would make it inherently impossible for the significance of some events for the inner life of the spirit to be greater than that of others? That this is so is indeed another historical fact which the historian must take into account in his historical reckoning. From the fact that the history of man is such that his life and being are determined by the historical conditions of his time and age, " it does not follow that the entire course of history is a field without heights and depths." [1] Of course, if one considers only outer, objective facts, unrelated to their significance for man's inner life and experience, all historical facts are radically equalized. There would, in that case, be no difference between a Socrates and a Hitler. Both lived and died, and did a host of things in between. But it would be a strangely arbitrary and even superficial historiography that thus radically equalized all facts. When we speak of history, we are talking not of things but of human beings. We are talking of inner, personal life (the realm of meanings and values) as well as objective catalogable facts. In this sense there are differences in historical phenomena, historical figures, and historical events. Caesar crossed the Rubicon, Hitler marched against Austria, Socrates was tried for heresy, and Jesus was crucified. The meanings of these events do not lie on the same level and are not of equal weight in the shaping of future history; and it is from what follows in the process of history subsequent to an event that its significance must be determined.

That the historic Christian community has found itself constrained to recognize Jesus to be organically related to the center of its view of life, death, and all things, is indeed another actual historic fact. No historian can be " objective " should he fail to register this as a historical fact.

In dealing with theology's reply to this objection, it should be noted also that it is an erroneous philosophy of history which leads one to view history as a process of life that can be explicated by the same principle of cause and effect that controls the process of nature. This was the fallacy of the ancient Greek view, which threw history into the same hopper as nature and thereby wrongly applied to history the natural, cyclical law of periodicity. The category of process is one basic (and valid) category for understanding history; but a second is of equal importance, namely, the category of personality. " Whence comes the fact," Adolf Harnack asked, " that a fruitful insight, a saving idea, transmitted from one generation to another, remains as fruitless and worthless as a dead stone until someone seizes upon it and brings intellectual light from it? " [2] From whence comes the faith and courage of spirit to overcome the evil of the world? Indeed, without the personal power and deed of the individual, no great advance of humanity in history is possible. Here, in the mystery of personality, said Harnack, lies the real lever (*Hebel*) of history.[3]

We believe that Harnack at least pointed in the right direction for an adequate understanding of history. The historicism of nineteenth-century historiography was correct, of course, in contending that every present situation grows out of the past. This was the dominating evolutionary concept of historicism. It was concerned to ferret out the causal interconnectedness of events. But when it conceived the historian's task to be simply that of establishing the facts and determining what the laws of their interconnectedness are, after the analogy of natural causation, it went astray, for in this way it capitulated to naturalism and failed to take into account the existential dimension of personality.

Historicism misunderstands *the nature of the determination* of the present by the past, for it construes it, after the analogy of nature, as a *purely causal* determination. It thereby fails to understand the dynamic, determinative factor of man's freedom, his power for decision, in the present situation. The real " hinge " of history lies just here. For it is this existential freedom which finally decides *how* one responds to the past and *how,* in such response, one thereby also determines his future. Because historicism misunderstands the relation between past and present, it also misunderstands the future. Restricting the notion of causality to the principle of natural causation, it developed a blind spot to the *openness* of the future as a potential to be grasped and shaped by the freedom of the present.

Harnack pointed to this existential dimension of the present moment when he insisted that the " Word " was not only " in the beginning," the " Word " which is at once both deed and life, but always in history the energetic Word (that is, the person) has reigned in and above the pressing difficulty and distress of life.[4]

In the inner spiritual life, then, man does not live by the bread of historical causality alone, " but by every word that proceeds from the mouth of God " (Matt. 4:4) . As Bultmann says, " Personality experiences its own history within the frame of universal history and interwoven within it, but nevertheless as a history which has its own meaning and is not merged into universal history." [5]

The character of man's existence in freedom means that the uniqueness of spiritual insight and power of personality must stand as a basic category of historical understanding, alongside the notion of the process of events. By recognizing this character of human existence we overcome the error of historicism, the error of attempting to understand history after the analogy of the causality of nature.

But if we lump all the seers, prophets, and men of religious genius together by the general category of personality, it would seem that once again the solitary uniqueness of Jesus (in the Christian faith) would disappear. He would now be regarded simply as one in the series (*a primus inter pares*) of prophetic personalities. Certainly he is that. But how can he be more than that? The answer is: Why not? There is no general category that can really comprehend the spiritual diversity of those we call " prophets." Each one is a great soul in and of himself. There is no rule by which we can predict ahead of time in what measure the Spirit will reign in a personality.[6]

Here, in man as person, as one who is characterized by the freedom of self-transcendence, we are confronted by the dimension of mystery, which transcends the so-called chain of historical causality. In view of the imaginable possibilities inherent in this transcendental dimension of man as person, why should it be regarded as a historical impossibility that even the early Christians, those who ate and drank with Jesus, were led, under the impact of his life, death, and resurrection, to look to him as the " Son of God " ? The impact was so great that they obviously felt that here, in the fields of time and history, one appeared who was greater than all the prophets, so great that they found the usual terms — prophet, leader, teacher — inadequate to express the significance of their experience of Jesus. Here was one in whom " grace and truth " were embodied in such fullness that they could only say that " the Word became flesh and dwelt among us " (John 1:14), the Word which was "in the beginning with God," and who indeed was God (John 1:1).

When Christian faith bears witness, however, that this historical figure is unique, it does not mean that as a figure in purely objective history (sometimes called world history) Jesus was unique. There is nothing unique in Jesus' being a carpenter in Nazareth; there were doubtless plenty such. There is nothing unique in his joining the religious movement of John the Baptist; many others did the same. Nor is there anything unique in the objective fact that Jesus was crucified under the reign of Pontius Pilate, for two others were crucified at the same time, on either side of him. Joseph Klausner argues, quite convincingly, that " throughout the Gospels there is not one item of ethical teaching which cannot be paralleled either in the Old Testament, the Apocrypha, or in the Talmudic and Midrashic literature of the period near to the time of Jesus." [7]

By the methodology of nineteenth-century historiography it would be impossible to ascertain the *kind* of uniqueness that Christian faith claims for the historical figure of Jesus. For nineteenth-century historiography labored under the positive influence of the emphasis on factual objectivity in the new natural sciences. It was, therefore, preoccupied with concern for brute facts. As a mere brute fact to be simply cataloged in relation to other brute facts, in an objective time series and by the rule of purely natural causation, the historical figure of Jesus could obviously not be regarded as unique; for at this level of historical research we are dealing with what Lord Acton called " the mere grammar of the work." [8]

With the twentieth century, however, this objectivistic historiography has given way to a historiography with dialogical and existential dimensions. This deeper dimension of historical understanding was indicated by Lord Acton when, at the turn of the century, he said: " We want brains for the higher objects of history — the difference between knowledge of facts and the energetic understanding of their significance is so serious." [9] This new note of " significance " in twentieth-century historiography involves the important insight that history is inadequately understood when viewed merely as that which happened once upon a time, for present human existence is related to the past in a much more organic way. The past is wrongly understood when construed as a happening which one merely views as a spectator, and which therefore holds for him no personal significance or involvement.

The new historiography thus moves beyond the level of mere cataloging and preoccupation with facticity to a concern for penetrating the intentions, meanings, and values held by persons in the past. This leads to personal dialogue with history. Through such dialogical encounter with persons of the past one's own being is called into question. A man sees himself in a new light and as a result perhaps alters his own existence, even in a profound way. It is this personal encounter with history that Lord Acton had in mind when he wrote that " history convinces more people than philosophy." [10] Further, " the lesson of modern history is that Religions enjoy (are endowed with) the prerogative of perpetual youth," whereas philosophic systems " seldom outlast a generation." [11]

The new twentieth-century historiography finds itself equipped with more adequate categories of historical understanding than those of the nineteenth century. The science of history is thus brought into close relation with the Christian faith, for it is the main concern of this faith to understand the deeper (existential) meaning of the event of Jesus of Nazareth. In a formal sense thus the new historiography and Christian theology approximate each other in their central concern.

In this way the developments in the science of history itself have led to a dissolution of the nineteenth-century cleavage between the *kerygmatized* Gospels of the New Testament and the purely factual character of the historian's objective. Indeed, in witnessing to the inner truth or meaning or existential relevance of the historical Jesus (as the Christ), the author of the Gospels did in theology the same sort of thing that modern historians are seeking to do in their own way, in the study of history.

As a result of these developments we are now able to see that due doubtless to the intellectual climate in which they operated, nineteenth-century theologians erred in attempting to locate the revelation of God in purely objective history. At this point, both orthodoxy and liberalism committed the same mistake, in principle, a mistake that orthodoxy still perpetûates in the twentieth century. As is evident in the contemporary debate between Bultmann and the orthodox Lutherans, orthodoxy stresses the historical objectivity of the historical referent in the faith relation, insisting that the mighty acts of God " are set before all human existence, indestructibly, indissolubly, and irremoveably." [12] It is the contention of the orthodox that the objective act of God is *Historie;* that is, it precedes all the being and doing of man, precedes it by way of " objective factualness."

Nineteenth-century liberalism tended to make the same mistake, with a different twist, when it placed dominant emphasis on " the Jesus of history," to such an extent and in such a manner that this historical Jesus was often set in sharp contrast to the "Christ of faith." Hence the antipathy of nineteenth-century liberals to Paulinism and their fondness for the Synoptic Gospels. They wished to go *behind* faith's witness to Jesus as Christ and Lord, and lay hold of the real Jesus, " Jesus of Nazareth as he actually was." In this way it was felt that we could establish, through the method of historical criticism, a solid historical foundation, an objectively verifiable body of words and deeds, in which faith could at last find security.[13] This obviously meant, however, that what was being sought was not the security (and risk) of faith, but a security *in history*. What was sought was reliable knowledge of " a solid nucleus of bare fact " that modern man could interpret as he wished "without regard to the interpretation given by the early Church." [14]

Bultmann fears that some of his followers are at the present time doing something highly similar when the new quest for the historical Jesus which has made itself manifest among them seeks to establish the truth value of the Christian kerygma by an appeal to the historical Jesus. It is the exact opposite, says Bultmann: "The history of Jesus is legitimized as messianic, because it is seen in the light of *kerygmatic* Christology." [15]

What both the orthodox and liberal seem to have forgotten is that the Christian faith did not emerge with the birth of the historical Jesus, however accurately or inaccurately the date and place of his birth can be determined, or other purely factual aspects of his life. Nor yet did Christian faith emerge with Jesus' vocational development in Nazareth. The Christian faith had its beginning in another kind of "event" than the event of brute fact, though to be sure not unrelated to historical factuality. Christian faith had its beginning when those who were drawn to this figure were led to make the affirmation of faith: that Jesus was Messias, that Messias had come, and that therefore the new age of righteousness had already begun, in the life, death, and resurrection of Jesus, whose spiritual significance is apprehended by eyes of faith (revelation).

In thus talking about an objective, historical Jesus (unrelated to faith), both orthodoxy and liberalism are not talking about the "historical Jesus" of the Biblical witness, for the latter is inseparable from the meaning that he possesses for faith *as the Christ*. It is Jesus *as the Christ* who is the *actual* Jesus in which Biblical faith is interested. When we point to the central and unique figure of Jesus, in Christian faith, it must be borne in mind that this central "event" is existential-historical in character. It is twofold: (1) the historical fact of the person of Jesus of Nazareth, born under the reign of Herod and crucified under Pontius Pilate, together with the antecedents of this fact in the history of Israel; and (2) the reception of the redemptive meaning (revelation) of this person *as the Christ of God*. Beyond all doubt, the central Christian confession "that Jesus is the Christ" shows that fact and faith, history and interpretation, are held indissolubly together in the primary " event " to which the Christian faith is forever anchored.

It is important to note that the nature of the " event " on which faith rests would be greatly misunderstood should it be labeled " subjective " or " mythological," meaning the *kind* of subjectivity or mythology that stands in contrast to objectively historical fact. The difference between the nineteenth-century interest in the " Jesus of history " and faith's interest in " Jesus as the Christ " is not a difference between objectivity and subjectivity. It is, rather, a difference in *the way in which* the concrete, historical figure of Jesus is regarded. In the one case, *he is viewed* from the outside (of the community of faith) by a nonparticipating observer. In the other, *he is viewed* from within the context of faith. In both cases *Jesus* is apprehended. The difference lies in the frame of reference in terms of which he is regarded. Nor is the technical historian's account of what *really* happened any more accurate than (perhaps not so accurate as) the account of faith found in the Gospel witnesses. As Paul Meyer aptly says, " To speak of the ' historical ' Jesus is precisely to raise the challenge whether the ' true,' the ' real ' Jesus, Jesus himself, is to be found in the historian's reconstruction or in the theological tradition." [16] The difference lies in the point of view of the observer. In the one case the event of Jesus' life is seen from the point of view of one who stands *outside* the community of faith. In the other, this event is seen from the point of view of one who stands *inside* this community. When apprehended from the inside, as H. Richard Niebuhr expressed it, these events are apprehended " as items in the destiny of persons and communities. . . . They belong to a life-time and must be interpreted in a context of persons with their resolutions and devotions." [17]

THE PROBLEM OF THE RELATIVELY UNKNOWN JESUS OF THE PAST BECOMING THE VITALIZING CENTER OF FAITH TODAY

We turn now to the second two objections raised against the Christological focus of the Christian faith: (1) as a historical figure Jesus belongs to the past and therefore cannot constitute the vitalizing center for religious faith today, and (2) even if he could do so, historical criticism of the New Testament sources has rendered any certain knowledge of Jesus impossible. Due to the kerygmatic character of our sources, our knowledge of the historical Jesus is so thoroughly intertwined with the devotion of faith, so profoundly interpretive in character, that they simply will not yield any certain, objective knowledge of the historical Jesus. We can perhaps arrive at probabilities here, but historical probabilities about what Jesus said and did are much too precarious and contingent to serve as a foundation for a victorious religious faith, which in any case ought to be oriented not to history but to the Eternal.

These two objections are so closely interrelated that we shall consider them together. The problem of the central historical referent in Christian faith, the figure of Jesus, has assumed new dimensions in our day.

For the older Catholic and Protestant theology, the dogma of the verbal inerrancy of the Scriptures buttressed the belief that the Gospel testimony about Jesus was entirely accurate historically. The only problem was how to " harmonize " the " apparent " contradictions in the different accounts.

For liberal Protestantism of the eighteenth-century Enlightenment, the relation of faith both to the historical Jesus and to the Christ of the church's dogma became problematical. For nineteenth-century liberalism, the problem was not so much the historical Jesus, save for a few radical minds like Ferdinand Christian Bauer and David Friedrich Strauss. Bauer's research was carried on under Hegelian presuppositions, which led him to see in Jesus' consciousness the unity of God and man. Bauer thus saw in the theology of German idealism " a Gnosticism of a higher order." Following Bauer, Strauss became highly skeptical in his attitude toward the historical reliability of the Gospels. The important thing (Hegel's influence) , however, as he saw it, is the Christ idea, the God-manhood idea. Strauss asked: " Is not the idea of the divine and human nature a real one in a far higher sense, when I regard the whole race of mankind as its realization than when I single out one man as such a realization? " [18] Secure as he believed himself to be in Hegelian idealism, Strauss felt that it was unimportant what or who the historical Jesus was.

However, this skepticism toward the historical Jesus was short-lived. The crisis that it precipitated in Christian theology led to an intensification of concern for the historical Jesus, a concern that resulted in the famous " life of Jesus " research. Out of this new impetus sprang a whole array of " Lives of Jesus." This chapter in the modern historical concern of theology regarding the figure of Jesus reached its negative conclusion around the turn of the century. Two books appeared in 1901 which marked the end of this " quest of the historical Jesus ": Albert Schweitzer, *Quest of the Historical Jesus;* and Wilhelm Wrede, *The Messianic Secret in the Gospels.* We shall deal with the outlook represented by these works in more detail later, but just here we should indicate that Schweitzer showed that in this nineteenth-century quest each epoch tended to rediscover its own moral ideal in the character of Jesus. It was as if one looked into the " well " of history: he thought he saw Jesus, when in truth it was but a reflection of his own self. Bauer thus saw in Jesus' consciousness a historical reflection of Bauer's Hegelian ideal of the unity of God and man. Ritschl saw a Jesus who embodied his Kantian moralism. Schleiermacher saw a Jesus who mirrored his concept of the essence of religion, centering in the God-consciousness. Strauss persistently argued that such a Christ as Schleiermacher depicted " never existed but in idea." [19]

Schweitzer's point was well taken, for such pictures of Jesus would seem to be projections back into history, by means of creative imagination, of a religious idea derived elsewhere. The authors of the Lives of Jesus were doubtless unaware of what they were doing, yet this does not nullify the judgment which we must make: they failed to discover the historical Jesus.

The twentieth century thus began with a resolute scholarly attempt to terminate the nineteenth-century method of " modernizing " Jesus, and to return Jesus to history.[20] " Jesus was not a Christian: he was a Jew." (Julius Wellhausen.) Jesus was not a Kantian moralist, nor a democratic American. As a historical figure he stood within Judaism. Even though his life and death mark the beginning of a break with Judaism and laid the foundations for the emergence of the Christian religion, nevertheless his speech and concepts were Jewish, and his own set of religious ideas were an organic part of the eschatological theology of Judaism in general. This is why it seems perfectly logical for modern Jewish theologians to claim Jesus as belonging to the history of Judaism. "How could it have been otherwise?" asks the Hebrew scholar Joseph Klausner. "Jesus derived his entire knowledge and point of view from the Scriptures and from a few, at most, of the Palestinian *apocryphal* and *pseudepigraphical* writings and from the Palestinian *Haggada* and *Midrash* in the primitive form in which they were then current among the Jews." [21] Historically, thus it is quite understandable that Klausner insists that "Jesus was a Jew and a Jew he remained until his last breath. His one idea was to implant within his nation the idea of the coming of the Messiah, and, by repentance and good works, hasten the 'end.'" [22]

Christian theology today is thoroughly historical-minded in rejecting the modernizing method of understanding the historical Jesus. But to draw the conclusion that Jesus is therefore of no religious relevance for our day is possible only on grounds of an outdated philosophy of historical time, which derives from the Greek view. Aristotle lumped space and time together under the category of "quantity." Time for him was a continuous quantity. Like a line in space thus the time line is made up of measurable parts. The time line is made of a quantitatively measurable succession of moments; though unlike a line, the parts of time have no abiding existence. [23] In this way Aristotle viewed time as something static; it was not characterized by movement. [24]

By failing to differentiate between historical time and cosmic time (the time of nature's movements), Aristotle was misled into thinking that there is no flow, no *durée*, in historical time. Time was thereby geometrized. It was mistranslated by the use of the analogy of space. Hence, historical time could be measured by clocks and mechanical devices. Historical time, so viewed, stretches out into a one-directional line, made up of discrete temporal units of equal magnitude.

This is why Augustine found the historical dimension of the Christian faith a bit of a problem. His own religious experience was, of course, shaped in good measure by ahistorical, Neoplatonic mysticism, which fused with the Pauline ideal of "life in the Spirit."

But on the basis of his Greek presuppositions, he wrote: "Who denies that future things do not exist as yet? . . . And who denies that past things now exist no longer?" [25] It was interesting to hear this affirmation of Augustine echoed (quite unconsciously) by a highly regarded American philosopher of religion who said: "The past is gone, the future is not yet, the present alone is real." It is easy to see, in such a view of historical time, how it would create intellectual difficulties to regard the Jesus of *past* history, in any significant sense, as the Lord of the Christian *present*.[26]

Although nineteenth-century historiography came to see history as a process rather than a mathematical series of temporal moments, some of the latter view still qualified nineteenth-century historiography. The ideal of objectivity in historical research often led to a kind of academic stance in which the historian attempted to avoid any personal encounter with the data of his study. It was not adequately seen that the past is far from something dead and gone. Through the power of memory, it enters into the present as a dynamic determinant.

As pointed out above, the new historiography of the twentieth century has corrected this weakness in nineteenth-century historiography by stressing the factor of significance. This "new" factor has operated as a constitutive element in the Christian view of Jesus Christ from the beginning of the Christian movement. How is it possible for the historical Jesus to become the living Lord of the ongoing Christian community? Theology replies that the answer lies in the kerygma, which stands at the heart of the continuous aspect of revelation. The apostle Paul expressed this revelatory (or kerygmatic) dimension of the church's proclamation of Jesus as the Christ when he contended that he who is "in Christ" is a new creation. "All this is from God," he wrote, "who through Christ reconciled us to himself and gave us the ministry of reconciliation; . . . entrusting to us the message of reconciliation. So we are

ambassadors for Christ, God making his appeal through us."
(II Cor. 5:18-20.) And in the Roman letter he wrote that he
was eager to preach the gospel to the Romans also, for this
preached gospel " is the power of God for salvation to every
one who has faith " (Rom. 1:15-16), the gospel of " Jesus
Christ and him crucified " (I Cor. 2:2).

Through the kerygma of church proclamation thus the
proclaiming one (Jesus) becomes the one proclaimed. The
kerygma transforms the onceness (*ephapax*) of Jesus' own
activity and proclamation into a once-for-allness. The particular historical Jesus is transformed into the universal presence
in Spirit. This is what is meant by calling the history of Jesus
" the decisive eschatological event," [27] which does not recede
into the past but is contemporized, is present in the proclamation of the ongoing church. That is, the eschatological event
of the crucifixion and resurrection is not only *proclaimed by*
the kerygma; it *happens continuously* in the proclamation itself. To borrow the words of James Robinson, " The act of
proclaiming Jesus' death and resurrection becomes God's act
calling upon me to accept my death and receive resurrected
life. Believing about God's past action in Christ coincides with
the occurrence of this divine action in my present life." [28]

The doctrine of the resurrection of Christ, which in the
kerygma is inseparable from the cross of Christ, means the victory of Jesus *as Christ and Lord* over the transitoriness of history. " It is the overcoming of his disappearance from present
experience and his consequent transition into the past except
for the limits of memory." [29] In the resurrection experience
of the disciples, what happened thus is that the concrete picture of the historical Jesus became indissolubly united with
the resurrected One, the Lord of life. Hence, the kerygma declares that *through the resurrection* " God has made him both
Lord and Christ, this Jesus whom you crucified (Acts 2:36).
He has been " designated Son of God in power according to
the Spirit of holiness by his resurrection from the dead, Jesus
Christ our Lord " (Rom. 1:4). In this way death was unable
to conquer the Christ reality of Jesus; it was not able to force
Jesus into the past. Though, to be sure, there is discontinuity
here as well as continuity, for as a physical, bodily individual

Jesus is, of course, no longer present. The character of the risen Lord is not the historical particular, but the universally spiritual. That the Christ reality of the risen One has the character of " Spirit " is clear in Paul's statement: " Now the Lord is the Spirit, and where the Spirit of the Lord is, there is freedom. And we all, with unveiled face, beholding the glory of the Lord, are being changed into his likeness from one degree of glory to another; for this comes from the Lord who is the Spirit " (II Cor. 3:17-18).

The center of the Christian faith is clearly indicated in the basic confession of the Christian community. It is stated in a simple form in the kerygma of the New Testament, in Simon Peter's confession at Caesarea Philippi: " You are the Christ, the Son of the living God " (Matt. 16:16). More fully developed, it appears in Peter's Pentecostal sermon, for then *on the basis of Christ's resurrection* he declares that " God has made him both Lord and Christ, this Jesus whom you crucified " (Acts 2:36). It appears in Paul's kerygmatic hymn, in which the apostle depicts the self-emptying of Jesus, his humiliation and obedience unto death, and his exaltation by God who " bestowed on him the name which is above every name, that at the name of Jesus every knee should bow, in heaven and on earth and under the earth, and every tongue confess that Jesus Christ is Lord, to the glory of God the Father " (Phil. 2:6-11).

This central confession eloquently shows that in the kerygma Jesus' earthly humiliation and the exalted Lordship of the risen, ever-present Christ are held indissolubly together. The " object " of faith thus embraces these two dimensions: the historical and the transcendental, the temporal and the eternal, the finite and the infinite. It follows that Christian theology must live in the dialectical tension of this paradox. It must refuse two erroneous ways of resolving the tension that has tempted the church through the centuries.

As we have seen, some have sought to resolve this paradox by not only demythologizing but also dehistoricizing the object of faith. To transform the object of faith into the " Christ of faith," separated from " the historical Jesus," is to *substitute* a mythological " heavenly Lord " for the Jesus Christ of

faith. This, of course, was the temptation to which many
Christians in the second century (but not that century only)
succumbed under the corrupting influence of the Greek mystery religions and of Gnosticism (Valentinus, Basilides, Cerinthus, and their followers). Indeed, it seems that the Johannine
canonical writings were, in part, aimed directly or indirectly
at this incipient, ahistorical corruption of the faith, perhaps
as Irenaeus suggests, against Cerinthus of Ephesus.[30] In the
Johannine reply, the historical dimension of faith receives
bold and unmistakable emphasis. "The Word *became flesh*"
(John 1:14, italics added). The author of I John suggests a
concrete test: "By this you know the Spirit of God: every
spirit which confesses that Jesus Christ has come *in the flesh*
is of God, and every spirit which does not confess Jesus is not
of God" (I John 4:2-3, italics added). The ahistorical Christology against which these Johannine passages were directed
came to be labeled "Docetism," from the Greek *dokeō,* which
means "to seem." This "heretical" version of the church's
Christology held that Jesus only *appeared* to be a human
being, he only *seemed* to be born of Mary and crucified on the
cross, but in reality was wholly free from all the sufferings of
finitude. Christianity thus became, in this heretical movement, a religious cult of an ahistorical, heavenly Christ. The
inward struggle of Christianity against the docetic Christology
of Gnosticism led ancient Catholic Christianity to a more profound appreciation of the importance of the historical dimension of the church's Christology.

The fact that there is thus the solid historical foundation
(and content) for faith does not mean, of course, that mythological concepts are not used by the New Testament writers
themselves to explicate the meaning of Jesus Christ. They are
indeed used, though demythologized when baptized into
Christ, so to speak; for new historical meanings burst the historical limits of the old mythological concept of the "heavenly
Lord," for example, borrowed from the intellectual frame-
work of the Greek mystery religions. But *what* are being proclaimed are not mythological ideas, but by means of such, *what*
is proclaimed is the redemptive significance of a concrete historical person, "born of woman, born under the law," [31] to

cite the apostle Paul's emphasis on the historical reality of Jesus.

On the other hand, theology must guard against the opposite but equally fallacious distortion which shifts in the opposite direction by transforming the "object" of faith into the historical Jesus, separated from "the Christ of faith." To resolve the paradox in this fashion is to *substitute* a "historical figure" for the Jesus Christ of faith. In the early period of the life of the church this distortion of Christology first made itself manifest in the particular form it assumed among the Ebionitic Jewish Christians, who denied as much as possible the "divinity" of Jesus and practically reduced his soteriological significance to that of giving a true interpretation of the Mosaic law.

In principle, the Ebionitic error was repeated by the nineteenth-century liberals who sought to eliminate the transcendental dimension signified by the Christ character of Jesus Christ and resolve the object of faith solely into the historical Jesus *as such*. If the former way of resolving the paradox resulted in mythology, this way resulted in Jesusology. This historism which would substitute Jesusology for the Christology of the kerygma could only end by restricting the meaning of Jesus to a noble exemplar of religious devotion and to his ethical ideals. For Jesusology, of course, the doctrine of the resurrection of Christ constituted a painful embarrassment, for it held no significance for its understanding of the object of faith.

Eventually, however, such historism is driven from its base, not only by the failure of the quest for the historical Jesus, but also by the thrust of the religious impulse toward the Eternal, as is evident in the theology of Albert Schweitzer. Even if the figure of Jesus as a teacher and moral example is retained, it tends to move to the periphery of the *object* of religious devotion, which is God. The final result is once again the religion of immediacy, a sort of mysticism that wants an immediate "religious experience" which is really "independent of anything belonging to the past." [32] Reference to the figure of Jesus finally becomes a sort of illustrative appendix to a religious experience which in fact has its main roots elsewhere.

A history of the church's Christology reveals the fact that in substance the early Christological confession has remained the norm down through the centuries: the kerygma that proclaims Jesus *as* Christ and Lord. The theological battles have been fought against a Christology that is too " low " or too " high." The form that the problem has assumed has varied from century to century. In the second century it was Ebionitism versus Gnostic Docetism. In the latter fourth and first half of the fifth century the Christological conflict developed into the clash between the two major schools of Christian thought then current: one centering in Alexandria, the other in Antioch. The conflict reached its major crisis in the fifth-century battle between Nestorius (an Antiochene), Bishop of Constantinople (A.D. 428–431), and Cyril (an Alexandrian), Bishop of Alexandria (A.D. 412–444). Though after the temporary settlement of this struggle by the Formula of Union at the Ecumenical Council of Ephesus in A.D. 431, it broke out anew in the following decade, thanks to Eutyches' noisy polemic against Nestorianism, and his advocacy of an extreme Cyrillianism.

Nestorius stressed the *ethical* significance of Jesus as a genuine human being, and interpreted the relation between the human and divine natures in the person of Jesus as a harmony of two wills (not two persons, as sometimes alleged). Hence, Nestorius was deeply concerned to maintain the thesis that the two natures in Jesus' person remained completely distinct, although, of course, conjoined and in will completely harmonious. He contended that " the essential characteristics in the name of the divinity and in the humanity are from all eternity distinguished." He affirmed faith in " both natures which by the highest and unmixed union are adored in the one person of the only begotten."

By way of contrast to Nestorius, Cyril emphasized the *soteriological* significance of Jesus, arguing that the assumption of the human nature by the divine was complete and entire, so that after the union there remained only one divine-human nature — two natures before the union, but only one after it. Only thus, Cyril felt, could the then current notion of salvation as the divinization of human life have a certain and secure basis. So complete is this assumption of the human by the divine that, as Eutyches (Cyril's theological successor) argued, it was analagous to the "assumption" of one single drop of honey by the entire ocean. Eutyches carried Cyril's doctrine of the *complete fusion* of the two natures to its logical conclusion. What happened to the human nature in the incarnation, said Eutyches, is comparable to what happens to the drop of honey when dropped into the ocean. This, however, has a docetic smell! Hence, Theodoret (Nestorius' theological successor) published a tractate entitled "Eranistes" in which he set forth, in the strongest possible way, the logical implications of Cyrillian Monophysitism (the doctrine of one divine-human nature). Such a Christology, said Theodoret, cannot escape the heresy of representing God himself as subject to change and suffering (the heresy of *Patripassianism*). In a pagan way it confounds the human with the divine, takes on docetic qualities, and thereby repeats the Apollinarian heresy.

The fifth-century Christological struggle finally precipitated the famous Chalcedonian formula of A.D. 451, which resolutely held the two dimensions together; though due to the "nature" category with which the theologians then operated, the statement was in the form of a powerful paradox: two unmixed natures in one person. The Chalcedonian Creed affirms one Lord Jesus Christ "the same perfect in deity and perfect in humanity, God truly and man truly." It recognizes "two natures . . . without confusion, without change, without division, without separation, the distinction of the natures being by no means taken away because of the union." The Latin text speaks of Christ acknowledged "*in duabus naturis.*" The Greek wording is *ek duo physeōn*. In view of the fact that there is no hint in the creed of any fusion of the two natures, and that the emphasis falls upon their distinction rather than their union, the theory is probably correct that the Latin represents the original text, whereas the Greek was probably altered to bring it more into line with the Cyrillian view.

The Chalcedonian formula remained the creedal norm in the church's Christology through the Middle Ages, the Reformation, orthodox Protestantism, right down to modern times.

In the nineteenth century we are confronted by the same basic problem in modern dress. Here the struggle was between the ahistorical Christology of German idealism (Hegel, Bauer, Strauss) and the subsequent reactionary historism that proceeded to substitute the historical Jesus per se for the Jesus Christ of the traditional faith.

For the most part, twentieth-century theology seems to have gotten free from this nineteenth-century error, due in part to the failure of the quest of the historical Jesus. It is one of the universally accepted insights of contemporary theology that the historical Jesus cannot be isolated from the Christ of faith in the way in which the nineteenth-century quest for the historical Jesus attempted to do. Yet it must be recognized with equal clarity that according to the kerygma neither can the Christ of faith be separated from the historical dimension designated by the word " Jesus."

VII

The New Quest for the Historical Jesus

In view of what Paul Tillich calls " the Jesus-character of Jesus as the Christ " [1] in the central strand of the church's Christology through the centuries, it is not too surprising that during the past few years a new quest for the historical Jesus has manifested itself among the followers of the Bultmann school of kerygma theology. Vigorous debate and research are at the present moment in process, but it is too early to predict how much momentum this new impulse will generate or how much positive value will accrue to contemporary theology.

THE NOVELTY OF THE NEW QUEST

To understand the significance of the new quest it is important that it be clearly distinguished from the nineteenth-century quest, for the two quests have different points of departure, different motivations, and different objectives. The earlier quest, it is usually said, began with Hermann Samuel Reimarus, Professor of Languages in Hamburg, Germany, who launched the quest on the basis of his deistic religious presuppositions. Reimarus' critique [2] set the aims of the historical Jesus in sharp contrast to those of his followers, and portrayed Jesus as a political, Messianic pretender who failed utterly in his ambitions.

Reimarus' radical view of the historical Jesus, however, found only a small following. The classic nineteenth-century period of the " Life of Jesus " research that followed, it is true, was motivated by the effort, inspired by Enlightenment rationalism, to get free from the Christ dogma of the church. It was anticlerical in its bearings. Yet at the same time there was present in it a strong desire to affirm the genuinely religious significance of Jesus.[3]

The colorful variety of the many Lives of Jesus that resulted from the critical-historical research generated a sense of uncertainty toward the close of the nineteenth century. About the same time the devotional, nonbiographical character of the Gospels began to come to light. In his book *The Messianic Secret in the Gospels* (1901), Wilhelm Wrede pointed out that Mark did not write in the spirit of a modern historian but, rather, as a theologian. Mark was dominated by a devotional interest. It was the faith perspective that led Mark to interpolate the " Messianic secret " into the tradition. Hence, Wrede eliminated this secret entirely from his portrait of Jesus. The organizing principle that shaped the writing of the Gospels was thus not historical objectivity but ecclesiastical usefulness. As they stand, the Gospels give us reliable information about the faith of the early church rather than about the historical Jesus. Their basic character is that of faith's witness. It was the faith of the church at work on the traditional materials that gave shape and content to the Gospels.

It represented another step in the dissolution of the quest of the historical Jesus when, a generation later, form criticism crystallized and further developed these earlier insights into the interpretative character of the Jesus tradition. If, as form criticism disclosed, the Gospels were originally intended to be an interpretative proclamation of Jesus as Christ, then they will not yield to the nonkerygmatic, historical reconstruction attempted by nineteenth-century Jesus research, which carried on its study on the basis of deliberate repudiation of the Christ of faith. It is an error to regard them " as historical sources from which the story of Jesus behind them could be extracted." [4] The school of form criticism thus made it forever clear *why* a historically accurate life of Jesus simply cannot be written.

The unanswerable thesis of form criticism marked the end of the nineteenth-century quest of the historical Jesus. If it sang its swan song at the opening of the twentieth century, it was crucified and buried by the school of form criticism. However, this by no means implies any denial of the *existence* of the historical Jesus. Indeed, as Meyer observes, the period of form criticism marked " the end of modern attempts to deny the existence of Jesus of Nazareth, not a new beginning of them." [5] Hence, there is here full recognition of the fact that the kerygma of the early church stands in close relation to the concrete historical figure of Jesus.

What is the reason for the new quest of the historical Jesus? Part of the reason evidently lies in the creative intellectual curiosity of Biblical scholars. The major impetus behind the new quest, however, does not seem to derive from mere intellectual curiosity, though to be sure this element is present in its motivation. Nor does the major impetus derive from the discovery of new historical sources that would now make it possible to revive the nineteenth-century quest. Ethelbert Stauffer seems to be spurred to the new quest by what he regards to be " new sources " which throw " new light on the accounts of the Gospels." [6] According to Stauffer, these new sources are: increased knowledge of Palestinian life and thought,[7] Rabbinical polemics against Jesus,[8] and the late-Judaistic apocalyptic writings.[9] Robinson correctly reminds Stauffer that none of these sources are really " new," even though in such sources there is " a quantitative increase of accumulated research." [10]

The major impetus that has generated the new quest is three-fold. First, among Bultmann's own followers a historical reaction has appeared against what has come to be regarded the too exclusively existential interpretation of the object of faith held by Bultmann. This phase of the impetus is dominant in the position of Nils Dahl. For Bultmann, the only thing of substantial consequence for faith is the fact of Jesus' life and death, and the proclamation of the meaning of this fact, a meaning to be grasped by faith.[11] If carried out consistently, Dahl holds that such kerygma theology leads " not only to a de-mythologizing, but also a de-historicizing of the New Testament." Such an ultra-Pauline extreme cannot do justice to the Gospels.[12]

Bultmann himself, however, stops considerably short of a

thoroughgoing dehistoricizing. His position is that "the message of Jesus" is a presupposition for the theology of the kerygma, even though Jesus' message cannot be regarded as "part of that theology itself," since Christian faith did not exist "until there was a Christian *kerygma,* i.e. a *kerygma* proclaiming Jesus Christ — specifically Jesus Christ the Crucified the Risen One — to be God's eschatological act of salvation." [13] Though Bultmann feels "that we can now know almost nothing concerning the life and personality of Jesus," [14] he still holds that it is "overwhelmingly probable" that Jesus was "the bearer of the word, and in the word he assures man of forgiveness of God." [15] At this point, Dahl poses the question: Must it not be an extreme existential theology which would argue that it is illegitimate to go further in research into the *how* and *what* of Jesus' life and teaching? [16] Even Bultmann, it seems, *in principle* establishes the legitimacy of such further research.

Günther Bornkamm, James Robinson, and Joachim Jeremias are motivated in their Jesus research by this same conviction, that the Gospels "point us directly to the earthly Jesus," [17] though, of course, in the perspective of faith in him as the Christ, and that "the primitive tradition of Jesus is brim full of history." [18] Hence, Bornkamm's book here cited is consciously intended to help fill the recent vacuum (in German theology) of inquiry into the message and history of Jesus of Nazareth.[19] This historical concern is equally strong in Robinson who argues that the new research can help to overcome a deficiency in the kerygma which "obscures formally the concreteness of his *historical* reality." [20] Yet at the same time, it is part of the "inner logic" of the kerygma to embrace real concern for the historical Jesus. It is this, says Robinson, which "necessitates a new quest." [21]

The second phase of the threefold impetus is one that is emphasized by Robinson, namely, the new twentieth-century concept of history and the self. As we have seen, the failure of the nineteenth-century quest was due to the fallacious, objectivistic historiography in terms of which it carried on its work. But with that failure, it has now become "a completely open question" as to whether a new research into the life and history of Jesus is possible by methods and aims of the new historiography.[22] Robinson believes that this is possible since the new historiography is formally analogous to the kerygma itself.[23] That is, both seek existential understanding in actual encounter with history.

The impetus toward the new quest supplied by the possibilities of the new historiography is dominant in Robinson's advocacy of the quest. He insists that in the parables of Jesus, his Kingdom sayings, the beatitudes, Jesus' remarks about John the Baptist and the Law, we have "sufficient insight into Jesus' intention to encounter his historical action, and enough insight into the understanding of existence presupposed in his intention to encounter his selfhood." [24]

The third phase of the major impetus behind the new Jesus research comes from Bultmann's demythologizing program. This may help to explain why the new quest has arisen among the exponents of the Bultmann school of thought. The call to demythologize the kerygma, even when recognized as a valid hermeneutical method, at once raises the questions: What remains as the substantial content of faith after the work of demythologizing has been completed? What is it that the kerygma interprets by means of mythological symbols and concepts?

It is possible, of course, to answer this question by returning, in principle, to the rationalism of the Enlightenment and say that the abiding substance which is mythologically explicated in the kerygma is some general, philosophical principle, some abstract metaphysical idea. Some have adopted this alternative. But this solution obviously moves away from the historical rootage of the Christian faith and ignores the Jesus character of the kerygma, which is not a part of its mythological set of concepts but concrete historical fact. A concrete historical figure is no myth. Demythologizing the kerygma is certainly a legitimate hermeneutical procedure, since the interpretative conceptual framework of theology varies from age to age. But dehistoricizing the kerygma is quite another matter. That the latter runs directly counter to the basic concern of the Christian message is obvious from the first basic part of the Christian confession: " God has made *this Jesus*

whom you crucified both Lord and Christ." What is encountered when the mythological interpretation is removed is the
historical figure of Jesus and the impact of his life and death
on his disciples.

It is not difficult thus to perceive why a new impetus toward
a greater understanding of Jesus would logically follow in the
wake of the demythologizing program of New Testament
studies, even though Bultmann contends that " the *kerygma*
is not interested in ' objective historicity' beyond the fact *that*
Jesus lived and died." [25] Bultmann admits, however, that
strictly speaking this is true only of Paul and John, and
that the Synoptics do reflect more interest in the history of
Jesus, though of course in the faith perspective.[26]

The new quest operates in a perspective different from that
of the old. The point of departure of the old quest (its driving
power) was the rationalism of the Enlightenment, the motivation was to discover the historical Jesus *behind* the Gospels,
and the objective was to get free from the Christ dogma of the
kerygma. The point of departure of the new quest (its driving
power) is the kerygma itself; the motivation is to discover more
about the Jesus *within* the kerygma; and the objective seems,
for the most part, to be greater understanding of what Robinson calls " the historical section " of the kerygma,[27] though it
is the question of the objective of the new quest that disturbs
not only Bultmann but other New Testament scholars as well.
It is obvious, however, that the new quest is far more integrally
bound up with the major Christological concern of faith than
was the case with the old quest.

There is some semantic confusion in the comparison of the
two quests due to the fact that both make use of the phrase
" the historical Jesus," yet mean different things by the phrase.
This confusion is unfortunate and can be the source of considerable difficulty in the new quest unless it is carefully borne
in mind that the phrase does not mean the same thing in the
two quests. In the old quest, the " historical Jesus " referred
to the objective figure in history prior to and independent of
the kerygma, a figure whose character and life it was the intention of critical-historical research to discover *behind* the
Gospels. In the new quest, the " historical Jesus " refers to the

factual (historical) element *in* the event of Jesus as the Christ. As Tillich says, " The term in this sense raises the question of faith and not the question of historical research." [28] It is this question of the factual aspect of the faith to which the new quest addresses itself.

That the new quest is highly problematical and at best can never yield more than historical probabilities is generally recognized even by those engaged in it. It is not possible to arrive at any " distinct and sharp separation " between what Jesus said and what the kerygma says he said. We can know Jesus " only as the disciples remembered him." [29]

A crucial example of these historical difficulties concerns the question of how Jesus understood his own death. The widely accepted view, of course, is that Jesus consciously and deliberately went to his death as the organic conclusion of his life's work. Hans Conzelmann, for example, argues that the passion sayings attributed to Jesus represent not Jesus' shrewd foresight of the final crisis, but rather the " divine necessity of his suffering." That is, they already contain the meaning of the passion and resurrection.[30] In a similar argument, Robinson holds that Jesus' selfhood was " not a selfish selfhood, but by its very constitution a selfhood for others." Hence, his death " was the ultimate realization of his eschatological selfhood." His selfhood " was interpreted as *pro nobis* not first by the Church, but already by Jesus himself," [31] whereas Bultmann contends that on this question everything is really a matter of conjecture.[32] That subsequent to the death of John the Baptist Jesus must have come to see that his own life would end in a similarly violent way, as Ernst Fuchs argues,[33] is, says Bultmann, " a psychological construction," and not very convincing, since Jesus formed a different conception of his ministry from that of John the Baptist, from whom he separated.[34]

Why was Jesus drawn to Jerusalem at the end of his life? Bornkamm repudiates the idea that Jesus " sought only his death in Jerusalem." Says Bornkamm, the repeated prophecies of suffering and resurrection " were clearly first formulated in retrospect in view of the passion." It cannot be doubted, says Bornkamm, that the reason for Jesus' final journey to Jerusa-

lem was "to deliver the message of the coming kingdom of
God in Jerusalem also," the Holy City.[35] If this was Jesus' reason for the final journey, says Bultmann, then Conzelmann's
theory that the passion sayings reveal Jesus' conviction of the
divine necessity of his suffering on the cross is placed in question. If we accept Bornkamm's theory, Jesus was hardly reckoning with his own execution at the hands of the Romans,
"but rather with the imminent incoming of the reign of
God." [36]

The truth is, Bultmann contends, there is only conjecture
on this crucial question. The only sure historical fact here is
that Jesus was indeed crucified by the Romans, and as a crimi-
nal.[37]

We cannot agree with Joachim Jeremias when he contends
that Jesus' interpretation of his own death is such a crucial
issue for faith that it takes precedence over all others.[38] Faith
can have only a *secondary* interest in this historical problem.
The really crucial issue for faith, its *primary* concern, lies instead in the revelatory meaning of Jesus' death, a meaning
generated in faith's experience of the resurrection, namely,
that he died *for us*. This basic truth of the gospel message is
not dependent on Jesus' own interpretation of his death, whatever it may have been; just as faith's belief in his Messiahship
is not dependent on the truth of the historical theory that
affirms his Messianic self-consciousness. The crucial issue for
faith, that which takes precedence over all others, is faith's
own personal decision in response to the message of the gospel.
Objective scientific arguments do not necessarily lead to faith.
Indeed, recognition of the historical truth of such arguments
can and does join with unbelief.

Theology must leave to New Testament scholars engaged
in the critical-historical study of the new quest the problem
of its details and findings. How far the new quest will be able
to illuminate our knowledge of the Jesus character of the
Jesus Christ of faith, how much it will be able to discover of
the *how* and *what* of the historical Jesus, and the relativities
and certainties of such discovery — all this must be left to
the critical-historical scholars. Theology's main concern in
the new quest has to do with its relevance for the life of faith.

The Question of the Theological Relevance
of the New Quest

As already indicated, Jeremias adopts a very bold view of the positive, theological significance of this new quest. He contends that the "full authority" of the gospel message rests upon the ability of critical-historical analysis to establish "the very words of Jesus himself." [39] The center of gravity in revelatory authority here seems to shift from the proclamation of the gospel to something historically objective. What Jeremias feels we need is "to hear once more the original tones of the utterances of Jesus, and to experience anew the vital qualities of force, conflict and authority in the historical events." [40] Hence, Jeremias believes that critical-historical reconstruction can bring us into the very presence of God.[41] If we followed out this line of reasoning, the church should dismiss its preachers and employ in their stead critical-historical scholars.

Should the objective of the new quest be consistently construed along the lines here suggested by Jeremias, and should the full theological implications of such an objective be carried out, it would lead us, in principle, into the same fallacy that characterized both nineteenth-century liberalism and also orthodoxy. That is, as its basic authority it will *substitute* the historical Jesus for the Jesus Christ of faith. The object of faith would thus again come to be something historically objective (Jesus) instead of the living Word of God heard in the eschatological event summed up by the phrase "Jesus Christ." Instead of eschatological event we would get objective historical fact. This would erase the distinction between faith's affirmative response to the saving meaning of Jesus' life and death, and historical familiarity with what Jesus said and did. Faith would thereby be *reduced* to "knowledge of the historical Jesus." [42] Meyer correctly perceives the theological danger in the new quest. And Bultmann is persuaded that the effort will end in a theologically invalid attempt "to prove the legitimacy of the *kerygma*." [43]

So long as the new quest consciously restricts its aims and objectives to arriving at greater understanding of the concrete character of the historical Jesus, his message, activities, and

intentions, we would argue that it does hold some positive significance for faith itself. A faith that moves in the direction in
which it becomes oriented to an ahistorical mystical or rational
object certainly veers from the Word of God in the gospel
message of the New Testament, for the latter is organically
related to and rooted in the concrete, historical figure of Jesus,
which it cherishes through the power of memory and tradition.
For this reason, because of the Jesus character of the Jesus
Christ of faith, faith cannot rightly manifest total distin-
terestedness in the new quest.

When we contend, therefore, that not objective historical
fact but eschatological event constitutes the center of gravity
of Christian faith, this is not to be construed as a radical
wrenching of faith away from the historical and a reduction of
faith to an existential " flight from history." Strauss ended up
in a similar, though rationalistic flight from history. He came
to the view that when the mind has " entered the domain of
the absolute," history ceases to be essential and becomes " as
the faint image of a dream which belongs to the past." [44] To
interpret the kerygma in this fashion would reflect a terrible
misunderstanding of the nature of *this* eschatological event,
which indeed *gathers up into itself* the entire impact of the
historical Jesus; hence, the portraits of Jesus, his deeds and
words, in the Gospels. Hence also the perpetuation of the
sacred memory of Jesus in the ongoing life of the church.

This, of course, does not mitigate the historical judgment
that the faith of the authors of the Gospels in Jesus' Messiahship naturally resulted in the fact that creative, religious
imagination constituted a determinative factor in the working
up of the materials of the oral tradition about Jesus. It must
be clearly seen that the historical life of Jesus was really
gathered up and transmuted in the Gospel story. As Bornkamm
has finely said, " Were we to accept uncritically everything
handed down to us as historical (in the usual sense), we
would be subjecting the Gospels to an investigation alien to
them, and forcing upon them an understanding of history
quite unsuited to them." [45]

It is this devotional character of the Gospels which makes it
impossible for us to eliminate all historical skepticism and

establish beyond all doubt a one-to-one correspondence between the message of Jesus and the message of the Jesus portrait in the Gospels, even though most New Testament
scholars would likely agree that in a number of areas we can
arrive at a high degree of probability in determining the main
substance of Jesus' actual teaching: in the Kingdom sayings,
his parables, his utterances about God's providence and righteousness.

There is then an organic continuity between the historical
Jesus and the kerygma of the church. Diem is correct when he
contends [46] that two basic phases in the revelatory act must be
differentiated, though they cannot be historically separated:
(1) Jesus' message and activity, and (2) the proclamation
about Jesus. These cannot be separated because the former is
"the basis for the reality and knowledge" of the latter.
Though in view of the problematical character of our knowledge of Jesus' own message, Diem would seem to be a bit arbitrary when he goes ahead to affirm [47] that the preaching *about*
Jesus is "identical" with Jesus' own preaching. This, it would
appear, would be very difficult to prove.

What must be said is that while there is certainly a basic
continuity between the historical Jesus and the original proclamation of the church about him, discontinuity is also present in Christian faith. This discontinuity becomes most evident when we raise the question of the relation between the
historical Jesus, on the one hand, and Christ the living Lord
of the ongoing church, on the other. The latter is no historical
phenomenon and cannot therefore be continuous with the historical phenomenon of the figure of Jesus, in the strict sense of
the term "continuous." Continuity between the message of
Jesus and the message of the kerygma, yes; for these are historical phenomena which stand in close historical relation to each
other. But "Christ the living Lord" is a form of the eternal
God himself, in his revelatory mode of being. Here there appears a break, a discontinuity, a rupture in the smooth continuity of historic process.

There is discontinuity also between the message of Jesus and
the message of the kerygma. For even unbelief can hear and
objectively describe the message of Jesus. Discontinuity makes

its appearance in the " leap " of faith. There is no continuous
development from an objective study of the Jesus of history to
the decision of faith that, through the cross and the resurrection, God has made him " my " Christ and Lord. Karl Löwith
is correct: " No historian as such can possibly discover that
Jesus is the Son of God." [48] To speak of discontinuity here is
precisely to say that the " event " of faith is eschatological in
nature. Therefore, the proclamation of the church is wrongly
regarded when interpreted as a *mere repetition* of past history
through the power of memory. What happens through the
proclamation is, rather, a *genuine contemporizing* of the past
Jesus of history, who is now seen anew in the light of his
eternal meaning of faith, a meaning born out of faith's experience of his death and resurrection.

It is, however, true that by its very nature faith can have
only a limited and secondary interest in the new historical
quest of Jesus. At the level of mere historical description of
Jesus and his death the question of faith has not yet arisen.
Furthermore, a historian qua historian could never perceive
the disclosure of God's love in the event of Jesus' life and
death. This is a higher-than-historical truth which is visible
only to eyes of faith. Due to this central concern of Christian
faith, the position that theology must take in regard to a sci-
entifically-historical research into the life of Jesus is that such
research does not lie at the heart of faith's interest, yet neither
can faith be totally disinterested in it. Though the two dimensions of faith and history are organically interrelated, it is the
eschatological meaning of the Jesus event that is really decisive for faith. Whatever detailed facts about Jesus are discovered by historical research, they can neither create nor destroy faith in the crucified and risen One as " the Son of God."

The problem of the theological relevance of the new quest
remains, however, due to the fact that Christian faith binds
the two dimensions of the historical and the transcendental
together. Faith must therefore maintain a position somewhere
between an ahistorical mysticism or rationalism on the one
hand, and the fallacious historism of nineteenth-century liberalism on the other. It can settle neither for a purely mythological Christology nor for a Jesusology. These represent the

distortions of the object of Christian faith, against which theology must protect itself in the controversy centering in the new quest of the historical Jesus.

That in between these extremes — mythology and Jesusology — there is ample room for a variety of emphases is evident by the different expressions of the gospel message in the New Testament itself. The apostle Paul dwelt upon the crucified and risen Lord, so that what is sometimes called " Christ mysticism " stands at the center of the Gospel according to Paul. To experience the eschatological power of the new being " in Christ " is the powerful note that stands at the center of the Pauline message. Paul manifested little concern for the details of the *what* and *how* of the life of the historical Jesus.

On the other hand, the authors of the Synoptic Gospels manifested a much greater interest in the church's memory of the words and deeds of Jesus, though these are, to be sure, viewed in the light of the resurrection that makes possible insight into their redemptive meaning.

It is not without significance that when the church finally compiled the canon of the New Testament and established its limits, the contrast between Paul and John, on the one hand, and the Synoptics, on the other, was felt to be a legitimate one. The very canonization of the New Testament writings thus reflects the " ecumenical " consciousness of the church and its awareness that the two dimensions — the historical and the transcendental — belong together in the experience of salvation. The key phrase " Jesus Christ " remained the norm.

The history of the church's thought, however, shows that it is not an easy matter for faith to live in this tension between time and eternity, between history and transcendence. The positions adopted today, in the problem with which we are dealing, once again reflect the difficulties of the tension. For many, the fact of the life, message, and death of Jesus is but a " presupposition " of the gospel. So far as the vitalizing center of faith is concerned, this historical fact tends to fade into the background. The vitalizing center is seen to be the eschatological event of hearing the living, contemporaneous Word of God, through the proclamation of the gospel. That this is Bultmann's position seems evident when he writes that if the kerygma proclaims Jesus as the Christ, as the eschatological event, if it claims that Christ is present *in the* kerygma, then the kerygma is established " in the place of the historical Jesus." [49]

For others, the emphasis of faith's concern shifts toward the historical Jesus. A splendid example of the shift in this direction is found in *The Riddle of the New Testament* by Edwyn Hoskyns and Noel Davey. While frankly recognizing that a historian can " help to clarify the issue, but no more," and that as such the historian is unable " to decide between faith and unbelief," [50] these authors nevertheless attach tremendous relevance of historical reconstruction of the life of Jesus for the life of faith. Unlike Bultmann, who holds that " we can now know almost nothing concerning the life and personality of Jesus," [51] Hoskyns and Davey not only believe that " a historical reconstruction " of the life of Jesus is possible,[52] but they proceed in the book cited to provide us with such. They are persuaded that the modern historical-critical method can and does yield results, " even assured results." [53] Furthermore, it is claimed that the Christian religion "demands " historical investigation and, indeed, that " its piety depends on it." [54]

It will be obvious that Hoskyns and Davey adopt a position on the question of the theological relevance of historical reconstruction of the life of Jesus considerably to the right of the position adopted by the author of this volume. It is our position that although faith cannot be totally disinterested in such critical-historical study, such is not a *primary* concern of faith, while Hoskyns and Davey are adamant in their belief that " the critical and historical study of the New Testament is . . . the prime activity of the church." [55] This is obviously saying far too much; it leads to bad theology, as we have already pointed out, though their historical concern is duly appreciated.

In the past, of course, the shift of faith's concern toward the concrete historical Jesus moved so far that the decisive significance of the resurrection for faith faded into the background and tended to be ignored, being construed as a sort of appendix to the real substance of faith, the life of the historic

Jesus. Nineteenth-century liberalism, indeed, shifted so far in this direction that it simply dropped aside the resurrection of Christ and regarded it as excess theological baggage.

The important thing, then, is for contemporary theology to learn a lesson from the history of the church's Christology, to be able to recognize the old problem in twentieth-century dress, and to remain awake and be on guard against the temptation to eliminate the dialectical tension either by de-historicizing the kerygma or by dekerygmatizing the history, for both movements represent fallacious concepts of the " object " of Christian faith: Jesus as Christ and Lord.

Bibliographical Notes

I: The Eschatological View of History in the Biblical-Augustinian Tradition

1. Herbert Butterfield, *Christianity and History* (Charles Scribner's Sons, 1960), pp. 120–121.

2. Rudolf Bultmann, *History and Eschatology* (Edinburgh: The University Press, 1957), p. 154.

3. C. H. Dodd, *History and the Gospel* (London: James Nisbet & Co., Ltd., Publishers, 1952), pp. 35, 159, 171.

4. Erich Dinkler, *Early Christianity* (Yale University Press, 1955), p. 190.

5. William Manson, *The Epistle to the Hebrews* (London: Hodder & Stoughton, Ltd., 1951), p. 55.

6. *Ibid.*, p. 195.

7. Dinkler, *Early Christianity*, p. 199.

8. Manson, *The Epistle to the Hebrews*, p. 37.

9. Hans Conzelmann, *The Theology of St. Luke*, tr. by Geoffrey Buswell (London: Faber & Faber, Ltd., 1960), p. 136.

10. *Ibid.*, p. 132.

11. Probably toward the close of the first century or possibly in the first decade of the second.

12. John 14:18-21; cf. ch. 16:7-8, 13-16. The few verses that appear to reflect the traditional apocalyptic eschatology are regarded as later interpolations (Bultmann) or as a charitable recognition of the popular view (E. F. Scott). I incline to the view that these so-called "vestiges" of eschatology refer to the crucifixion "with its attendant circumstances of glorification and the giving of the Spirit" (Ernest Cadman Colwell and Eric Lane Titus, *The Gospel of the Spirit* [Harper & Brothers, 1953], p. 168).

13. The problem is implicit in Jesus' reply to Peter's confession: " Flesh and blood has not revealed this to you, but my Father who is in heaven " (Matt. 16:17).

14. Erich Frank, *Philosophical Understanding and Religious Truth* (Oxford University Press, Inc., 1945), p. 132.

15. Heb. 6:5; II Cor. 1:22; Rom. 14:17.

16. Irenaeus, *Against Heresies* III. iii. 1-2.

17. Eusebius, *Ecclesiastical History* III. iv, vi, xiv, xv, xxii.

18. Didache, xvi.

19. Ignatius, *Epistle to the Ephesians* xi and xvi; *Epistle to the Magnesians* v.

20. Polycarp, *Epistle to the Philippians* ii, v, xi; *The Martyrdom of Polycarp* xvi.

21. *The Epistle of Barnabas* iv, vi, vii, xv, xxi.

22. *Against Heresies* V, xxv–xxxvi.

23. *The Epistle of Barnabas* iv; cf. Hippolytus, *Commentary on the Prophet Daniel* II, 4.

24. Julius Africanus, *Fragments of the Five Books of the Chronography* I.

25. *Comm. Dan.* II, 4 ff.

26. Lactantius, *The Divine Institutes* VII. xxv.

27. Augustine, *The City of God* XII. xiii. Direct quotations from this work will be taken from the English translation by John Healey (London: J. M. Dent & Sons, Ltd., 1957).

28. Charles Norris Cochrane, *Christianity and Classical Culture* (Oxford University Press, Inc., 1944), p. 456.

29. Augustine, *The City of God* XIX. iv.

30. *Ibid.*, XI. ii.

31. *Ibid.*, X. xxxii; Epistle 102, part 12.

32. Augustine, *Enchiridion* VIII.

33. Augustine, *The City of God* I. xxxiv.

34. *Ibid.*, XIV. xi; cf. XII. iii.

35. *Ibid.*, V. xiii.

36. *Ibid.*, V. xiv.

37. *Ibid.*, V. xxiv.

38. Cf. Ernst Troeltsch, *Augustin, die christliche Antike und das Mittelalter* (München und Berlin: R. Oldenbourg, 1915), p. 17; Heinrich Hermelink, *Die Civitas Terrena bei Augustin* (Tübingen: J. C. B. Mohr-Paul Siebeck, 1921), pp. 308–309.

39. Augustine, *The City of God* XV. ii.

40. *Ibid.*, XIV. iii.

41. *Ibid.*, II. xiii.

42. *Ibid.*, XIX. xvii.

43. Frank, *Philosophical Understanding and Religious Truth,* p. 136.

44. Robert W. McLaughlin, *The Spiritual Element in History* (Abingdon Press, 1926), p. 46.

45. See for example, *The City of God* I. i.

46. Augustine, *Enchiridion* XI; cf. XII; *Confessions* VII. xiii.

47. Augustine, *Enchiridion* X, XI, XXVII.

48. *Ibid.,* XI.

49. *Ibid.,* XCVI.

50. *Ibid.,* XXVII.

51. *The Anti-Pelagian Works of Augustine,* tr. by Marcus Dods (Edinburgh: T. & T. Clark, 1871–1875), Vol. III, p. 145.

52. *Ibid.,* p. 49.

53. Augustine, *The City of God* XIII. xiv.

54. *Ibid.*

55. Cochrane, *Christianity and Classical Culture,* p. 167.

56. Augustine, *The City of God* XIX. xiv.

57. *Ibid.*

58. *Ibid.*

59. Augustine, *Enchiridion* LVI, LXI.

60. *Ibid.,* I, VIII.

61. *Ibid.,* XXXI, XXXII.

62. *Ibid.,* C; Augustine, *The City of God* XX. ii.

63. Karl Barth, *Church Domgatics,* ed. by G. W. Bromiley and T. F. Torrance (Edinburgh: T. & T. Clark, 1957), II. ii. 2 ff.

64. Augustine, *On Holy Virginity* xxiv.

65. Adolf Harnack, *History of Dogma,* tr. by James Millar (Oxford: Williams & Norgate, 1898), Vol. V, p. 168.

II: The Crisis of Faith in the Unhistorical Rationalism of the Enlightenment

1. J. B. Bury, *The Idea of Progress* (The Macmillan Company, 1932), p. 64.

2. Descartes, *Philosophical Writings,* selected and translated by Norman Kemp Smith (London: Macmillan & Co., 1952), pp. 200–201.

3. *Ibid.,* p. 203.

4. Karl Löwith, *Meaning in History* (The University of Chicago Press, 1949), p. 118.

5. See the third Meditation.

6. Bury, *The Idea of Progress,* p. 65.

7. *Ibid.,* pp. 78 ff.

8. *Ibid.*, p. 81.

9. *Ibid.*

10. *Ibid.*, p. 83.

11. *Ibid.*, p. 92.

12. Voltaire, *Philosophical Dictionary*, tr. by H. I. Woolf (London: George Allen & Unwin, Ltd., 1929), p. 20.

13. Voltaire, *Philosophical Dictionary*, tr. with an introduction and glossary by Peter Gay, 2 vols. (Basic Books, Inc., Publishers, 1962), Vol. I, p. 62.

14. *Ibid.*, Vol. II, p. 404.

15. *Ibid.*, Vol. I, pp. 322–323.

16. Voltaire, *Philosophical Dictionary*, tr. by H. I. Woolf, p. 303.

17. Voltaire, *The General History and State of Europe* (London: J. Nourse, 1754–1757), Part I, p. 38.

18. Voltaire, *Philosophical Dictionary*, tr. by H. I. Woolf, p. 303.

19. Matthew Tindal, *Christianity as Old as the Creation* (London, 1731), p. 218.

20. *Ibid.*, p. 58.

21. *Ibid.*, p. 52.

22. *Ibid.*, p. 2.

23. *Ibid.*, p. 3.

24. *Ibid.*, the thesis of Chapter VI.

25. *Ibid.*, p. 52.

26. Norman L. Torrey, *Voltaire and the English Deists* (Yale University Press, 1930), p. 110.

27. Voltaire, *Philosophical Dictionary*, tr. by Peter Gay, Vol. II, p. 445.

28. Edwin Ewart Aubrey, *Secularism a Myth* (Harper & Brothers, 1954), p. 55.

29. Alfred Cobban, *In Search of Humanity* (George Braziller, Inc., 1960), p. 105.

30. *Ibid.*

31. Carl L. Becker, *The Heavenly City of the Eighteenth-Century Philosophers* (Yale University Press, 1946), pp. 93–94.

32. Voltaire, *The General History and State of Europe*, Part I, Introduction. Cf. *Philosophical Dictionary*, tr. by H. I. Woolf, p. 159.

33. Voltaire, *The General History and State of Europe*, Part I, Introduction.

34. *Ibid.*, Part III, p. vi.

35. *Ibid.*, Part I, p. 1.

36. *Ibid.*, p. 7.

37. Löwith, *Meaning in History*, p. 107.

38. Voltaire, *The General History and State of Europe*, Part I, p. 12.

39. *Ibid.*, Part V, pp. 7–8.

40. *Ibid.*

41. Voltaire, *Philosophical Dictionary*, tr. by H. I. Woolf, p. 157. This sorry state of human history is the motif of Voltaire's *Candide*, the sad tale of a young man's multitudinous misfortunes: an eloquent piece of philosophical banter, yet profound as a reply to Rousseau and Pope's doctrine that " whatever is, is right " and to Leibniz' teaching that " this is the best of all possible worlds."

42. Voltaire, *The General History and State of Europe*, Part III, p. 168.

43. *Ibid.*, Part I, Introduction.

44. Löwith, *Meaning in History*, p. 107.

45. Voltaire, *The General History and State of Europe*, Part V, p. 9.

46. Cobban, *In Search of Humanity*, p. 107.

47. *Ibid.*

48. Cf. R. G. Collingwood, *The Idea of History* (Oxford: At the Clarendon Press, 1946), p. 78.

49. *Ibid.*, p. 77.

50. Becker, *The Heavenly City*, p. 103.

51. David Hume, in *Essays, Moral, Political, and Literary*, ed. by T. H. Green and T. H. Grose (London: Longmans, Green & Co., Inc., 1907), Vol. II, pp. 389–390.

52. *Ibid.*, p. 391.

53. Cobban, *In Search of Humanity*, p. 107.

54. Peter Gay in *The Present-Day Relevance of Eighteenth-Century Thought*, ed. by Roger P. McCutcheon (American Council of Learned Societies, 1956), p. 41.

55. Blaise Pascal, *Pensées*, tr. with an introduction by Martin Turnell (Harper & Row, Publishers, Inc., 1962), p. 211.

56. David Hume, *Dialogues Concerning Natural Religion* (London: William Blackwood and Sons, 1907), p. 40.

57. *Ibid.*, p. 33.

58. David Hume, *An Enquiry Concerning the Human Understanding, and an Enquiry Concering the Principles of Morals*, ed. by L. A. Selby-Bigge (Oxford: At the Clarendon Press, 1894), p. 76.

59. *Ibid.*, p. 77.

60. *Ibid.*, p. 148.

61. Hume, *Dialogues Concerning Natural Religion*, p. 76.

62. *Ibid.*, p. 78.

63. *Ibid.*, p. 79.

64. The French Encyclopedists such as La Mettrie, Étienne Bonnot de Condillac, and Baron Holbach were, of course, more thorough in their revolt against religion. It was their view that man is nothing but a "machine" and that morals are nothing but "public opinion." The editor of the *Encyclopédie,* Denis Diderot, is rather to be classed as an ardent moralist who sought to replace Christian morality with natural, humanistic morality. See Becker, *The Heavenly City,* pp. 80–81; also Joseph Edmund Barker, *Diderot's Treatment of the Christian Religion in the Encyclopedie* (King's Crown Press, 1941), pp. 30–31, 128.

65. Becker, *The Heavenly City,* p. 31.

66. As quoted by Becker, *ibid.,* p. 45.

67. *Ibid.*

68. Collingwood, *The Idea of History,* p. 78.

69. *Ibid.,* p. 80.

70. David Friedrich Strauss, *The Life of Jesus,* tr. by Marian Evans, 4th ed. (Calvin Blachard, 1860), p. 895.

71. Immanuel Kant, *Religion Within the Limits of Reason Alone,* tr. by Theodore M. Greene and Hoyt H. Hudson (The Open Court Publishing Company, 1934), p. 15.

72. *The Philosophy of Kant, ed. by Carl J. Friedrich* (Modern Library, Inc., 1949), p. 116.

73. *Ibid.,* p. 118.

74. *Ibid.,* p. 132.

75. *Ibid.,* p. 138.

76. Kant, *Religion Within the Limits of Reason Alone,* p. 54.

77. *Ibid.,* p. 91.

78. *Ibid.,* p. 106.

79. *Ibid.,* p. 112.

80. Kant himself used this description, *ibid.,* p. 109.

81. Edward Caird, *The Critical Philosophy of Immanuel Kant,* 2d. ed. (Glasgow: James Maclehose and Sons, 1909), Vol. II, p. 537.

82. Friedrich, ed., *The Philosophy of Kant,* p. 191.

83. *Ibid.,* p. 192.

84. Kant, *Religion Within the Limits of Reason Alone,* p. 43. Italics mine.

85. Kant, *Religion Within the Limits of Reason Alone,* p. 24.

86. *Ibid.,* p. 33.

87. *Ibid.,* p. 49.

88. *Ibid.,* p. 92.

89. *Ibid.,* p. 41.

90. John Oman, *The Problem of Faith and Freedom in the Last Two Centuries* (A. C. Armstrong and Son, 1909), p. 186.

91. Georg Wilhelm Friedrich Hegel, *Philosophy of Right,* tr. by

S. W. Dyde (London: George Bell and Sons, 1896), p. xxx.

92. Georg Wilhelm Friedrich Hegel, *Lectures on the Philosophy of Religion,* tr. by E. B. Speirs and J. Burton Sanderson, 2d. German ed. (London: Kegan Paul, Trench, Trubner & Co., Ltd., 1895), Vol. I, p. 4.

93. Hegel, *Philosophy of Right,* p. 341.

94. *Ibid.,* p. xxix.

95. John Baillie, *The Interpretation of Religion* (Charles Scribner's Sons, 1928), p. 195.

96. Hegel, *Lectures on the Philosophy of Religion,* Vol. I, p. 153.

97. *Ibid.,* p. 154.

98. *Ibid.*

99. Baillie, *The Interpretation of Religion,* p. 195.

100. Oman, *The Problem of Faith and Freedom,* p. 252.

101. Adolf Harnack, *Das Christentum und die Geschichte,* Dritter Aufl. (Leipzig: J. C. Hinrichs'sche Buchhandlung, 1896), p. 4.

102. Pascal, *Pensées,* p. 189.

103. *Ibid.,* p. 192.

104. *Ibid.,* p. 209.

105. *Ibid.,* p. 287.

106. Though Mill felt that " the adaptations in Nature afford a large balance of probability in favor of creation by intelligence " (*Three Essays on Religion* [Henry Holt & Co., 1884], p. 174).

107. *Ibid.,* p. 245.

108. *Ibid.,* p. 74.

109. Thomas H. Huxley, *Science and Christian Tradition* (London: Macmillan and Co., Ltd., 1909), p. 249.

110. Thomas H. Huxley, *Evolution and Ethics and Other Essays* (D. Appleton and Company, 1929), p. 146.

III. The Modern Development of the Idea of History

1. Johann Gottfried von Herder, *Ideen zur Philosophie der Geschichte der Menschheit* (Leipzig: Johann Friedrich Hartknoch, 1785–1792), Erster Theil, Vorrede, p. 14.

2. *Ibid.,* Dritter Theil, p. 387.

3. *Ibid.*

4. *Ibid.,* p. 396.

5. *Ibid.,* p. 392.

6. *Ibid.,* Zweiter Theil, pp. 85–86.

7. *Ibid.*

8. *Ibid.,* Dritter Theil, p. 87.

9. *Ibid.,* Erster Theil, Vorrede, p. 15.

10. *Ibid.,* Dritter Theil, p. 395.

11. *Ibid.*, p. 458.

12. *Ibid.*, p. 459.

13. *Ibid.*, Zweiter Theil, p. 232; cf. Erster Theil, Vorrede, p. 3.

14. *Ibid.*, Dritter Theil, p. 393; Vierter Theil, p. 415.

15. *Ibid.*, Zweiter Theil, p. 248.

16. *Ibid.*

17. Friedrich Schleiermacher, *Soliloquies,* tr. by Horace Leland Friess (The Open Court Publishing Company, 1926), p. 30.

18. *Ibid.*, p. 31.

19. *Ibid.*, pp. 31–32.

20. Benedetto Croce, *History, Its Theory and Practice,* tr. by Douglas Ainslie (Russell & Russell, 1960), p. 265.

21. Schleiermacher, *Soliloquies,* p. 17.

22. Ludwig W. Kahn, *Social Ideals in German Literature, 1770–1830* (Columbia University Press, 1938), p. 93.

23. Schleiermacher, *Soliloquies,* p. 39.

24. Kahn, *Social Ideals,* p. 58.

25. Friedrich, ed., *The Philosophy of Kant,* p. 117.

26. First Principle of Kant's " Idea for a Universal History."

27. Second Principle of Kant's " Idea for a Universal History."

28. Friedrich, ed., *The Philosophy of Kant,* p. 119.

29. *Ibid.*, p. 128.

30. *The Popular Works of Johann Gottlieb Fichte,* tr. by William Smith (London: John Chapman, 1849), Vol. II, p. 4.

31. *Ibid.*, p. 15.

32. *Ibid.*, p. 3.

33. *Ibid.*, p. 5.

34. *Ibid.*, p. 33.

35. *Ibid.*, p. 9.

36. *Ibid.*

37. *Ibid.*, pp. 9–10.

38. *Ibid.*, p. 158.

39. Georg Wilhelm Friedrich Hegel, *Vorlesungen über die Philosophie der Geschichte,* herausgegeben von D. Eduard Gans (Berlin: Duncker and Humblot, 1837), pp. 3 ff.

40. *Ibid.*, p. 4.

41. *Ibid.*, p. 11.

42. *Ibid.*, p. 436.

43. Georg Wilhelm Friedrich Hegel, *Die Vernunft in der Geschichte,* herausgegeben von Johannes Hoffmeister (Hamburg: Felix Meiner, 1955), p. 28.

44. *Ibid.*, p. 30.

45. Hegel, *Vorlesungen über die Philosophie der Geschichte,* p. 20.

46. Hegel, *Die Vernunft in der Geschichte,* pp. 50–51.

47. *Ibid.*, p. 105; also, *Vorlesungen über die Philosophie der Geschichte,* p. 32.

48. Hugh Ross Mackintosh, *Types of Modern Theology* (Charles Scribner's Sons, 1937), p. 102.

49. Georg Wilhelm Friedrich Hegel, *Encyclopedia of Philosophy,* tr. by Gustav Emil Mueller (Philosophical Library, Inc., 1959), Par. 449.

50. Hegel, *Die Vernunft in der Geschichte,* p. 32.

51. Hegel, *Vorlesungen über die Philosophie der Geschichte,* p. 32.

52. See, for example, Collingwood, *The Idea of History,* pp. 116–117.

53. Robert Flint, *The Philosophy of History in Europe* (Scribner, Welford & Armstrong, 1875), p. 505.

54. Croce, *History, Its Theory and Practice,* p. 58.

55. Morris R. Cohen, *The Meaning of Human History* (The Open Court Publishing Company, 1947), p. 286.

56. *Ibid.*

57. *Ibid.*

58. *Ibid.*, p. 33.

59. *Ibid.*, p. 285.

60. Hegel wrote: " *Existence* is the immediately appearing unity of immediacy and mediation, of being and seeming to be, of essential and non-essential, of being unproblematic in being problematic " (*Encyclopedia of Philosophy,* Par. 82) .

61. Flint, *The Philosophy of History in Europe,* p. 510.

62. Hegel, *Encyclopedia of Philosophy,* p. 279.

63. *Ibid.*, Par. 452.

64. Paul Tillich, *Systematic Theology,* 2 vols. (The University of Chicago Press, 1957), Vol. II, p. 25.

65. *Ibid.*

66. Georg Wilhelm Friedrich Hegel, *The Science of Logic,* tr. by W. H. Johnston & L. G. Struthers (London: George Allen & Unwin, Ltd., 1929), Vol. II, p. 467.

67. Hegel, *Die Vernunft in der Geschichte,* pp. 61–62.

68. Hegel, *Encyclopedia of Philosophy,* Par. 454.

69. Hegel, *Lectures on the Philosophy of Religion,* Vol. III, p. 303; cf. *Ibid.*, Vol. II, p. 327; also, *Encyclopedia of Philosophy,* Par. 565.

70. Hegel, *Lectures on the Philosophy of Religion,* Vol. III, p. 303.

71. Hegel, *Die Vernunft in der Geschichte,* pp. 149, 153.

72. *Ibid.*, p. 149.

73. *Ibid.*, p. 45.

74. *Ibid.*, p. 54.

75. Hegel, *The Science of Logic*, p. 375.

76. Hegel, *Vorlesungen über die Philosophie der Geschichte*, p. 22.

77. Hegel, *Die Vernunft in der Geschichte*, p. 62.

78. *Ibid.*, p. 155.

79. Reinhold Niebuhr, *Faith and History* (Charles Scribner's Sons, 1949), p. 3.

80. Hegel, *Die Vernunft in der Geschichte*, p. 64.

81. *Ibid.*, p. 48.

82. R. Niebuhr, *Faith and History*, p. 108.

83. Collingwood, *The Idea of History*, p. 126.

84. Jacob Burckhardt, *Force and Freedom: Reflections on History* (Pantheon Books, Inc., 1943), p. 94.

85. Croce, *History, Its Theory and Practice*, p. 293.

86. Theodor Mommsen, *The History of Rome*, tr. by William Purdie Dickson (Charles Scribner's Sons, 1895), Vol. I, p. 8.

87. *Ibid.*, Vol. V, p. 313.

88. *Ibid.*, Vol. V, pp. 309 ff.

89. Charles Darwin, *The Origin of Species* (Frederick Ungar Publishing Co., 1956), p. 27.

90. *Ibid.*, p. 27.

91. *Ibid.*, p. 36.

92. *Ibid.*, p. 133.

93. *Ibid.*, pp. 133–134.

94. Collingwood, *The Idea of History*, p. 129.

95. Auguste Comte, *The Positive Philosophy*, tr. by Harriet Martineau (William Gowans, 1868), p. 30.

96. *Ibid.*, p. 25.

97. *Ibid.*, p. 27.

98. *Ibid.*, p. 26.

99. *Ibid.*, p. 27.

100. Leopold Ranke, *Geschichten der romanischen und germanischen Völker von 1494 bis 1935* (Berlin: G. Reimer, 1824), Vol. I, p. vi.

101. *Ibid.*, p. viii.

102. *Ibid.*, p. vi.

103. *Ibid.*, p. vii.

104. Hegel, *Die Vernunft in der Geschichte*, p. 31.

105. Bury, *The Idea of Progress*, pp. 334–335.

106. B. A. G. Fuller, *A History of Philosophy* (Henry Holt & Co., 1938), p. 526.

107. Bury, *The Idea of Progress*, p. 335.

108. The full title is: *Social Statics, or, the Conditions Essential to Human Happiness Specified, and the First of Them Developed.*

109. Herbert Spencer, *Social Statics*, (D. Appleton and Company, 1896), p. 28.

110. *Ibid.*

111. Herbert Spencer, *First Principles of a New System of Philosophy* (D. Appleton and Company, 1865), p. 216.

112. *Ibid.*, p. 148.

113. Spencer, *Social Statics*, p. 8.

114. *Ibid.*, p. 32.

115. *Ibid.*

116. *Ibid.*

117. *Ibid.*, p. 238.

118. *Ibid.*

119. *Ibid.*, p. 253.

120. Collingwood, *The Idea of History*, p. 144.

121. Mommsen, *The History of Rome*, Vol. I, p. 5.

122. Huxley, *Evolution and Ethics*, p. 81.

123. *Ibid.*, p. 85.

124. *Ibid.*, p. 83.

125. *Ibid.*, p. 82.

126. Friedrich Nietzsche, *Beyond Good and Evil* (The Modern Library, Inc., 1917), p. 43.

127. *Ibid.*, p. 188.

128. *Ibid.*, p. 97.

129. Burckhardt, *Force and Freedom*, p. 80.

130. *Ibid.*, p. 81.

131. *Ibid.*

132. Cf. Collingwood, *The Idea of History*, p. 213.

133. Burckhardt, *Force and Freedom*, p. 83.

134. *Ibid.*, p. 82.

135. *Ibid.*, p. 355.

136. *Ibid.*, p. 149.

137. *Ibid.*, p. 352.

138. *Ibid.*, p. 358.

139. *Ibid.*, p. 355.

140. *Ibid.*, p. 354.

141. *Ibid.*, p. 358.

142. *Ibid.*, p. 97.

143. *Ibid.*, p. 98.

144. Croce, *History, Its Theory and Practice*, p. 24.

145. Burckhardt, *Force and Freedom*, p. 82.

146. *Ibid.*, p. 85.

147. Frank, *Philosophical Understanding and Religious Truth*, p. 121.

IV: Recent Developments in Historiography

1. Benedetto Croce, *History as the Story of Liberty,* tr. by Sylvia Sprigge (London: George Allen & Unwin, Ltd., 1941), p. 289.

2. Croce, *History, Its Theory and Practice,* p. 25.

3. *Ibid.*

4. *Ibid.,* p. 100.

5. *Ibid.,* p. 12.

6. *Ibid.,* p. 19.

7. *Ibid.,* p. 12.

8. *Ibid.,* p. 13. Morris R. Cohen objects to Croce at this point. Cohen quotes Croce's statement that "nothing exists outside of thought" and then adds the comment: "The notion that Caesar or my great-grandfather exists, gets born, marries, enters business, dies, only when I think of him is an absurdity" (*The Meaning of Human History,* p. 50). I think that Cohen fails to realize that his quarrel with Croce at this point is largely a semantic problem. Even Croce is able to use the word "history" in the loose sense of "what has happened" when he refers to "history" without relation to a document as "unverifiable history" (*History, Its Theory and Practice,* p. 14). But surely Croce is correct in underscoring the vital distinction between all that has happened and all that has verifiably happened. Croce would not say that Caesar did not once exist merely because Cohen fails to know it. What he would say is that Caesar's existence can only become history, in the genuine sense of this word, if and when Caesar's existence is *rethought* by Cohen. Croce would perhaps add that the idea of Caesar's existence is utterly unthinkable apart from somebody's thought of it, at least Caesar's thought of his own existence, and perhaps that of those who knew him personally.

9. Croce, *History, Its Theory and Practice,* p. 12.

10. *Ibid.,* p. 98.

11. *Ibid.,* p. 100.

12. *Ibid.,* p. 13.

13. *Ibid.,* p. 64.

14. *Ibid.,* p. 75.

15. *Ibid.,* p. 65.

16. *Ibid.,* p. 67.

17. *Ibid.,* p. 73.

18. *Ibid.,* p. 75.

19. *Ibid.*

20. *Ibid.,* p. 69.

21. *Ibid.,* p. 62.

22. *Ibid.,* p. 78.

23. *Ibid.,* p. 72.

24. *Ibid.,* p. 76.
25. *Ibid.,* p. 58.
26. *Ibid.,* p. 59.
27. *Ibid.,* p. 85.
28. Croce, *History as the Story of Liberty,* p. 52.
29. *Ibid.,* p. 51.
30. Croce, *History, Its Theory and Practice,* p. 85.
31. Croce, *History as the Story of Liberty,* p. 59.
32. Bultmann, *History and Eschatology,* pp. 125–126.
33. Croce, *History as the Story of Liberty,* p. 54.
34. Arnold J. Toynbee, *A Study of History,* abridgement of Vols. I–VI by D. G. Somerville (London: Oxford University Press, 1946), p. 8.
35. *Ibid.,* pp. 43–44.
36. Collingwood, *The Idea of History,* p. 163.
37. *Ibid.,* p. 162.
38. *Ibid.,* p. 163.
39. *Ibid.,* p. 164.
40. Toynbee, *A Study of History,* p. 48.
41. *Ibid.,* p. 48.
42. *Ibid.,* p. 60.
43. Arnold J. Toynbee, *Civilization on Trial* (Oxford University Press, Inc., 1948), p. 12.
44. Bultmann, *History and Eschatology,* p. 87.
45. Arnold J. Toynbee, *An Historian's Approach to Religion* (London: Oxford University Press, 1956), p. 1.
46. *Ibid.,* p. 3.
47. *Ibid.,* p. 4.
48. Toynbee, *A Study of History,* p. 67.
49. *Ibid.,* p. 70.
50. *Ibid.,* p. 248.
51. Toynbee, *Civilization on Trial,* p. 12.
52. Toynbee, *A Study of History,* p. 254.
53. *Ibid.*
54. Toynbee, *Civilization on Trial,* p. 39.
55. Toynbee, *A Study of History,* p. 275. Reinhold Niebuhr feels that Toynbee here says too much, for history shows that sometimes a " good " nation may be overwhelmed by superior power. " A strategic mistake may be the cause of the defeat of a just by an unjust force " (*Faith and History,* p. 130).
56. Toynbee, *A Study of History,* p. 578.
57. *Ibid.,* pp. 307 ff.
58. Toynbee, *Civilization on Trial,* p. 16.
59. *Ibid.*

60. *Ibid.,* p. 90.
61. *Ibid.,* p. 55.
62. *Ibid.,* p. 249.
63. *Ibid.,* p. 235.
64. R. Niebuhr, *Faith and History,* p. 111.
65. Toynbee, *Civilization on Trial,* p. 236.
66. *Ibid.,* p. 240.
67. *Ibid.,* p. 260.
68. *Ibid.,* p. 251.
69. *Ibid.,* p. 263.
70. *Ibid.*
71. Collingwood, *The Idea of History,* p. 266.
72. *Ibid.,* p. 232; cf. R. G. Collingwood, *An Autobiography* (London: Oxford University Press, 1939), pp. 79, 88.
73. Collingwood, *The Idea of History,* p. 213.
74. *Ibid.*
75. Hans Meyerhoff, ed., *The Philosophy of History in Our Time* (Doubleday & Company, Inc., 1959), p. 154.
76. Collingwood, *The Idea of History,* p. 303.
77. *Ibid.,* p. 215.
78. *Ibid.*
79. Collingwood, *An Autobiography,* p. 79.
80. R. G. Collingwood, *An Essay on Metaphysics* (Oxford: At the Clarendon Press, 1940), p. 58.
81. Collingwood, *An Autobiography,* p. 45.
82. Collingwood, *The Idea of History,* p. 218.
83. See Julian N. Hartt's criticism, *Journal of Religion,* Vol. XXXIII (July, 1953), p. 207.
84. Collingwood, *The Idea of History,* p. 215; *An Autobiography,* p. 110.
85. Collingwood, *The Idea of History,* p. 227.
86. *Ibid.,* p. 305.
87. Collingwood, *An Autobiography,* p. 111.
88. *Ibid.,* p. 113.
89. Collingwood, *The Idea of History,* p. 288.
90. Collingwood, *An Autobiography,* p. 113.
91. *Ibid.*
92. Collingwood, *The Idea of History,* p. 286.
93. *Ibid.,* p. 287.
94. *Ibid.*
95. *Ibid.,* p. 294.
96. *Ibid.,* p. 312.
97. *Ibid.,* p. 313.
98. *Ibid.,* p. 246.

99. *Ibid.*, p. 234.

100. *Ibid.*, p. 303.

101. One finds an expression of such Platonic realism in the debate on the problem of universals by the medieval theologians. Realism, as opposed to conceptualism and nominalism, was championed by Anselm, William of Champeaux, and John Wycliffe. Anselm, for example, criticized the nominalism of Roscellinus in which universals were regarded as mere breathings of the voice (*flatus vocis*). The ontology of the realists stressed the need to probe behind the appearance of individuals and lay bare the universal, which should be considered in itself, prior to and independent of its corporeal, individual manifestations.

102. In Meyerhoff, *The Philosophy of History in Our Time*, p. 299.

103. Collingwood, *The Idea of History*, p. 10.

104. *Ibid.*

105. *Ibid.*, p. 332.

106. *Ibid.*, p. 317.

107. *Ibid.*, p. 215.

108. *Ibid.*, p. 318.

109. *Ibid.*

110. Collingwood, *An Autobiography*, p. 100.

111. *Ibid.*

112. *Ibid.*, p. 101; cf. p. 114.

113. Meyerhoff, *The Philosophy of History in Our Time*, p. 155.

114. Collingwood, *The Idea of History*, p. 308.

115. *Ibid.*, pp. 10, 315.

116. *Ibid.*, p. 220.

117. *Ibid.*, p. 265.

118. *Ibid.*

119. In Meyerhoff, *The Philosophy of History in Our Time*, p. 141.

120. R. G. Collingwood, *An Essay on Philosophical Method* (Oxford: At the Clarendon Press, 1933), p. 198.

121. *Ibid.*, p. 191.

122. *Ibid.*

123. *Ibid.*, p. 192.

V: Implications of the Modern Idea of History for Theology

1. To borrow a phrase from Karl Barth, *Evangelical Theology: An Introduction,* tr. by Grover Foley (Holt, Rinehart and Winston, Inc., 1963), p. 130.

2. *Ibid.*, p. 16.

3. See for example, Robert McAfee Brown's comments in Georges Casalis, *Portrait of Karl Barth*, tr. by Robert McAfee Brown (Doubleday and Company, Inc., 1963), p. 32; Daniel Day Williams, *What Present-Day Theologians Are Thinking* (Harper & Brothers, 1952), p. 49; Tillich, *Systematic Theology*, Vol. I, p. 61; Vol. II, p. 14; Rudolf Bultmann, *Essays: Philosophical and Theological*, tr. by James C. G. Greig (The Macmillan Company, 1955), pp. 259 ff.; H. Richard Niebuhr, in *The Christian Century*, March 2, 1960.

4. Karl Barth, *The Humanity of God*, tr. by John Newton Thomas (John Knox Press, 1960), p. 18.

5. Tillich, *Systematic Theology*, Vol. I, p. 5.

6. Cf. Gerhard Ebeling, in *The New Hermeneutic*, ed. by James M. Robinson and John B. Cobb, Jr. (Harper & Row, Publishers, Inc., 1964), p. 81.

7. To borrow a phrase from Roland H. Bainton, *The Reformation of the Sixteenth Century* (The Beacon Press, 1952), p. 45.

8. *Luther's Works*, ed. by E. Theodore Bachmann (Muhlenberg Press, 1960), Vol. 35, p. 362.

9. *Ibid.*, p. 398.

10. *Ibid.*, p. 397.

11. *Ibid.*, p. 398.

12. Ernst Troeltsch has forcefully described this universal law of historical relativity in his *Christian Thought, Its History and Application*, ed. and with an introduction and index by Baron F. von Hügel (A Living Age Book, Meridian Books, Inc., 1957), p. 44.

13. Friedrich Schleiermacher, *On Religion*, tr. by John Oman (London: Kegan, Paul, Trench, Trübner & Co., Ltd., 1893), p. 214.

14. *Ibid.*, p. 217.

15. *Ibid.*

16. Ernst Troeltsch has disclosed the sociological factors that are at work in the historically diversified forms of church existence. See his *The Social Teaching of the Christian Churches*, tr. by Olive Wyon, 2 vols. (The Macmillan Company, 1931).

17. Numerous modern thinkers have recognized the finite historical limitations that characterize the work of metaphysics. Paul Tillich, for example, points out the fact that the philosopher's "existential situation" is an inescapable positive influence in the shaping of his vision of reality (*Systematic Theology*, Vol. I, p. 25). Similarly, R. G. Collingwood underscores the historical character of the absolute presuppositions that have characterized the work of philosophers in different ages (*An Essay on Metaphysics*, pp. 49, 71).

18. See the brilliant study by H. Richard Niebuhr, *The Social Sources of Denominationalism* (Hamden: The Shoe String Press, 1929).

19. H. Richard Niebuhr, *The Meaning of Revelation* (The Macmillan Company, 1946), p. 13.

20. Tillich, *Systematic Theology,* Vol. III, p. 308.

21. Theodore Otto Wedel, *The Coming Great Church* (The Macmillan Company, 1945), p. 20.

22. James Moffatt, *The Thrill of Tradition* (The Macmillan Company, 1944), p. 178.

23. Troeltsch, *The Social Teaching of the Christian Churches,* Vol. II, p. 796.

24. Friedrich Schleiermacher, *The Christian Faith,* tr. by H. R. Mackintosh and J. S. Stewart (Edinburgh: T. & T. Clark, 1928), p. 3.

25. *Ibid.,* p. 52.

26. Friedrich Schleiermacher, *Brief Outline of the Study of Theology,* tr. by William Farrer (Edinburgh: T. & T. Clark, 1850), p. 102.

27. Barth, *Church Dogmatics,* Vol. I, Part 1, p. 1.

28. H. Richard Niebuhr, *The Meaning of Revelation,* p. 51.

29. Barth, *The Humanity of God,* p. 31.

30. Karl Barth, *The Epistle to the Romans,* tr. by Edwyn C. Hoskyns (Oxford: Oxford University Press, 1933), p. 6.

31. Barth, *The Humanity of God,* p. 30.

32. In Arnold S. Nash, *Protestant Thought in the Twentieth Century* (The Macmillan Company, 1951), pp. 22–23.

33. Barth, *The Epistle to the Romans,* p. B.

34. See Waldemar Gurian, *Hitler and the Christians,* tr. by E. F. Peeler (London: Sheed & Ward, Inc., 1936), p. 108.

35. Ernst Wolf, *Barmen: Kirche zwischen Versuchung und Gnade* (München: Chr. Kaiser Verlag, 1957), p. 92.

36. Karl Barth, *Theological Existence Today,* tr. by R. Birch Hoyle (London: Hodder & Stoughton, Ltd., 1933), p. 45.

37. *Ibid.*

38. In Ralph G. Wilburn, ed., *The Reconstruction of Theology* (The Bethany Press, 1963), p. 79.

39. In Robinson and Cobb, eds., *The New Hermeneutic,* pp. 164–167.

40. *Ibid.,* p. 182.

41. *Ibid.,* p. 183.

42. *Ibid.,* p. 204.

43. Bultmann, *Essays: Philosophical and Theological,* p. 251.

44. *Ibid.*

45. In Robinson and Cobb, eds., *The New Hermeneutic,* p. 251.

46. Tillich, *Systematic Theology,* Vol. I, p. 7.

47. Emil Brunner, *The Christian Doctrine of God,* Dogmatics: Vol. I, tr. by Olive Wyon (The Westminster Press, 1950), pp. 141 ff.

48. In Robinson and Cobb, eds., *The New Hermeneutic,* p. 154.

49. H. Richard Niebuhr, *Christ and Culture* (Harper & Brothers, 1956), p. 14.

50. John A. T. Robinson, *Honest to God* (The Westminster Press, 1963), p. 115.

51. John Baillie, *The Sense of the Presence of God* (London: Oxford University Press, 1962), p. 161.

52. Dietrich Bonhoeffer, *Letters and Papers from Prison,* tr. by Reginald H. Fuller (London: SCM Press, Ltd., 1953), p. 124.

VI: Christological Problems Posed by the Modern Historical Understanding of Human Existence

1. Bultmann, *History and Eschatology,* p. 144.

2. Harnack, *Das Christentum und die Geschichte,* p. 8.

3. *Ibid.*

4. *Ibid.,* p. 8.

5. Bultmann, *History and Eschatology,* p. 146.

6. Harnack, *Das Christentum und die Geschichte,* p. 10.

7. Joseph Klausner, *Jesus of Nazareth,* tr. by Herbert Danby (The Macmillan Company, 1925), p. 384.

8. As quoted in Herbert Butterfield, *Man on His Past: The Study of the History of Historical Scholarship* (Cambridge: Cambridge University Press, 1955), p. 96.

9. *Ibid.*

10. *Ibid.,* p. 96.

11. *Ibid.*

12. Ernst Kinder, ed., *Ein Wort Lutherischer Theologie zur Entmythologisierung* (München: Evang. Presseverband für Bayern, 1952), p. 93.

13. Cf. Erich Dinkler, *Bibelautorität und Bibelkritik* (Tübingen: J. C. B. Mohr-Paul Siebeck, 1950), p. 19.

14. Dodd, *History and the Gospel,* p. 11.

15. Rudolf Bultmann, *Das Verhältnis der urchristlichen Christusbotschaft zum historischen Jesus* (Heidelberg: Carl Winter-Universitätsverlag, 1960), p. 13.

16. Paul W. Meyer in *Novum Testamentum,* Vol. IV (1960), p. 123.

17. H. Richard Niebuhr, *The Meaning of Revelation,* p. 63.

18. Strauss, *The Life of Jesus,* p. 895.

19. *Ibid.,* p. 887.

20. See Ernest Cadman Colwell, *The Study of the Bible* (The University of Chicago Press, 1937), pp. 104 ff., 121 ff.; also Henry Joel

Cadbury, *The Peril of Modernizing Jesus* (The Macmillan Company, 1937).

21. Klausner, *Jesus of Nazareth,* p. 363.

22. *Ibid.,* p. 368.

23. *Categoriae,* Ch. 6.

24. *Topica,* Bk. III, 6.

25. *Augustine: Confessions and Enchiridion,* tr. by Albert C. Outler (The Westminster Press, 1955), pp. 266–267.

26. Related to this question Carl Michalson writes: "It does not seem strange that theologians should have denied Christ is historical. For by that denial they intended to affirm the reality of Christ as present" (*The Hinge of History* [Charles Scribner's Sons, 1959], p. 171).

27. Bultmann, *Das Verhältnis der urchristlichen Christusbotschaft zum historischen Jesus,* p. 25.

28. James M. Robinson, *The New Quest of the Historical Jesus* (Alec R. Allenson, Inc., 1959), pp. 42–43.

29. Tillich, *Systematic Theology,* Vol. II, p. 157.

30. Irenaeus, *Against Heresies,* III. xi. 1; cf. I. xxvi. 1; III. xvi. 5. Irenaeus records an interesting rumor, which he said derived from the famed Polycarp. According to the rumor, "John, the disciple of the Lord, going to bathe at Ephesus, and perceiving Cerinthus within, rushed out of the bathe-house without bathing, exclaiming 'Let us fly, lest even the bathe-house fall down, because Cerinthus, the enemy of the truth, is within'" (*ibid.,* III. iii. 4).

31. This passage in Paul should not be forgotten in interpreting the difficult passage in which he said, "Though we once regarded Christ from a human point of view, we regard him thus no longer" (II Cor. 5:16). By the phrase "from a human point of view" Paul possibly meant, as Robinson suggests, "a historically proven Lord" (Robinson, *The New Quest of the Historical Jesus,* pp. 87–88).

32. Emil Brunner, *The Scandal of Christianity* (The Westminster Press, 1951), p. 13.

VII: The New Quest for the Historical Jesus

1. Tillich, *Systematic Theology,* Vol. II, p. 142.

2. Published posthumously by Lessing between 1774 and 1778.

3. Cf. Strauss, *The Life of Jesus,* p. 879.

4. Hermann Diem in *Kerygma and History,* ed. by Carl E. Braaten and Roy A. Harrisville (Abingdon Press, 1962), p. 201.

5. Meyer, *Novum Testamentum,* Vol. IV, p. 126.

6. Ethelbert Stauffer, *Jesus and His Story*, tr. by Richard and Clara Winston (Alfred A. Knopf, Inc., 1960), p. 6.

7. *Ibid.*, p. viii.

8. *Ibid.*, p. ix.

9. *Ibid.*, p. x.

10. James M. Robinson, *The New Quest of the Historical Jesus*, pp. 59 ff.

11. Bultmann, *Das Verhältnis der urchristlichen Christusbotschaft zum historischen Jesus*, p. 9.

12. As quoted in Diem, *Kerygma and History*, p. 163.

13. Rudolf Bultmann, *The Theology of the New Testament*, tr. by Kendrick Grobel (Charles Scribner's Sons, 1954), Vol. I, p. 3.

14. Rudolf Bultmann, *Jesus and the Word*, tr. by Louise Pettibone Smith and Erminie Huntress Lantero (Charles Scribner's Sons, 1958), p. 8.

15. *Ibid.*, p. 217.

16. As quoted in Diem, *Kerygma and History*, p. 165.

17. Günther Bornkamm, *Jesus of Nazareth*, tr. by Irene and Fraser McLuskey (London: Hodder & Stoughton, Ltd., 1960), p. 24.

18. *Ibid.*, p. 26.

19. *Ibid.*, p. 19.

20. Robinson, *The New Quest of the Historical Jesus*, p. 86.

21. *Ibid.*, p. 88.

22. *Ibid.*, p. 67.

23. *Ibid.*, p. 69.

24. *Ibid.*, pp. 69–70.

25. Bultmann, *Das Verhältnis der urchristlichen Christusbotschaft zum historischen Jesus*, p. 13.

26. *Ibid.*

27. Robinson, *The New Quest of the Historical Jesus*, p. 48.

28. Tillich, *Systematic Theology*, Vol. II, p. 107.

29. Dahl, as quoted in Diem, *Kerygma and History*, p. 153.

30. Conzelmann writes: " *Man kann ihre* (the passion sayings) *Echtheit nicht damit verteidigen, J. habe einen kommenden Zusammenstoss auf Tod und Leben vorausssehen müssen. Denn diese Worte sprechen nicht eine scharfsichtige Analyse der Lage aus, sondern eine göttlich Notwendigkeit des Leidens. Dh. sie enthalten bereits die Deutung der Passion von Ostern her* " (*Die Religion in Geschichte und Gegenwart*, 3. Aufl., Dritter Band [Tübingen: J. C. B. Mohr-Paul Siebeck, 1959], p. 630).

31. Robinson, *The New Quest of the Historical Jesus*, pp. 106–107.

32. Bultmann, *Das Verhältnis der urchristlichen Christusbotschaft zum historischen Jesus*, p. 12.

33. Ernst Fuchs, in *Zeitschrift für Theologie und Kirche,* 53 (1956), p. 222.

34. Bultmann, *Das Verhältnis der urchristlichen Christusbotschaft zum historischen Jesus,* p. 12.

35. Bornkamm, *Jesus of Nazareth,* p. 154. Cf. Conzelmann: "*Sicher ist jedenfalls, dass J. nach Jerusalem zog . . . um sein Volk im Zentrum, am Sitz des Tempels und der obersten Behörde, vor die letzte Entscheidung zu stellen*" (*Die Religion in Geschichte und Gegenwart,* p. 647).

36. Bultmann, *Das Verhältnis der urchristlichen Christusbotschaft zum historischen Jesus,* p. 12.

37. *Ibid.;* cf. the remark of Dahl: "A historical description of the death of Jesus is still a most difficult and complicated task. . . . One must be extremely cautious about employing them [the passion narratives] in the service of historical reconstruction" (quoted in Diem, *Kerygma and History,* p. 158).

38. Joachim Jeremias, "The Present Position in the Controversy on the Problem of the Historical Jesus," in *The Expository Times,* ed. by A. W. Hastings and E. Hastings (Edinburgh: T. & T. Clark), LXIX, p. 336.

39. Joachim Jeremias, *The Parables of Jesus,* tr. by S. H. Hooke (Charles Scribner's Sons, 1955), p. 7.

40. *Ibid.,* p. 20.

41. Jeremias, "The Present Position in the Controversy on the Problem of the Historical Jesus," in *The Expository Times,* LXIX, p. 338.

42. So Meyer, *Novum Testamentum,* Vol. IV, p. 131.

43. Bultmann, *Das Verhältnis der urchristlichen Christusbotschaft zum historischen Jesus,* p. 14.

44. Strauss, *The Life of Jesus,* p. 896.

45. Bornkamm, *Jesus of Nazareth,* p. 15.

46. Diem, *Kerygma and History,* p. 203.

47. *Ibid.,* p. 204.

48. Löwith, *Meaning in History,* p. 186.

49. Bultmann, *Das Verhältnis der urchristlichen Christusbotschaft zum historischen Jesus,* p. 26.

50. Edwyn Hoskyns and Noel Davey, *The Riddle of the New Testament* (London: Faber & Faber, Ltd., 1931), p. 179.

51. Bultmann, *Jesus and the Word,* p. 8.

52. Hoskyns and Davey, *The Riddle of the New Testament,* p. 172.

53. *Ibid.,* p. 12.

54. *Ibid.,* p. 10.

55. *Ibid.*

Index

237